GREAT AMERICAN WARTIME
SURVIVAL STORIES

GREAT AMERICAN WARTIME SURVIVAL STORIES

EDITED BY TOM MCCARTHY

LYONS
PRESS

Essex, Connecticut

An imprint of The Globe Pequot Publishing Group, Inc.
64 South Main Street
Essex, CT 06426
www.globepequot.com

Distributed by NATIONAL BOOK NETWORK

British Library Cataloguing in Publication Information available

Library of Congress Cataloging-in-Publication Data
Names: McCarthy, Tom, 1952– editor.
Title: Great American wartime survival stories / edited by Tom McCarthy.
Description: Essex, Connecticut : Lyons Press, an imprint of Globe Pequot, the trade division of The Rowman & Littlefield Publishing Group, Inc., [2024] | Includes bibliographical references.
Identifiers: LCCN 2024013732 (print) | LCCN 2024013733 (ebook) |
ISBN 9781493084302 (paperback) | ISBN 9781493084319 (epub)
Subjects: LCSH: Soldiers—United States—Biography. | Civilians in war—United States—Biography. | United States—History, Military—Anecdotes. | Survival—United States. | BISAC: HISTORY / Military / United States
Classification: LCC U52 .G73 2024 (print) | LCC U52 (ebook) |
DDC 355.0092/273—dc23/eng/20240715
LC record available at https://lccn.loc.gov/2024013732
LC ebook record available at https://lccn.loc.gov/2024013733

♾️™ The paper used in this publication meets the minimum requirements of American National Standard for Information Sciences—Permanence of Paper for Printed Library Materials, ANSI/NISO Z39.48-1992.

Contents

Contents

Introduction

Great American Wartime Survival Stories is an extraordinary collection.

Within, you will find indefatigable human beings caught in circumstances, I truly believe, that summoned the resilience and strength we are all capable of.

The flip side, of course, is that while each story is a great read, none of us would want to be tested as these heroes were. We can only hope that reading is as close to such tests as we will ever get.

One's first reaction upon reading each of the stories in this collection would instinctively be admiration. How can anyone go through such trials and continue? The heroes within these stories are unflappable, one might think. They all benefit from some otherworldly gift to be able to face, for example, a plane crash in the jungles of Burma, or a Pacific typhoon, or a dangerous flight from Confederate soldiers intent on shooting, capturing, and killing.

Look closer and you will find that each of the survivors who persevered is as normal as the rest of us—perfectly human individuals thrown into unexpected and trying circumstances.

And that is why these stories have persevered. Within each is an uplifting lesson on the human condition.

The stories in this stunning collection are indelible proof that within each of us there is an untapped strength to live and persevere under the most suffocating circumstances—and therein lies hope.

Take, for example, the group of imprisoned American sailors trapped in a foul Philippine jail at the turn of the nineteenth century so vividly described by author Matthew Westfall:

> The greatest risk now to the Gillmore party was not the violence of war, but the impoverished landscape of the Philippines itself. Pathogens swirled in their midst, encouraged by a trying climate that bred infection. Dysentery, typhoid, and malaria stood as ever-present killers. One recalled, "In the daytime we had to put up with great swarms of flies, and at night the mosquitoes gave us no peace. We also had a full allowance of bedbugs, lizards, rats, and mice.
>
> Sonnichsen was the first to fall violently ill, with bloody diarrhea, abdominal cramps, and fever, leaving him curled up in agony on the bamboo-slat bed in his dank, fetid cell.
>
> And if the threats of bacteria, parasites, and malnutrition were not enough, the high heat and humidity presented a final, almost insulting blow to their health. All the men suffered from severe skin irritations and Dhobie itch—a persistent skin ailment of the crotch. Some battled tropical, or phagedenic, ulcers, often originating from small, even innocuous wounds around the ankle or lower leg, caused by something as simple as a brush against a sharp rock, swiping a barbed plant, or the bite of an insect. The small abrasion quickly became infected from exposure to an anaerobic bacterium, Fusobacterium ulcerans, found in the island's muddy, stagnant water. The wound then swelled into a blister that would eventually burst, leaving a raw, festering ulcer that refused to heal. A necrotic black coating formed, emitting the stench of rotten flesh. On some of the prisoners, the depth of the putrid ulcers revealed tendon and bone. In these desperate conditions, the prisoners were starting down the slow spiral path toward early death.

These poor souls, malnourished and exhausted from their long imprisonment, were about to be marched into the steaming and impenetrable mountains and executed. None gave up hope for rescue.

You'll find here Alf Wilson's account of his audacious plan to escape the confines of a Confederate jail and make his way safely through Rebel territory to Union warships he hoped would be anchored hundreds of miles to the south. Hungry, weak, and worn, Wilson and his colleague persevered, even in the midst of a swamp, while Confederate soldiers searched for them.

> But the 'gators were cowardly fellows, and, on the least demonstration on our part, would scramble into the water. Still we feared that they might steal upon and lay hold of us with their powerful jaws while we were asleep. We had learned that they were not apt to attack, except when the object of their voracious appetites lay quiet; but, when once they did lay hold, that they were hard to beat off. They will drag their victim, be it man or beast, instantly under the water, where the struggle soon ends.

Here also are two U.S. Navy officers on the bridge of a ship being battered by a Pacific typhoon during World War II, recounted vividly by author Buck Melton.

> The task group's screen commander, Captain Mercer, riding out the storm on the bridge with Calhoun, tried to keep up his own spirits, but he doubted his flagship would come through the typhoon. By now the rolls were beyond the range of the bridge inclinometer, which stopped at seventy-three degrees, and even that of the engine room instrument, which maxed at seventy-five. During one of them, while Calhoun and Mercer hung from a stanchion facing each other, the starboard pilothouse window directly below them, they had a remarkably calm conversation.
>
> "If we go over and end up in this sea," asked Mercer, "do you think you can make it?"
>
> Calhoun, in his early thirties, was fit, and he had a wife and son to live for.

"Yes," he replied. "I think I can."

Mercer disclosed that he himself was a poor swimmer. "I don't feel too badly about it," he said nevertheless. "I've had a good life and my insurance is all paid up," he continued with a smile.

The ten stories in this inspirational collection are filled with quiet heroics of everyday people who refused to be cowed. They each had obligations—to themselves and the greater cause for which they had enlisted.

That is the essence of this collection.

Mary Loughborough, a young mother caught in the vicissitudes of the siege of Vicksburg, took to a cave bombarded daily. John Ransom survived the hell that was Andersonville. William Diebold was shot down over the impenetrable jungles of Burma, and the crew of the USS *Indianapolis* spent days floating in shark-infested waters, not knowing whether anyone knew they were missing.

Paul Joseph Travers's excellent oral history of the bombing of Pearl harbor brings to life the stories of men who were there and what they saw.

Courage is not the absence of fear but rather the ability and pluck to face fear and move into the fight.

The horrors of war offer countless ways for soldiers, sailors, and Marines to die, unfortunately.

The heroes in this collection met their challenges and survived.

Readers are fortunate to hear their stories and to be inspired by each of these survivors and the gifts they offer.

Defying the Odds

Matthew Westfall

THIS MOMENT WAS ONE TO BE CAPTURED FOR POSTERITY.

Twenty-three gaunt, starving men approached a gray boulder that punctuated the rock-strewn bank of the river. Wracked by disease and riddled with sores, the haggard souls mustered their last reserves of energy to hoist each other up and jostle into position. A small American flag was handed to the dazed senior naval officer of the party, Lieutenant James C. Gillmore Jr., who weakly held it aloft.

That a camera was present there and then, in the war-ravaged Philippines, two weeks shy of the close of the nineteenth century, defied all odds. Brought along by a forward-thinking army lieutenant, the Kodak folding pocket camera had been introduced in the United States just eight months earlier, in April 1899. The hand-sized marvel of photographic innovation had survived a transpacific ocean journey to the Philippines, a grueling months-long march into northern Luzon, pitched battles against insurgents, and a daring mission into the uncharted hinterlands of the Cordilleras to rescue the men now assembled.

The Captives

In the squalid Vigan jail, the health of the prisoners with Lieutenant James C. Gillmore Jr. began to fail. Insufficient food, poor sanitation, and exposure to disease drained the color from their faces and carved away their weight. A few fell violently ill. Gillmore wrote a series of urgent letters to the town's mayor, the presidente, and the Filipino military command, demanding medical attention for his increasingly listless prisoners. The entreaties fell on deaf ears.

Sonnichsen, the civilian quartermaster, suffered from festering tropical ulcers on his right foot that completely disabled him. Landsman Edwards, battling violent diarrhea, visibly wasted away.

Vigan's residents, and surprisingly, the alcalde (prison warden), took pity on the prisoners. It could have been the novelty of American captives, or the cultural importance to hardworking Ilocanos to be seen as gracious hosts. Or maybe, given that American forces were rumored to be on the advance, they thought a demonstration of compassion might pay dividends in the future.

Whatever the motivation, the alcalde visited the men, accompanied by wealthy local merchant Pedro Rivera. Trailing behind was Rivera's servant, his arms overflowing with a stack of clothes. Rivera cheerfully explained that he had collected the items from his many friends about town, all of whom were eager to give what they could. "Help yourself," he urged. The grateful prisoners rummaged through the pile, sorting coats, shorts, pants, and pajamas in all sizes and colors.

News of the unusual delivery trickled back to the Filipino officer in command of the region, General Manuel Tinio, and it enraged him. That same evening, he summoned Rivera to his office and threatened the merchant with imprisonment if he ever again attempted to help the enemy. For good measure, Tinio declared the prisoners incommunicados, and posted additional guards. The threat of death hung over anyone who engaged the prisoners. From then on, even casual passersby avoided going anywhere near the jail.

General Tinio, almost twenty-two, was now in control of the Gillmore party's survival. Appointed governor of the Ilocos province and commanding general of northern Luzon nine months earlier, the handsome ladies' man had rapidly ascended among the ranks to become one of four senior commanders of Aguinaldo's Army of Liberation. Now, Tinio had a band of American prisoners who might one day have value. For the time being, the youthful general was happy to leave his enemies to rot in prison.

The greatest risk now to the Gillmore party was not the violence of war, but the impoverished landscape of the Philippines itself. Pathogens swirled in their midst, encouraged by a trying climate that bred infection. Dysentery, typhoid, and malaria stood as ever-present killers. One recalled, "In the daytime we had to put up with great swarms of flies, and at night the mosquitoes gave us no peace. We also had a full allowance of bedbugs, lizards, rats, and mice."

Sonnichsen was the first to fall violently ill, with bloody diarrhea, abdominal cramps, and fever, leaving him curled up in agony on the bamboo-slat bed in his dank, fetid cell.

And if the threats of bacteria, parasites, and malnutrition were not enough, the high heat and humidity presented a final, almost insulting blow to their health. All the men suffered from severe skin irritations and Dhobie itch—a persistent skin ailment of the crotch. Some battled tropical, or phagedenic, ulcers, often originating from small, even innocuous wounds around the ankle or lower leg, caused by something as simple as a brush against a sharp rock, swiping a barbed plant, or the bite of an insect. The small abrasion quickly became infected from exposure to an anaerobic bacterium, Fusobacterium ulcerans, found in the island's muddy, stagnant water. The wound then swelled into a blister that would eventually burst, leaving a raw, festering ulcer that refused to heal. A necrotic black coating formed, emitting the stench of rotten flesh. On some of the prisoners, the depth of the putrid ulcers revealed tendon and bone. In these desperate conditions, the prisoners were starting down the slow spiral path toward early death.

THE EXPEDITION

On December 5, 1899, flush with their victory at Tangadan, the two American battalions—one led by Colonel Luther R. Hare and the other by Lieutenant Colonel Robert Lee Howze—moved out at first light, advancing beyond the overrun fortifications of the Filipinos.

Breaking over the mountain pass, the 350-man column dropped into the Abra River valley. Following orders from General Young, who had returned to Vigan to oversee operations with the balance of American forces, Hare and Howze's soldiers proceeded together up the wide expanse of the river course, torching insurgent barracks and food stores in their wake.

By mid-morning, a thick, heavy fog had rolled in, reducing visibility to just yards and casting an eerie pall over the march. The sun broke through in the late afternoon, moments before descending as a glowing red ball over the distant sea. After a ten-mile hike, the column reached the town of San Quintin where they camped for the night.

The next morning, while marching to the settlement of Pidigan, the Americans encountered several hundred starved Spanish prisoners who had been abandoned by their captors at Bangued. Brought before the command, the emaciated Spaniards excitedly explained that Lieutenant Gillmore and twenty-five other prisoners had been seen in the town just days earlier. The news grabbed the command's attention, and likely triggered wide-eyed glances among the officers.

Hare and Howze pressed the Spaniards for details. What they got were disheartening rumors. While the Spanish prisoners had been left behind, the Gillmore party captives, obviously more valuable, had been marched into the mountains. And then this, which the Spaniards had only heard secondhand: General Tinio had issued specific orders that under no circumstances were the Gillmore party prisoners to fall back into American hands. To ensure this did not happen, Tinio had commanded that Lieutenant Gillmore and his men were to be marched to a desolate location, deep in the mountains, and executed.

Runners were sent back to Vigan to share the grim news with Young. And now it dawned on Hare, Howze, and their officers: What had begun as an operation to capture Aguinaldo, and then shifted to the fight with his rear guard under Tinio, was about to become something else altogether. The forward advance of the northern campaign was no longer chasing the elusive rebel general or even focused on pacifying the country; it was now directed exclusively toward saving the lives of a navy lieutenant and his cutter crew.

As the expedition prepared to chase the American prisoners of war, Hare, as the ranking officer, assembled his fellow officers, rallying them around the probable challenges and possible payoff that lay ahead. And then, unable to contain himself, he punched the air, proclaiming, "I will find Gillmore if I have to follow him to hell."

Yet, with little more than unsubstantiated rumors in hand, it was unclear what route the Gillmore prisoners had followed into the Cordilleras. Trail upon trail cut into the mountains, an informal and age-old zigzagging network of foot-worn paths of mud, rock, and ruts that linked the lowlands to the uplands, towns to mountain villages, barrios to the Isneg *rancherias*. Had the Gillmore party prisoners gone south along the winding Abra River toward San Jose? Or north from Bangued toward La Paz and the high mountains of Ilocos Norte? No one knew.

The two commanders held differing opinions about the most likely route to follow. The discussion edged toward an argument as the senior-ranking Hare argued for the southern route, while dismissing Howze's views on the merits of going north.

Hare summed it up: If Howze wanted to run off in another direction and waste precious time, that was just fine with the old colonel. The two American commanders, unable to reconcile, decided to split up and cover both scenarios. Hare's 33rd Infantry—with 220 men—would take the San Jose trail to the south, the most probable route, while Howze's 34th Infantry—with 130 men—would take the trail north toward Bangued and La Paz. Hopefully, one of them would pick up the route taken by the prisoners.

Howze, perhaps driven by a touch of competitive spirit, moved out at speed. By late afternoon, traipsing through rich, tilled land, he and his men could see the town of Bangued a few miles ahead. Along the rutted dirt road, a trickle of emaciated Spanish soldiers staggered toward them, warily at first, unsure if the Americans were liberators or about to become their new captors. Informed that they were free, the former prisoners burst into shouts of joy. The trickle grew by tens and scores until it was a large crowd, hobbling, limping, and being helped down the road, an unceasing stream of gaunt men that swamped the American column.

Inspired by their own elation, the Spaniards turned in their tracks and joined the American column heading to Bangued. All told, roughly one thousand impoverished and ailing Spanish prisoners who had been abandoned by Tinio's forces came to the Americans over the course of the day.

The residents of Bangued greeted the mobbed American column with a brass band and the ringing of the church tower's bells. Howze marched into the town plaza to set up camp and ordered his men to question residents about the American prisoners. The locals had little to share but led Howze and a handful of his officers to the prison where the captives had been held.

The officers poked about, kicking abandoned jars and cookware scattered about the yard, searching for clues. An officer ducked out of one of the cells and called for Howze to come have a look. Howze entered the dark chamber where his senses were assaulted by the lingering stench of the long-unwashed and ailing, a caustic mix of sweat, feces, and rot hanging heavy in the air. The officer pointed to the wall. Howze stepped forward, squinting to make out the words.

Crudely etched onto the wall with bits of charcoal was a list of names of the Gillmore party. But this time, the addition of a grim skull and crossbones suggested that a pall of hopelessness had fallen over the men. This was palpable evidence that the prisoners had been here, and just days ago. A chill raced through Howze. He would need to move at even greater speed, as soon as daylight offered the opportunity to resume the hunt.

Howze once again took up his pursuit of the Gillmore party, moving out at noon. Traveling north across the Abra River and east through San Gregorio to La Paz, nine miles distant, they hoped they might learn of the prisoners' movements. The column arrived at nightfall to little news, however. A few houses near the center of town were sequestered for the night, with strong outposts set and rotating patrols organized to guard against the remote chance that insurgents might double back from their retreat to attack.

Later in the evening, one of the American patrols came upon a Filipino who claimed to be a deserter from Tinio's Brigade. Upon close questioning, he advised that the Gillmore party had been taken north, with orders from Tinio to "dispose of them where the Americans will never find them." Howze and his command could only listen, frustrated at the turn of events.

Around 3:45 a.m., in the absolute dead of night, two weary guards on outpost duty heard rustling in the pitch-black brush. Two shadowy forms stumbled toward them. The guards raised their rifles and shouted challenges. The response could not have been more startling. The senior officer on duty raced back to the command to awaken Howze to the news: Two of the American prisoners had just staggered into the camp, and reportedly a third was close behind.

A groggy but excited Howze approached the rail-thin, bleary-eyed captives. Questions were rattled off in quick succession. Under the cool moonlit night, the prisoners began to recount their incredible escape.

Rushed out of Bangued three days earlier, the Gillmore party had been marched fifteen miles to a small mountain barrio called Danglas. Arriving just as darkness fell, they were quartered in a two-room bamboo shack lifted up on stilts. Most of the prisoners, including Gillmore, stayed in one large room of the hut; soldier Bruce, sailor Edwards, and civilian O'Brien occupied the small adjacent room. All three men were suffering from fever and dysentery, and believed that whatever was under way—most likely a protracted hike up into the mountains—was not survivable. They were slowly deteriorating, sliding toward death.

The possibility of escape had been discussed among the group before, but Gillmore had angrily dismissed the idea each time with the same response: "Why man, that would be suicide, just like jumping off a bluff!" By now, Bruce, Edwards, and O'Brien felt they had no other choice but to act on their own. This time, they would not bring it up with Gillmore, knowing he would merely attempt to overrule them. This was no longer about following orders; it was about survival.

Lying awake with churning stomachs, the three prisoners listened to Tinio's soldiers straggling about the town and waited for the right moment. Unfortunately, too many people were up and about. If their escape was to be successful, the prisoners would need to rethink their plan. They needed to add the element of a ruse. It was agreed that Edwards would take an empty water jar, climb down the ladder, and ask the guards for permission to go to the river to refill it. Presumably, he would be escorted by a contingent of armed guards, as had happened in the past. Edwards was to make plenty of noise during all of this, to cover the exit of Bruce and O'Brien down the back ladder. The two would escape into the brush, quickly take the narrow trail through the tall canebrake to the river, and wait for Edwards and his escort. When they passed, Bruce and O'Brien would club the guards senseless, and Edwards would join his comrades to make their getaway to freedom.

The plan was put into motion. This time, to the great surprise of the prisoners, Edwards was sent to the river for drinking water without an escort. Bruce and O'Brien were nearly incredulous; there would be no need for violence. They slipped down the ladder and rushed into the brush. Breathless with adrenaline, hearts pumping, the three escapees regrouped and waded into the swift Abra River. They swam across, setting the water jug adrift at midstream.

Reaching the opposite bank, they climbed out and stealthily made their way down along the riverbank. As the first rays of morning light broke over the horizon, they frantically searched for somewhere, anywhere, to hide. Out of time, they scrambled to the top of the promontory and wedged themselves among the rocks and brush. High and hidden from view, they had a sight line on the possible approaches by their guards from their camp. Sopping wet and chilled by the cool mountain air, the three ailing men dropped into fitful sleep, their stomachs gnarled with cramps caused by the dysentery. There they lay in silent agony until the sun rose completely, removing their cloak of darkness.

With the full morning light came the reverberating alarm of a gong, followed by excited shouts. The hunt was on. Rebel patrols moved out, searching the scrub brush and riverbanks. The three escapees lay as still as possible, until a gaggle of chattering crab-eating macaques swarmed the tree branches overhead, squealing in consternation at the intruders in their habitat. Convinced that the monkeys' din would attract a patrol, the prisoners tried to silence the excited primates with handfuls of thrown rocks. The assault only ratcheted up their volume. The men finally tried turning away and ignoring them, praying for silence. Thankfully, their novelty wore off and the monkeys settled.

Sunlight warmed the rocks throughout the day, and the three men lay completely still, wedged in place. But soon, thirst began to parch their throats. They berated themselves for not bringing water; to think they had even had a jug in their hands and discarded it in the river. Down below, the insurgent teams were busy patrolling suspected sections of brush, hoping to flush their prey. After a few hours, the frustrated search teams gave up their quest and returned to camp. The three prisoners remained silent, still.

Finally, the harsh tropical sun moved toward the horizon and began to set. The air cooled. The three men had survived the day. They made their way down from their rocky promontory, covering their tracks, and kept moving. Edwards and O'Brien were barefoot; Bruce had barely serviceable shoes that soon fell apart. They worked their way back to a tributary of the Abra River, slaked their severe thirst, and then quietly slid into the water. Carried along on the current, they half-floated and half-swam for about a mile, arriving at a rocky shoal, an ideal location to climb ashore without leaving any footprints.

Out in the night, again, wet to the bone, stomachs afire with infection, the three prisoners headed to the distant sea coast. As the trails became wider and more worn, they stopped worrying about the footprints they were leaving behind. At one point, moving at a jog, the prisoners froze at the sound of approaching horses. They dove into a muddy ditch just seconds before a Filipino cavalry patrol passed, their mounts snorting, possibly aware of the breathless forms hiding just yards away. To the Americans' amazement, the soldiers passed unaware of their presence. Within moments, the three escapees were again on the run down the dark road, barefoot, anxiously glancing over their shoulders.

Bruce, Edwards, and O'Brien finally arrived at the ferry crossing at Bangued and slipped back into the river. Holding hands, they fought the current together. But by mid-river, it was clear that it needed to be every man for himself. Separating, each called upon a final burst of energy, tapping unknown reserves for the very hope of survival.

"We landed almost a mile below where we started in and climbed out on the bank looking like three drowned rats," Edwards recounted. "It was some time before we could go on, as we were all nearly exhausted by the long swim. It was only the thought of freedom and home that buoyed our spirits and gave us the strength to go on."

Sitting in the darkness, the three escaped prisoners assessed the decreasing menu of options before them. There was no place to hide, and in their current state of hunger, weakness, and pain, it was unlikely they could cover much more distance on foot. They needed to eat. The decision was made: They would risk going into town in search of food and, perhaps more importantly, information.

They entered Bangued from the northeast, moving as quietly as they could through the unlit narrow streets toward the plaza. If American forces had bivouacked in the town, that's where they would be found. White flags of surrender hung from every house, though every structure they passed appeared deserted.

Stepping into the shadows of the empty plaza, the three escapees stopped to confer. They could move up into the mountains to hide and wait for the Americans, with the hope that they would come soon. Or they could gather up some bamboo poles, fashion a makeshift raft, and attempt to float thirty miles down the Abra River to Vigan, where they were sure Americans were encamped. Or, thirdly, they could try to find at least one friendly resident in Bangued of whom they could inquire about the location of American forces. They knew the local population had an uncanny ability to track the movements of American forces, and with a striking level of accuracy.

"Hunger got the best of the argument, and we decided to seek out the house of our former jailer, who had been friendly to us," recalled Edwards. They stumbled through the town's narrow, cobblestone streets to the house of Señor Mateo, the man responsible for their captivity for the past three months. A faint light danced in the window. Someone was home.

It was a huge gamble to approach the enemy for a hiding place and sustenance. It could easily go badly, and quickly—especially if American forces had passed through and caused any suffering to the town's residents. O'Brien pushed for a consensus, saying, "Let's take a shot at it." Bruce and Edwards agreed. They devised a plan: Edwards would go up the stairs and knock on the door. Bruce and O'Brien would stand guard at each end of the street. If it was safe, they would join him. Edwards made his way up the creaky wooden stairs, barefoot and still drenched from his swim across the river. He paused, took a breath, and rapped on Señor Mateo's door.

"*Quién está?*" came the response.

"It's Edwards, one of the American prisoners."

The door opened slowly. His former prison warden stood before him, smiling, graciously inviting him in. In the *sala*, the living room, several other men sat silently, barely illuminated by the flicker of candlelight. Edwards explained that he had two companions waiting down below. Bring them up, Mateo urged, and Edwards gave the signal. O'Brien entered slowly, surveying the room. Spying a large chest by the door with several bolos casually placed on top, he moved toward it and sat down, the weapons within reach in the event things went awry. With two bolos, O'Brien figured, he could surely dole out some damage.

Señor Mateo was effusive. He explained that a large American *El Kapitan*, on a huge horse—much larger than their native ponies—had ridden into town with more than a hundred American soldiers on foot. Mateo then turned his attention to the men, commenting in Spanish, "You must be hungry, and all I have is some cold rice and fish."

The famished men smiled gratefully and were soon devouring the stale food as the warden continued his tale. That enormous horse—the sheer size of it was truly incredible, he gushed. More surprising, Mateo added, was that the Americans had treated the Filipinos well. They had arrived at noon, the same day the prisoners had been marched out to Danglas.

After spending several hours in the town, the Americans—and that huge horse—had left for La Paz, heading northwest, in pursuit of Tinio and his prisoners. By Mateo's estimate, the American soldiers were now likely camped up the road, just a few miles from where the three men had escaped. The prisoners savored the irony: Had they stayed where they were, they would have reached the American forces long ago. Now, they would need to double back, covering thirty arduous miles in total, all of it unnecessary.

Mateo assigned a guide to lead Bruce, Edwards, and O'Brien through the night toward La Paz. They pushed forward with every ounce of their strength. As they neared the foot of the hill where it was believed the American forces were camped, O'Brien, the once-fearless world adventurer, simply quit. He lay down on the ground and refused to move. No more, not another step, he sighed. He was done; there was nothing left. Bruce and Edwards desperately encouraged him on. Go ahead, leave me, O'Brien argued. No, they responded, if they did that, he might be captured and killed. "What of it," he exhaled. "That would be a relief."

Left without much choice, Bruce and Edwards turned to the guide, who pointed to the crest of a distant hill. "You will find the Americans there," the guide said. "Now, I am going. Thank you." The guide disappeared in one direction and the two exhausted prisoners staggered in another, leaving O'Brien sprawled out on the ground between them.

Bruce and Edwards pressed forward, making one last push. Halfway up the hill, they were confronted by the startled American sentries settled behind a rock, rifles drawn. The soldiers demanded that the intruders halt and identify themselves.

And now here they were, telling their story.

Lieutenant Colonel Howze immediately sent a squad of five soldiers to bring in O'Brien, who quickly regained his will to live. The battalion commander then ordered everyone back to sleep for the few hours before daylight. In moments, under a blanket of stars and a half-crescent moon, the three exhausted, aching former prisoners of war slipped into deep, heavy sleep. Their ordeal was over.

Escape had come as a natural impulse to Bruce, Edwards, and O'Brien, who at great risk and against all odds had made their dramatic break from captivity. The balance of the prisoners, under armed guard, had at times conspired to make a similar exit, but had been either thwarted in their attempts or talked out of their proposed brash behavior by an ever-cautious Lieutenant Gillmore.

At daybreak on December 8, 1899, Howze's column and their three new additions were eating breakfast. Despite having only a few hours of slumber, Edwards remembered the meal as the best he had ever eaten—Swift's premium bacon, piping-hot coffee, and hardtack. The starved prisoners consumed all the bacon on hand and even tried to gnaw through some of the tough *carabao* meat the column had been holding in reserve.

After breakfast, the column marched on to Danglas, following a winding river for eleven miles into the mountains. Here, they encountered a community of long-haired, non-Christian tribal people who made the mountains of Abra their home. Dressed in loincloths, armed with spears, head axes, and shields, they appeared to the Americans as wild warriors from another world. The soldiers had heard tales from their native guides and scouts about these tribal people—tales of head-hunting and bizarre pagan rituals in the untamed Cordilleras. Now, meeting these fascinating warriors firsthand, the Americans gaped at them with a mix of caution and wonder.

Scattered about the settlement was indisputable evidence of a mad scramble into the mountains by Tinio's men. Eighty bull carts and sleds had been abandoned, while farther afield, where the trails grew narrow and more difficult to climb, other supplies had been dumped. Howze ordered the property burned and rallied his men to push on. They were close, right on Tinio's tail. But now they would also need guides to lead them through the uncharted territory they were about to enter. Arrangements were made with the native tribesmen, the Tinggians, for several guides. These hunters knew the terrain intimately and they could track; their knowledge and skills would be invaluable to the Americans.

With several Tinggian warriors on point, the column marched into the mountains, leaving smoldering piles of abandoned supplies in their wake. Over the next few miles, they stumbled across more ditched materiel: several hundred rifles, thousands of rounds of crated ammunition, reloading tools, cartridge presses, sheet copper, lead, and clothing. The rebels had jettisoned anything not absolutely critical for escape and survival. The retreat of Tinio's forces had become a rout.

Throughout the afternoon, the column followed a grassy trail along a knife-edged ridge. Their route gradually climbed into the main divide of the Cordillera mountain range and then spectacularly opened onto a richly forested promontory. Even at this altitude, the trail was still littered with abandoned pack animals and an odd assortment of jettisoned baggage. Penn recalled that the stunning old-growth forest, the inspiring vistas, and the chaos of a rout, "would have delighted a Remington or a Zogbaum," the two famous war artists of the day.

Before dusk, the American column passed through a stunning grove of majestic pine. In the crisp, biting air of high altitude, it was an environment of otherworldly beauty. Having covered more than twenty miles over rough, mountainous terrain, Howze ordered camp to be set in a deep canyon near the summit.

Colonel Hare's column, leading the chase from another direction, was also in aggressive pursuit of the Gillmore prisoners. They had camped overnight in San Jose, traversed the Abra River outside the settlement the following morning, and hiked to the settlement of Dolores. Arriving before midnight, they had found three Spanish women left behind by Tinio's men, former prisoners who helpfully advised that the insurgent column had passed by just two days prior, with the American captives in tow. Their best guess: Tinio's rear guard and the remaining prisoners were now somewhere near La Paz.

This critical information confirmed for Hare that he and his five companies of 33rd Infantry had actually gone in the wrong direction. They now needed to catch up to Howze and his three companies of the 34th Infantry, who were on the right trail. The lives of Gillmore and the rest of the prisoners, he knew, hung in the balance.

Early on December 9, Howze's men broke through a steep, pine-covered slope and spilled onto a sunlit, grassy summit. Whipped by a fierce wind, the men paused to take in a stunning view of Laoag Valley and the glistening blue sea below. Ahead, they traced the trail, a winding path etched into the grassy ridge, which ominously dropped into another deep, thickly forested canyon. Into that abyss, Tinio's rear guard had disappeared.

They pressed on. At one point, the advance stopped and huddled around a rock. Howze and the officers were called forward. Before them, the advance pointed out the oddest of signs. Scrawled on a boulder was a slogan, an advertisement, chalked out in smudged white letters: DRINK PABST BEER—AGGIE DRINKS IT. It had to have been written by one of the prisoners, but which one? Howze's soldiers could not have known, but it was the beer merchant George W. Langford, leaving a trail, albeit half-erased by irritated insurgents who passed after him, to guide his rescuers.

As the trail had become almost impossible to track, the inveterate marketer and salesman was making sure the American rescue stayed on course.

The terrain once again shifted from wooded forest to waist-high cogon grass land. Moving through the dry, golden field, the American column found more abandoned carts, rifles, ammunition, and several dead *carabao* that had collapsed under the duress of Tinio's forced retreat. The soldiers broke up the guns, bending their barrels and smashing their stocks. Ammunition was scattered into the canyons. The freshly expired *carabao*, chilled by the cool mountain air, were butchered to augment the Americans' diminishing rations. In pockets of trammeled grass, the soldiers also stumbled over several bodies. Apparently, they were Filipino fighters who had died of their wounds along the way and were left behind. Without the time or inclination to pursue a proper burial for these unfortunate casualties of war, the Americans left the dead where they lay.

By the afternoon, at the western edge of the plateau, the American column dropped into a rocky draw that snaked into a deep canyon rutted by a creek.

As the sun began to set, they emerged from the canyon and descended into the foothills that overlooked the fertile Ilocos valley. In a final firefight at a large granary, they jumped a squad of twelve rebels, leaving one wounded and dispersing the rest. Howze ordered camp again to be set and the granary's rice divided among his men. Now near Banna, the exhausted column hunkered down to sleep, having covered another punishing twenty miles along the Cordillera's formidable mountain trails.

Some twenty-three miles to the southeast at the town of Dolores, Hare and his men had also pitched camp, after staggering in past midnight. The colonel surveyed his 270 men. Nearly all had worn through their footwear and were now barefoot, with some beginning to succumb to malaria, dengue, and dysentery. Hare knew his column was breaking down. If he was to catch

Howze, his column would need to march at a forced pace, but less than half of the men were in any condition for such a march. It was time to cull his men. Hare ordered each company commander to select twenty men, who, in their judgment, would hold up under the rigors of the chase to come.

With the men chosen, a start was made the following afternoon, December 10, with one hundred men from the five companies, along with thirteen officers. Each soldier carried two days' worth of rations. The balance—some 150 men who were assessed to be either too sick, injured, or otherwise unable to press on— were ordered back to Vigan. Challenged to catch his counterpart and still lagging several days behind, Hare rallied his men forward.

On the same day, farther north, Howze and his men were also forging on. Daylight had found them moving down the river, burning warehouses and barracks in their wake. Somewhere before the town of Banna, a group of ponies they had chanced upon were pressed into service for a number of the barefoot men.

As night fell in Solsona, having traversed another twenty-one tiring miles, the lieutenant colonel and his men collapsed into an exhausted slumber.

Unknown to Howze at the time, additional American forces had in fact landed at Laoag. They had failed, however, to move beyond the town to close off the unguarded mountain routes to the east. With these passes remaining open, Tinio's rear guard had easily retreated into the Cordilleras without resistance. It was later learned that Tinio, encircled at Solsona, had cleverly slid through enemy lines dressed as a peasant woman to make his way back to Banna.

With Hare and Howze's columns in aggressive pursuit and American forces holding the coast, the Army of Liberation had once again evaporated. General Tinio and his prisoners had simply vanished like smoke. Despite this setback, the Americans were not about to give up.

At daybreak on December 11, Howze and his column marched from Solsona to Maananteng, a nearby barrio that stood vigil at the head of a yawning canyon leading into the Cordilleras. Latest intelligence suggested their quarry had fled through this steep, narrow canyon, a sharp wedge of geology carved over the millennia by the Cura River, a tributary of the Laoag River. If reports were right, Tinio's force had entered the canyon no more than twenty-four hours before.

Howze and his officers clustered around an old Spanish map. The canyon, they could see, led into the heart of the Cordilleras' wildest country, territory that remained uncharted and untamed. Now, it seemed, they might be in luck: If the frayed map was accurate, Tinio and his men were trapped, hemmed in by a ring of nearly impassable mountains. It was inconceivable that the insurgents could climb the near-vertical mountains, which peaked at over five thousand feet, and escape east across the range. Cornered into what the tattered map portrayed as a dead end, Tinio's forces could be chased down and the prisoners liberated.

With this news, excitement rippled across the American column. The end was in sight; they were close to completing their mission. But the short, hard morning march had demonstrated to Howze that his men were at the very end of their tether. The lieutenant colonel conferred with his officers. Their men had been marching and fighting from dawn to dusk and rotating on outpost guard duty at night. Most were thoroughly spent following the 350-mile trek from San Fernando to Maananteng. Over the past six days, following the Battle of Tangadan Pass, they had covered a hundred miles that included an armed encounter with dogged bands of insurgents practically every day.

The last two days covered a hard march through a wild, mountainous, uninhabited country over a narrow pack-trail. A count revealed just twelve pairs of shoes among the 130 bone-weary men. Even scrounging what they could from captured stores and the settlements they passed, the column had little food. If they were to go forward, it would be exclusively on foot. The trail through the mountains was known to be absolutely impassable for ponies or other pack animals. Every man who entered the canyon would have to be prepared to live off the land. Was it possible?

Howze conferred with his officers. Like Colonel Hare had done, they decided they would need to cull their 130 men and take only the strongest forward. Howze had the men lined up and examined by the regimental surgeon. A quick medical inspection would determine who would proceed on the final dash after Gillmore and his band of prisoners; the balance would be sent to Laoag for much-needed medical care. The surgeon quickly made the cut, picking from among the cowboys and carpenters, mechanics and miners, blacksmiths and butchers, to select a fighting force that would continue the hunt.

As Howze's men sorted themselves at Maananteng, Hare's haggard column arrived on the scene, making good time but at a cost. Of the 113 soldiers who had started from Dolores, 18 had dropped out due to exhaustion or damaged feet. Hare now had a near-broken force of 95 men, and all were fast playing out. The colonel held council with his officers. It was agreed to cull the men once again, choosing from the eclectic mix of ironworkers and oil-mill operators, dairymen and druggists, bookkeepers and bridge men. The five companies were surveyed, and 74 enlisted men—the most physically able—were offered up for the job.

Together, the two joined columns comprised a force of men 151 strong, a fraction of the almost 400 soldiers who had started out together at Tangadan Pass just nine days earlier. Given Hare's seniority, it was agreed he would take the lead, with his force of 13 officers and 74 enlisted men. Howze and his column of hand-picked men—6 officers, 59 enlisted men, and 1 Ilocano scout—would follow, as soon as critically needed supplies arrived from the coast. On the afternoon of December 13, 1899, Hare marched his chosen contingent into the rocky canyon in a final push. Two of his men, too lame to keep up, dropped out after the first mile.

A few miles up the rock-strewn river, Hare's men were caught up in a light skirmish. They quickly scattered the insurgents, but the encounter put the column on edge. Rocks and boulders littered their path, a few defaced by George Langford's whimsical graffiti. Now the phrases took on a touch of biting sarcasm: In one place, DRINK PABST'S BEER—AGGIE DRINKS IT, and in another, GILLMORE AND PARTY—ON THE ROAD TO HELL. Hare and his men were closing in.

CORDILLERAS

Nine days before, the Gillmore party had begun its trek into the Cordilleras—Lieutenant Gillmore on horseback, twenty-five fellow captives on foot, and two pet macaques on the shoulders of Privates Huber and Honnyman.

The captives were now part of the chaotic retreat of Tinio's dwindling band of soldiers from Bangued, assigned their own guard under a Filipino officer, Lieutenant Yuson. Five miles to the northeast at the town of Tayum, Tinio's column was joined by another retreating force led by General Benito Natividad—crippled from a wound—and his family. "All about us were frightened native people," Gillmore recalled, "a jabbering, shouting rout of men, women, children, chickens, Natividad and his staff, crazy wooden carts, bellowing *carabao*, loads of ammunition and rifles carried in the arms of almost naked conscripts, sick and wounded men struggling painfully along and begging in vain for an ox or a pony." The prisoners fell into the procession, arriving at the small town of Dolores by late afternoon.

The logistics of the retreat were challenging, particularly feeding the five hundred–odd people of the eclectic column. In the center of each camp, large iron cauldrons were set up to prepare and distribute soup and rice. The prisoners soon learned they needed to muscle their way to the front of the hungry crowd if they wanted to eat; the Filipino soldiers, Chinese *cargadores*, and Tinggian guides were already in a scrum for their scant share.

After a lean supper the march continued, a short three-mile jaunt to the settlement of San Juan, where they arrived around midnight.

The next day, the prisoners were marched without breakfast. Shortly after getting under way, a Filipino soldier galloped madly to the head of the column and presented Natividad with a message that seemed to bewilder him. The general held counsel with his officers and they decided to turn back. The huge column retraced its steps halfway to Dolores, and then cut across rice and cane fields into open country. The column pushed at pace over hills and across a number of small tributaries along a wide swath of riverbed until it finally reached the deserted settlement of La Paz by afternoon.

Gillmore had had enough. He requested rest, but Natividad would not permit it. The march needed to continue, and it did, for another fifteen miles over rough stony roads, up and down hills, until they at last came to the Tinggian village of Danglas. Faced with the arrival of the massive column, the local Tinggians had fled to the surrounding forest. After the prisoners had settled into their assigned bamboo hut, Yuson advised that if they wanted to eat, they would need to hunt down their own dinner. The hungry prisoners gave chase to abandoned Tinggian livestock and, after an hour, managed to club two pigs senseless and tackle six squawking chickens. They cooked up a fine supper, and Gillmore and his men went to sleep on full stomachs for the first time in days.

That was the evening, December 6, when Bruce, Edwards, and O'Brien had made their escape. The following morning, Tinio arrived, heard the news, and fumed. There was also word that just the day before, seven Spaniards had also escaped, but had been successfully chased down by their guards. Five of the men had been executed on the spot by Tinio's soldiers, one had drowned, and the last, presumably, had made it to freedom. Poor odds indeed.

But the search for the American escapees proved futile, and so the march resumed. Less than a few hundred yards on, the lumbering column met a steep trail and the weather warmed. Several of the load bearers, sixteen water buffalo, were hauling heavy sleds weighed down with Mexican silver. The burden was too much, and when the narrow path turned rough, the sleds broke apart. The bags of currency were shifted onto the backs of the *carabao*, but the straining animals refused to move. As a clutch of pack-train drivers discussed their dilemma, a small boy walked by with a stick in his hands. Unable to resist, he sharply punched one of the animals in the flanks. The *carabao* heaved up, kicked, and went scrambling over the bank. The bags burst open and their precious treasure—some $4,000 worth of dollar coins—scattered down the hillside and into the canyon. An infuriated Tinio arrived upon the scene, angrily unholstered his pistol, and shot one of the civilian pack-train drivers dead in his tracks.

From there, the hills grew steeper, the trail narrowed, and the river became treacherous. Yuson, his own horse tied to Gillmore's, led the way across the raging river. Suddenly, Yuson's horse was swept away, plunging Gillmore and the officer into the water in a blur of kicking, panicked animals. Both men managed to swim to shore, soaked and exhausted, half a mile downstream. Quartermaster William Walton recounted, with a touch of sarcasm, "One of the Spanish officers with us kindly lent him a spare horse, so he was able to continue his journey."

At dusk, the retreating column and their captives stopped to camp in a deep canyon. The prisoners slaked their thirst in a nearby cool stream, which would have to suffice for their dinner, too. Temperatures dropped, the high altitude delivering bitterly cold weather. By morning, all the men—prisoners and guards alike—were huddled around a small fire, trying to draw warmth into their chilled limbs.

At daylight on December 8, the march resumed, but by dusk, as they dropped into a valley near the present-day town of Nueva

Era, Ilocos Norte, the last, seemingly endless miles had reduced the prisoners to a crawl. Staggering to a halt, they found several hundred more Spanish prisoners camped with their own guard.

Since leaving Bangued four days earlier, Gillmore and his band of prisoners had traversed about forty miles, much of it over strenuous mountain terrain. Fearing they could not go another day without food, they summoned up the courage to slaughter one of the weaker horses. Gillmore and his men took the choice front- and hindquarters and passed the rest to the glum Spaniards. The gamey meat was cut up, threaded on wooden sticks, and roasted over an open fire. "If it was prime beef, I could not have enjoyed it any better," recalled Private Harry Huber.

As the men ate their roasted pack-animal supper, a rebel officer raced into camp on a wheezing gray horse, its nostrils foaming. The officer had orders for the entire column to move immediately; there could be no delay. The prisoners assumed this meant that an American rescue was near, so they stalled for time. The guards waved their bayonets about to get the prisoners moving. Pushed to their feet and poked along, dinner still in hand, the weary men stumbled into the night, Gillmore following on his horse. Guided by moonlight, they marched north, following a swift, ink-black river that snaked along the foothills of the looming Cordilleras.

For those on foot, the hike was as miserable as ever. They tripped over boulders, bruising shins and knocking knees. At midnight, the prisoners began to drop from exhaustion. Yuson had little choice but to stop and allow the men to rest. Four hours later, however, they were slogging through swampy, low country, and by mid-morning, they limped into a settlement where a long, hungry line of rebel soldiers and ragged Spaniards were already jostling for breakfast. Gillmore and his party elbowed their way into the pack to secure their handful of boiled rice.

Incessant marching and meager food continued as they made their way through Banna and Dingras. Gillmore and his men vigorously protested. They would not go any farther without a proper meal and rest. An argument ensued. The guards were assembled to prod the prisoners again, now seriously, at bayonet point. Seeing that resistance was futile, the prisoners got back on their feet. Outside of Dingras, however, their guard quickly lost their way and led the column into an impassable swamp. For two hours the weakened column marched in confused circles.

In the absolute dead of night, the column finally made the lowland Ilocano settlement of Solsona, having covered an exhausting twenty miles over the previous twenty-four hours. The Gillmore party collapsed in a rice granary, while the rest of the weary column scattered themselves about the village. In just hours, the approaching dawn would reveal that they had reached the mouth of a canyon that led back into the jagged, dark peaks of the Cordilleras beyond.

On the morning of December 10, the men were hurried off into the canyon and marched along a rocky riverbed until noon. Gillmore and his sailors had hiked through the mountain domain of the Ilongots when leaving Baler, and the domain of the Tinggians when retreating from Bangued.

Now, they were about to pass into the lands of the Apayao—known more accurately as the Isneg—who eked out a hard life among the steep cliffs overlooking the turbulent Apayao River. For nearly three hundred years, the Isneg had successfully thwarted attempts by the Spaniards to Christianize their people, resorting to punitive raids into the coastal lowlands to drive the point home. And, like the many other tribes of the Cordilleras, the Isneg were not just warriors and staunch defenders of their ancestral domain; they were also inveterate hunters of human heads.

An oblivious Gillmore party pressed on, unaware that Howze and his soldiers were on their trail, less than a day behind. But the increasing anxiety of their Filipino captors was surely evident. That afternoon brought a change in circumstances, when Gillmore and the twenty-two other prisoners were separated from

Tinio's command, which itself had splintered into smaller groups, moving in different directions.

The senior Filipino officer, Major Joaquin Natividad, the brother of the general—seeing his own forces starting to dissolve, and perhaps feeling the futility of their retreat—approached Gillmore. "Don't be discouraged," he advised, saying they would all soon be free.

Separated from the massive column for good, Gillmore and his ragged, barefoot band broke off from the riverbed, turning up a narrow trail into the mountains, accompanied by several pack horses and a guard of fourteen armed soldiers, under the command of Yuson. Just a short distance later, they struck a swift, chilly river. They followed it into another canyon, crossing it at every sharp twist and turn. Progress slowed to a crawl. The strong current tugged at the men's tattered clothing, in one instance tearing the legs off Huber's disintegrating pants. After an afternoon of hurried marching, they came upon an open gravel bed along the river and lay down for the night.

The constant effort to keep moving had left the column spent; they moved even more slowly after the sun came up. Before noon, one of the overworked pack horses collapsed from exhaustion. The prisoners and guards stopped to kill the animal, carve up the carcass, and roast the meat on wooden sticks. They packed all the remaining meat they could carry and trudged along trails until darkness. Again, they camped among the rocks of the same river, dining on the balance of the horsemeat under a brilliant canopy of stars.

On the morning of December 12, the prisoners moved out slowly, making a gorge by noon. As they climbed higher up a narrowing ravine, it was clear they would need to abandon the remaining animals. Yuson shot his own pony. The prisoners killed another two before letting the rest go. They cut up and bundled the flesh, each man carrying horsemeat on his shoulders.

Moving on, their advance brought them to steeper and rougher trails. In places, the prisoners had to crawl hand over hand, helping each other over the large boulders. It was now obvious that the rebel lieutenant had been ordered to take the prisoners to a location so wild and inaccessible that no sane American soldier would ever attempt a rescue. At times they had to cling to the rock walls with fingers and toes to inch themselves along. Gillmore later recalled, "The penalty of a single misstep [would have been] to dash to death into the rapids perhaps a hundred feet below." They had entered, he colorfully described, "a veritable devil's causeway." Just before dusk, they reached the head of the dark canyon and camped for the night, "more dead than alive."

The thirty-seven-man column consumed the last remnants of the rancid pack animals the next morning. At this point, Gillmore began to lose his sense of time. Their narrow, muddy trail climbed steeply up a pinestudded mountain. Now, Private Smith began to stumble and lag behind. And then he stopped. The guards forced Smith up, but he only walked another hundred yards before sinking again to the ground. Dragged onward, Smith eventually collapsed in a delirious heap. The guards circled, shouting angrily and kicking the catatonic soldier about the head. "I was so far gone that I do not remember I felt anything," Smith recounted. At this point, another prisoner—his name was not recorded—fainted from fever.

After a time, Smith collected his strength and they were able to stagger on. Toward evening, the column came upon three Isneg who had just finished their supper and were preparing to leave. The Isneg offered the little leftover rice they had, as well as some fermented sugarcane juice, for two pesos. As Huber recalled, "We also got some tobacco which gladdened the old sailors' hearts." The group stopped to camp for the night, despite the site offering nothing more than a few *nipa* huts. It was, however, near a fresh-water stream that allowed the men to rehydrate.

The night came on cold, and sleep was almost impossible. By morning, the hungry band of prisoners, along with their shivering armed hosts, awoke to find the mossy ground dusted with white frost. The prisoners were exhausted, and most of them were ill with fever, dysentery, and infection. They were completely out of food. Exposed to the elements, their situation was dire and deteriorating.

If this continued, they would surely die.

At Maananteng, Lieutenant Colonel Howze and his men waited impatiently for supplies. The delay paid an unexpected dividend, however; just after midnight on December 13, several 4th Cavalry soldiers arrived with an officer from Tinio's Brigade, Major Natividad, who had surrendered at Solsona just hours earlier. Exhausted from the chase, fearing death in the mountains, and having learned that his own brother, General Benito Natividad, was also planning to give it up, the major had slipped away from Tinio after being ordered to backtrack on the trail to find stragglers who had become disoriented in the night. Seizing the opportunity, the major had ditched his uniform, changed into civilian clothes, and beat a path to American lines.

Pressed by Howze, Natividad confirmed what everyone had feared: Tinio had ordered the Gillmore party prisoners separated and marched into the mountains. If the Americans attacked and the prisoners were not able to escape, Tinio had ordered his guardsmen "to kill them one by one, quietly and without the others knowing anything about it, only the officer to be saved." Seeing the faces of his inquisitors harden, Natividad emphatically added, "When I heard this barbarous order, I told the officers not to commit such an act of savagery . . . and they promised me they would not carry out the orders."

Howze knew he had to move. As if on cue, early on the morning of December 14, long-awaited supplies finally arrived. Howze pulled his men together and ordered them outfitted.

Major Penn, Captains French and Russell, First Lieutenants Heaton and Decker, along with fifty-nine enlisted men, the liberated prisoners Bruce, Edwards, and O'Brien, and their faithful Ilocano scout Espino were each given five days' half-rations to pack. Most took advantage of the navy shoes that had arrived with the supplies. Edwards, his feet swollen, scabbed, and scarred, continued to go barefoot as he had done for the past several months. At 10:00 a.m., Lieutenant Colonel Howze ordered his column to enter the canyon. They were nineteen hours behind Colonel Hare.

At midday, Howze and his men came upon a small group of stragglers from Tinio's rear guard. A brief skirmish left one insurgent dead and drove the rest off. By late afternoon, Howze ran into the same difficult terrain as Hare had—the canyon bed had become too rough for the pack ponies to traverse. Howze ordered one killed for meat and the rest sent back. After an hour's halt for supper, they were back on the trail. The moon rose early, three days shy from full, illuminating the column as it navigated the canyon's rocky bed, scrambled over great masses of boulders, and wound in and out of the shadows of the sheer granite walls that enveloped them.

Four hours later, Howze's 34th caught up with Hare's 33rd at the point where the trail split off from the river and cut into the mountains. Combining their forces, the two commands agreed to alternate leadership each day. The united column of 152 American soldiers, augmented by a complement of guides, scouts, and *cargadores*, trudged on.

In the early morning of December 15, the rescue climbed a harrowing trail that weaved up an almost-perpendicular mountain face. Progress was tedious, compounded by the slick soles of their navy shoes, which made it nearly impossible to gain a foothold. The breathless men stopped frequently, but finally reached the summit—likely in the shadows of Mount Licud, at an elevation of 5,900 feet—which offered a magnificent view of the distant Laoag valley below. It was truly spectacular country. The trail then dropped down, and after ten miles on a steep, narrow path, they set up camp at the foot of a bluff, beside a dank, gloomy brook.

The column broke camp by sunrise, with Howze leading. The forest trail cut high in the mountains and later, led the men up, down, and along limestone cliffs of the oddest formations. Having crossed the principal range of the Cordilleras, the column came across the first human habitation they had seen since leaving Maananteng, where they once again ran into Tinio's rear guard. Several rebel soldiers were killed, a few captured, and two fled, abandoning their Mausers in a panic. The Americans assumed these soldiers would race ahead to warn their comrades that their pursuers were closing in. Every indication at this point suggested the rescue party was on track.

Late that day, as the sun disappeared beyond the range, the trail descended to a stony riverbed carved in a canyon, where it was again impossible to determine the route taken by the prisoners. The men fanned out, searching for clues, poking about the brush, studying impressions in the earth, and following their instincts. One of the men ran back to Hare, holding a single sheet of yellowed paper, torn on one edge. He had found it fluttering in the wind. Hare studied the sheet, his eyes narrowing. It was a page from a US Navy memorandum book with a cryptic entry, written in Gillmore's hand.

It explained that Gillmore expected to be killed.

Daybreak on December 17 found the rescuers making slow progress. Their one map was poorly drawn and outdated, offering only a rough approximation of where they were. Again studying the ground for clues, the men found a fresh path and footprints along the banks of the river, and followed it until the trail came to an end. Here, they could see that a footpath turned into the river and continued on the opposite bank. The river would need to be crossed. A quick scouting of the area located, oddly, several abandoned bamboo rafts.

The rafts were tied together with rope and assembled into a ferry. The soldiers stripped down, placed their clothes on the rafts, and waded across. On the northern bank of the river, they again found more of Langford's witticisms scratched out on the rocks, confirming they were on track. The first men over also found a message ominously etched into the sand: "Here we are, God knows where."

A day earlier, the Gillmore party prisoners had been on a relentless march through remote Isneg settlements, scrounging together, through purchase or theft, whatever sugarcane, sweet potatoes, and rice they could find. Then, they dropped down to a wide, turbulent river. The Filipinos, having earlier pressed several Isneg warriors into the role of guides, ordered the men to construct several bamboo rafts. Once completed, the column had floated across the frothy current in small groups. The rafts were then abandoned.

That afternoon, the prisoners and guards followed the course of the river on foot, along its banks, until they were overtaken by darkness. At that point, the group of twenty prisoners and fourteen guards arrived at a small gravel bed along the riverbank, hemmed in by sheer, granite cliffs.

That evening, the guards moved off about fifty yards and camped by themselves among the rocks at a distance. Every night prior, they had camped together with the prisoners. Something, the prisoners sensed, was not right. The prisoners were sitting around a fire discussing their predicament when Lieutenant Yuson approached with a grim look. He stopped, stuttered for a bit, and then blurted out in Spanish, "General Tinio gave me orders to shoot you when we reached the mountains." The startling message was slowly translated by the bilingual men in the group. The prisoners stood in alarm, dumbfounded at the turn of events. Hospital Corpsman Huber recalled, "It was terrible to think we had marched all that distance and suffered such privations, only to be shot down like dogs in the heart of the wilderness of northern Luzon."

After a moment's silence, one that seemed to take an age to pass, the lieutenant continued, saying, "But I do not want the stain of your blood upon my head, so I will abandon you here."

The prisoners immediately began to reason with him. In broken Spanish and with frantic gestures, several theatrically explained that they almost preferred to be shot than left to starve or be killed by the Isneg.

Yuson responded that American forces were on their trail and would arrive in days. He turned and started off. The prisoners called to him, begging not to be abandoned without at least a gun for their defense. Yuson stopped, said that he would check with his soldiers, and disappeared among the rocks.

He returned a minute later on the run, breathlessly exclaiming, "My soldiers have left me and it is my duty to follow them." In a final gasp of desperation, Gillmore yelled out to the lieutenant, offering every protection and $500 in gold if he would stay to guide them to American lines. It was not to be. In this remote wilderness, where each man's survival hung in the balance, the offer was meaningless. "Adios!" Yuson called back, waving good-bye, and disappeared for good.

Enveloped in darkness, and having never felt more alone, the prisoners regrouped, sat down, and tried to make sense of events. Their main concern now was the Isneg head-hunters, who they believed would soon rush the defenseless men. To be sure, their column had raided Isneg settlements and abused their inhabitants along the way; retribution would be only logical.

For now, to get through the night, they decided to divide the party. Half would stand guard while the others slept, and vice versa, in shifts. The only weapons at their disposal were two small axes and an old bolo, which one of the men had found at one of the *rancherias* and had concealed in his bundle. Each man collected a pile of stones for himself, which they agreed would serve as "formidable weapons in the hands of desperate men." Cold, hungry, and exposed to the elements, the twenty prisoners huddled together. Half of the men eyed the awful shadows, while the rest made their best effort to sleep.

At first light, the cold and weary prisoners awoke among the rocks on the riverbank, without their guard, alone in the unknown Cordillera wilderness. A weakened Gillmore convened a meeting to discuss their options again. Some spoke in favor of retracing the route back to the Ilocos coast, arguing that they already knew the country. Others suggested it would be better to build rafts and float down the nameless river; surely it had to bring them to the sea. The majority sided with taking rafts down the river. And while seniority and rank meant nothing in these mountains, the men still wanted structure and leadership. Gillmore, coughing, pale, and dazed, but still the only officer present, was elected their commander.

The abandoned prisoners began a march down the riverbank in search of a location to assemble a new flotilla of rafts. Several miles on, their trail terminated at a sheer rock face, which jutted into the swift, foaming rapids. Further passage was impossible. As the men searched for a way around this barrier, a group of Isneg arrived, armed with spears and bows and arrows. One let out a horrifying yell before retreating from view. Panicked, Gillmore and his men quickly took cover behind some rocks and tried to decide what to do.

Huber spied what looked like a grove of bamboo on the opposite bank and volunteered to swim over to scope it out. Gillmore agreed. Huber made the swim, confirmed his find, and motioned for the other men to join him. Ten more men swam over with the two axes and the dull bolo, cut a number of long poles, and pulled them back across the river. In time, they had a collection of one hundred poles, each about twenty feet long. Some quick math determined a raft composed of fourteen poles could accommodate three or so men. They would need at least six rafts.

The construction was laborious and slow. To their dismay, a full morning's effort resulted in a single raft. As the men rested, three unarmed Isneg appeared some two hundred yards out in the brush and began to make friendly signs. Gillmore suggested that Huber, who had picked up a few words of the Ilocano dialect, should parley and see what they wanted.

Huber walked out to meet one of the Isneg, who cautiously came down to the bank. Huber motioned that they had been left by the Filipino soldiers with nothing to eat and would like to buy some rice. Huber offered money, but the Isneg man was not interested. Instead, he pointed to Huber's shirt. The hospital corpsman quickly pulled it off and handed it over. The man smiled and nodded. Behind him, another Isneg ran off, returning minutes later with a supply of rice and several more companions.

Huber, thinking the Isneg might help with the rafts, gestured for them to follow him. The group arrived at the camp, saw the number of rafts under construction, and began negotiating: one shirt per raft. A deal was struck. Soon, the five muscular Isneg men were busy building the remaining rafts with their sharp axes and, within half an hour, the task was done. More rice and a few coconuts were delivered to the group. The Isneg, content with their day's work and the bountiful trade, disappeared into the forested mountains.

The abandoned prisoners watched as night again fell, worried that the Isneg might return to divest them of the last pieces of their wardrobe. The same guard arrangements were put into place for the night, working in shifts, to ensure that any attack would at least be preceded by an alarm.

Shortly after daybreak on December 18, a few of the men tested their new rafts. They were buoyant, but each was in fact only good for two men, not three. More rafts would be needed. Huber and Sackett started out to try to find the Isneg to help them once again; they knew their settlement had to be close.

A trail was located, but only a few steps along it, Sackett screamed and fell to the ground in agony. He had impaled his left foot on two sharpened bamboo stakes buried on the path. One razor-sharp stake had sliced into the ball of his foot and another into the heel, disabling him. Sackett had stumbled upon a typical Isneg defense set to protect their crops and villages. Huber carried Sackett back to camp, where the men were sitting around a small, crackling fire. Sackett's injuries, they felt, were an ominous sign, maybe even part of a trap to take them all down, one by one. It was decided they would immediately start down the river on what would be crowded, unstable rafts.

As the worried and weakened prisoners rushed to get onto the river, they heard the report of a revolver and loud shouts—an attack! Startled, the men instinctively closed together as a group, grabbing sticks and rocks to defend themselves.

Another yell, strangely familiar, and the men turned to one another in disbelief.

Salvation

With Lieutenant Decker and his scouts leading the way, the men commanded by Colonel Hare and Lieutenant Colonel Howze were once again on the move. The steep terrain brought progress to a crawl. Shortly after 8:00 a.m., the advance returned to report that the Gillmore party was in sight. Hare and Howze moved to the front of the column to verify the news, surveying the horizon with their field binoculars. Sure enough, the trail following the riverbank ran through a patch of cogon grass, about eight feet tall, and emerged on a rock-strewn gravel bar. Ahead, the two commanders could count the twenty-odd prisoners, perhaps 150 yards away, building rafts at the water's edge. But something was clearly wrong. Tinio's soldiers were missing. A few large boulders hid the lower end of the gravel bar from view. They concluded that the prisoners' captors must be there, out of their line of sight.

Hare sent three details of soldiers to approach from the front and both flanks, and surround the group without being detected. On an agreed-upon signal—a shot from the colonel's revolver—every man was to simultaneously rush the prisoners' location, but hold their fire. The last thing they wanted was to shoot any of the prisoners by mistake. Once his soldiers were in place, Hare gripped his pistol and squeezed off a shot. Rifles up and ready, the three details rushed the party while shouting, "Get down, get down!"

Gillmore and his men did everything *but* get down. Upon hearing the American soldiers, they dropped their rocks and sticks and rushed toward them in an eruption of joy. The anxious soldiers, rifles still raised, clumsily raced past them, charging the harmless boulders beyond, slowing into confusion at the absence of an insurgent defense.

Huber ran to Hare with tears streaming down his face.

"Are you all here?" the colonel shouted.

"Yes!" Huber cried.

"Is Lieutenant Gillmore here?" the colonel asked. Huber nodded yes.

"Thank God!" Hare gasped, keenly aware of his triumph. Hobbling forward, the famed Gillmore, visibly confused, weakly approached Hare. Slowly, the dazed lieutenant realized that he was free.

The prisoners embraced their rescuers, laughing and crying, overwhelmed with emotion. The soldiers, in return, gave the prisoners a series of rousing cheers, the commotion reverberating against the canyon's sheer walls, echoing across the heart of the Cordilleras.

Hare and Howze had pulled it off.

2

My Cave Life in Vicksburg

Mary Loughborough

SUNDAY, THE 17TH. 1863—THE MEMORABLE SEVENTEENTH OF May—as we were dressing for church and had nearly completed the arrangement of shawls and gloves, we heard the loud booming of cannon. Frightened, for at this time we knew not *what* "an hour would bring forth," seeing no one who might account for the sudden alarm, we walked down the street, hoping to find some friend that could tell us if it were dangerous to remain away from home at church. I feared leaving my little one for any length of time, if there were any prospect of an engagement.

After walking a square or two, we met an officer, who told us the report we heard proceeded from our own guns, which were firing upon a party of soldiers, who were burning some houses on the peninsula on the Louisiana shore; he told us, also, it had been rumored that General Pemberton had been repulsed—that many citizens had gone out to attend to the wounded of yesterday's battle—all the ministers and surgeons that could leave had also gone.

Still, as the bell of the Methodist church rang out clear and loud, my friend and I decided to enter, and were glad that we did so, for we heard words of cheer and comfort in this time of trouble. The speaker was a traveller, who supplied the pulpit this day, as the pastor was absent ministering to the wounded and dying on the battle field. This was a plain man, of simple, fervent words, but with so much of heart in all his exercises, that we felt, after the last hymn had been sung, the last prayer said, that we had been in a purer atmosphere.

After the blessing, he requested the ladies to meet and make arrangements for lint and bandages for the wounded. As we returned home, we passed groups of anxious men at the corners, with troubled faces; very few soldiers were seen; some battery men and officers, needed for the river defences, were passing hastily up the street. Yet, in all the pleasant air and sunshine of the day, an anxious gloom seemed to hang over the faces of men: a sorrowful waiting for tidings, that all knew now, would tell of disaster.

There seemed no life in the city; sullen and expectant seemed the men—tearful and hopeful the women—prayerful and hopeful, I might add; for, many a mother, groaning in spirit over the uncertainty of the welfare of those most dear to her, knelt and laid her sorrows at the foot of that Throne, where no earnest suppliant is ever rejected; where the sorrow of many a broken heart has been turned in resignation to His will who afflicts not willingly the children of men.

And so, in all the dejected uncertainty, the stir of horsemen and wheels began, and wagons came rattling down the street— going rapidly one way, and then returning, seemingly, without aim or purpose: now and then a worn and dusty soldier would be seen passing with his blanket and canteen; soon, straggler after straggler came by, then groups of soldiers worn and dusty with the long march.

"What can be the matter?" we all cried, as the streets and pavements became full of these worn and tired-looking men. We sent down to ask, and the reply was: "We are whipped; and the Federals are after us." We hastily seized veils and bonnets, and walked down the avenue to the iron railing that separates the yard from the street.

VIEW FROM THE COURTHOUSE

The next morning all was quiet; we heard no startling rumors; the soldiers were being gathered together and taken out into the rifle pits; Vicksburg was regularly besieged, and we were to stay at our homes and watch the progress of the battle. The rifle pits and intrenchments were almost two miles from the city. We would be out of danger, so we thought; but we did not know what was in preparation for us around the bend of the river. The day wore on; still all was quiet.

At night our hopes revived: the Federal troops had not yet come up—another calm night and morning. At three o'clock that evening, the artillery boomed from the intrenchments, roar after roar, followed by the rattle of musketry: the Federal forces were making their first attack. Looking out from the back veranda, we could plainly see the smoke before the report of the guns reached us.

Our anxiety was great, indeed, having been told by gentlemen the night before, that the works in the rear of Vicksburg were anything but of a superior kind.

It was amid the clump of trees on the far distant hillside, that the Federal batteries could be discerned by the frequent puffings of smoke from the guns. Turning to the river, we could see a gunboat that had the temerity to come down as near the town as possible and lay just out of reach of the Confederate batteries, with steam up.

Two more lay about half a mile above and nearer the canal; two or three transports had gotten up steam and lay near the mouth of the canal. Below the city a gunboat had come up and landed, out of reach, on the Louisiana side, striving to engage the lower batteries of the town—firing about every fifteen minutes. While we were looking at the river, we saw two large yawls start out from shore, with two larger boats tied to them, and full of men.

We learned that they were the Federal prisoners that had been held in the town, and to-day paroled and sent over to the Federal encampment, so that the resources of the garrison might be husbanded as much as possible, and the necessity of sustaining them avoided.

The idea made me serious. We might look forward truly now to perhaps real suffering.

Yet, I did not regret my resolution to remain, and would have left the town more reluctantly to-day than ever before, for we felt that now, indeed, the whole country was unsafe, and that our only hope of safety lay in Vicksburg.

Next day, two or three shells were thrown from the battle field, exploding near the house. This was our first shock, and a severe one. We did not dare to go in the back part of the house all day.

Some of the servants came and got down by us for protection, while others kept on with their work as if feeling a perfect contempt for the shells.

In the evening we were terrified and much excited by the loud rush and scream of mortar shells; we ran to the small cave near the house, and were in it during the night, by this time wearied and almost stupefied by the loss of sleep.

The caves were plainly becoming a necessity, as some persons had been killed on the street by fragments of shells. The room that I had so lately slept in had been struck by a fragment of a shell during the first night, and a large hole made in the ceiling. I shall never forget my extreme fear during the night, and my utter hopelessness of ever seeing the morning light. Terror stricken, we remained crouched in the cave, while shell after shell followed each other in quick succession.

Morning found us more dead than alive, with blanched faces and trembling lips. We were not reassured on hearing, from a man who took refuge in the cave, that a mortar shell in falling would not consider the thickness of earth above us a circumstance.

The next morning we heard that Vicksburg would not in all probability hold out more than a week or two, as the garrison was poorly provisioned; and one of General Pemberton's staff officers told us that the effective force of the garrison, upon being estimated, was found to be fifteen thousand men; General Loring having been cut off after the battle of Black River, with probably ten thousand.

One afternoon, amid the rush and explosion of the shells, cries and screams arose—the screams of women amid the shrieks of the falling shells. One man, after starting and coming back once or twice, his timidity overcoming his curiosity, at last gathered courage to go to the ravine near us, from whence the cries proceeded, and found that someone had been buried alive within a cave, he being alone at that time. Workmen were instantly set to deliver him, if possible; but when found, the unfortunate man had evidently been dead some little time.

This incident made me doubly doubtful of my cave; I feared that I might be buried alive at any time. Another incident happened the same day: A gentleman, resident of Vicksburg, had a large cave made, and repeatedly urged his wife to leave the house and go into it. She steadily refused, and, being quite an invalid, was lying on the bed, when he took her by the hand and insisted upon her accompanying him so strongly, that she yielded; and they had scarcely left the house, when a mortar shell went crashing through, utterly demolishing the bed that had so lately been vacated, tearing up the floor, and almost completely destroying the room.

The cave we inhabited was about five squares from the levee. A great many had been made in a hill immediately beyond us; and near this hill we could see most of the shells fall. Caves were the fashion—the rage—over besieged Vicksburg.

It was about four o'clock, one Wednesday evening—the shelling during the day had gone on about as usual—I was reading in safety, I imagined, when the unmistakable whirring of Parrott shells told us that the battery we so much feared had opened from the intrenchments. I ran to the entrance to call the servants in; and immediately after they entered, a shell struck the earth a few feet from the entrance, burying itself without exploding. I ran to the little dressing room, and could hear them striking around us on all sides. I crouched closely against the wall, for I did not know at what moment one might strike within the cave.

A man came in much frightened, and asked to remain until the danger was over. The servants stood in the little niche by the bed, and the man took refuge in the small ell where I was stationed. He had been there but a short time, standing in front of me, and near the wall, when a Parrott shell came whirling in at the entrance, and fell in the centre of the cave before us all, lying there smoking.

Our eyes were fastened upon it, while we expected every moment the terrific explosion would ensue. I pressed my child closer to my heart, and drew nearer to the wall. Our fate seemed almost certain. The poor man who had sought refuge within was most exposed of all. With a sudden impulse, I seized a large double blanket that lay near, and gave it to him for the purpose of shielding him from the fragments; and thus we remained for a moment, with our eyes fixed in terror on the missile of death, when a young boy rushed forward, seized the shell, and threw it into the street, running swiftly in the opposite direction.

Fortunately, the fuse had become nearly extinguished, and the shell fell harmless—remaining near the mouth of the cave, as a trophy of the fearlessness of the servant and our remarkable escape.

And so the weary days went on—the long, weary days—when we could not tell in what terrible form death might come to us before the sun went down.

Sitting in the cave, one evening, I heard the most heartrending screams and moans. I was told that a mother had taken a child into a cave about a hundred yards from us; and having laid it on its little bed, as the poor woman believed, in safety, she took her seat near the entrance of the cave. A mortar shell came rushing through the air, and fell with much force, entering the earth above the sleeping child—cutting through into the cave—oh! most horrible sight to the mother—crushing in the upper part of the little sleeping head, and taking away the young innocent life without a look or word of passing love to be treasured in the mother's heart.

At ten or twelve o'clock, we saw, in spite of the continual falling of the shells, gentlemen hurrying toward the river. Soon we heard the Confederate river batteries booming loudly, and then all was silent. What could it mean? I did not venture to look without; and so I sat waiting for some one to come to me. At last a friend appeared, who, in the most triumphant manner, told us that the Confederates had routed the Federal fleet.

A friend came soon after and told me that I would find my home on the battle field far more pleasant and safe than the one in town—that we were protected from the fragments only in our cave—that on the battle field the missiles were of far less weight, and in falling far less dangerous.

I was sitting near the entrance, about five o'clock, thinking of the pleasant change—oh, bless me!—that to-morrow would bring, when the bombardment commenced more furiously than usual, the shells falling thickly around us, causing vast columns of earth to fly upward, mingled with smoke. As usual, I was uncertain whether to remain within or run out. As the rocking and trembling of the earth was very distinctly felt, and the explosions alarmingly near, I stood within the mouth of the cave ready to make my escape, should one chance to fall above our domicile.

In my anxiety I was startled by the shouts of the servants and a most fearful jar and rocking of the earth, followed by a deafening explosion, such as I had never heard before. The cave filled instantly with powder smoke and dust. I stood with a tingling, prickling sensation in my head, hands, and feet, and with a confused brain. Yet alive!—was the first glad thought that came to me;—child, servants, all here, and saved!—from some great danger, I felt. I stepped out, to find a group of persons before my cave, looking anxiously for me; and lying all around, freshly torn, rose bushes, arbor-vitæ trees, large clods of earth, splinters, pieces of plank, wood, &c.

I stood dismayed, and surveyed the havoc that had been made around me, while our little family under it all had been mercifully preserved.

This, only breaking the daily monotony of our lives!—this thrilling knowledge of sudden and horrible death occurring near us, told to-night and forgotten in to-morrow's renewal!—this sad news of a Vicksburg day.

A young girl, becoming weary in the confinement of the cave, hastily ran to the house in the interval that elapsed between the slowly falling shells. On returning, an explosion sounded near her—one wild scream, and she ran into her mother's presence, sinking like a wounded dove, the life blood flowing over the light summer dress in crimson ripples from a death-wound in her side, caused by the shell fragment.

A fragment had also struck and broken the arm of a little boy playing near the mouth of his mother's cave. This was one day's account.

The next morning at four o'clock, I was awakened by a perfect tumult in the air: the explosion of shrapnell and the rattling of shrapnell balls around us reminded me that my dangers and cares were not yet over. How rapidly and thickly the shells and Minié balls fell—Parrott of various sizes—canister and solid shot, until I was almost deafened by the noise and explosions! I lay and thought of the poor soldiers down below in the ravine, with only their tents over their heads; and it seemed in this storm of missiles that all must be killed. How strange so few casualties occur during these projectile storms!

Our little home stood the test nobly. We were in the first line of hills in back of the heights that were fortified; and, of course, we felt the full force of the very energetic firing that was constantly kept up; and being so near, many that passed over the first line of hills would fall directly around us.

The hill opposite our cave might be called "death's point" from the number of animals that had been killed in eating the grass on the sides and summit. In all directions I can see the turf turned up, from the shells that have gone ploughing into the earth. Horses or mules that are tempted to mount the hill by the promise of grass that grows profusely there, invariably come limping down wounded, to die at the base, or are brought down dead from the summit.

I laughed heartily at the appearance of the cave. The logs of the roof were hung with festoons of jerked meat, that swung gracefully and constantly above us; and walking around under it, I felt, quite like an Indian, I suppose, after a successful chase, that starvation for a while was far in the background.

I heard, one night, a soldier down the ravine singing a weird, melodious hymn; and, amid the firing and crashing of projectiles, it floated up to me in soft, musical undertones that were fascinating in the extreme: the wailing of the earthly unrest—the longing for the glorious home that the warm imagery pictures to be glorious in golden lights and silvery radiance—of song and brilliant happiness! The voice was full and triumphant.

Then the rapid change, in low and mournful cadence, to the earth, the clay, the mire—to dearth, to suffering, to sin! "I wonder, Lord, will I ever get to heaven—to the New Jerusalem?" came with the ending of every verse. I bowed my face in my hands. Yes! Heaven was so far off! Yet—"he that cometh to me, I will in nowise cast out"—our grasp is firm, but our eyes are blind. Some day, after the earthly longings are stilled, we will know the exceeding glory.

I was sewing, one day, near one side of the cave, where the bank slopes and lights up the room like a window. Near this opening I was sitting, when I suddenly remembered some little article I wished in another part of the room. Crossing to procure it, I was returning, when a Minié ball came whizzing through the opening, passed my chair, and fell beyond it. Had I been still sitting, I should have stopped it. Conceive how speedily I took the chair into another part of the room, and sat in it!

The next day, the news came that one of the forts to the left of us had been undermined and blown up, killing sixty men; then of the death of the gallant Colonel Irwin, of Missouri; and again, the next day, of the death of the brave old General Green, of Missouri.

We were now swiftly nearing the end of our siege life: the rations had nearly all been given out. For the last few days I had been sick; still I tried to overcome the languid feeling of utter prostration.

I felt a strange unrest, the quiet of the day was so unnatural. I walked up and down the cave. The day was extremely warm, and came with a violent headache. I met an old soldier who told me that the Federal troops had acted splendidly; they were stationed opposite the place where the Confederate troops marched up and stacked their arms; and they seemed to feel sorry for the poor fellows who had defended the place for so long a time. Far different from what he had expected, not a jeer or taunt came from any one of the Federal soldiers. Occasionally, a cheer would be heard; but the majority seemed to regard the poor unsuccessful soldiers with a generous sympathy.

After the surrender, the old gray-headed soldier, in passing on the hill near the cave, stopped, and, touching his hat, said:

"It's a sad day this, madam; I little thought we'd come to it, when we first stopped in the intrenchments. I hope you'll yet be happy, madam, after all the trouble you've seen."

To which I mentally responded, "Amen."

Saturday evening, Vicksburg, with her terraced hills—with her pleasant homes and sad memories, passed from my view in the gathering twilight—passed, but the river flowed on the same, and the stars shone out with the same calm light!

But the many eyes—O Vicksburg!—that have gazed on thy terraced hills—on thy green and sunny gardens—on the flow of the river—the calm of the stars—those eyes! how many thou hast closed on the world forever!

3

A Prisoner's Diary

John L. Ransom

CAMP LAWTON, MILLEN, GA., NOV. 1.—ARRIVED AT OUR DES-
tination not far from midnight, and it was a tedious journey. Two
died in the car I was in. Were taken from the cars to this prison
in what they call ambulances, but what I call lumber wagons. Are
now congregated in the south-east corner of the stockade under
hastily put up tents.

This morning we have drawn rations, both the sick and the
well, which are good and enough. The stockade is similar to that
at Andersonville, but in a more settled country, the ground high
and grassy, and through the prison runs a stream of good pure
water, with no swamp at all. It is apparently a pleasant and healthy
location.

A portion of the prison is timber land, and the timber has
been cut down and lays where it fell, and the men who arrived
before us have been busily at work making shanties and places to
sleep in. There are about six thousand prisoners here, and I should
judge there was room for twelve or fifteen thousand. Men say they
are given food twice each day, which consists of meal and fresh
beef in rather small quantities, but good and wholesome.

The rebel officer in command is a sociable and kindly disposed man, and the guards are not strict, that is, not cruelly so. We are told that our stay here will be short.

Nov. 2.—Have seen many of my old comrades of Andersonville, among whom is my tried friend Sergt. Wm. B. Rowe; were heartily glad to see one another; also little Bullock who has improved wonderfully in appearance. Everyone is pleased with this place and are cheerful, hoping and expecting to be released before many weeks; they all report as having been well treated in Savannah and have pleasant recollections of that place; from what could be seen of the city by us prisoners it seems the handsomest one in America. Should judge it was a very wealthy place.

My duties as nurse are hard, often too much so for my strength, yet the enforced exercise does me good and continue to improve all the time. A cane will be necessary to my locomotion for a long time as am afraid myself permanently injured; my cane is not a gold headed one; it is a round picket which has been pulled off some fence.

Nov. 3.—About a hundred convalescents were taken outside to-day to be sent away to our lines the officials told us. At a later hour the commander came inside and said he wanted twelve men to fall into line and they did so, myself being one of the twelve; he proceeded to glance us over and on looking at me said: "Step back out of the ranks, I want only able-bodied men." I stepped down and out considerably chagrinned, as the general impression was that they were to go to our lines with the convalescents who had been taken outside before.

He marched off the twelve men and it then leaked out that they were to be sent to some prison to be held as hostages until the end of the war. Then I felt better.

Nov. 8.—All eager for news. Seems as if we were on the eve of something. So quiet here that it must predict a storm. Once in a while some pesky rebel takes it upon himself to tell us a lot of lies to the effect that our armies are getting beaten; that England joins the Confederacy to whip out the North; that there is no prospect of ending the war; that we are not going to be exchanged at all, but remain prisoners, etc., etc. If he is a good talker and tells his story well it makes us all blue and down-hearted.

Then, pretty soon, we are told more joyful news which we are ready to believe, and again take heart and think of the good times coming. Would like to hear the election news. Wonder who is elected? Feel stronger every day, and have a little flesh on my bones. As the weather gets cool, we are made painfully aware of the fact that we are sadly deficient in clothing. Will freeze if compelled to stay through the winter.

One good sign—the rebels are making no more improvements about this prison; they say we are not to stay here long. We hear that our troops are marching all through the South. Guess that is the reason why they think of moving us all the time. All right, Johnny Rebels, hope we are an elephant on your hands.

Nov. 15.—At about six or seven o'clock last night six hundred men were taken away, making in all twelve hundred for the day; another six hundred are ready to go at a moment's notice. I don't know what to think. Can hardly believe they go to our lines. Seems almost like a funeral procession to me, as they go through the gate. Rowe and Hub Dakin talk of going to-day, if any go, having decided to flank. I have concluded to wait until it is my turn to go.

Later.—Eight hundred have gone, with Rowe and Dakin in the crowd, and I am here alone as regards personal friends. Could not be induced to go with them. Have a sort of presentiment that all is not right.

Still Later.—Six hundred more have gone, making 2,600 all together that have departed, all heavily guarded.

Nov. 17.—It is now said that the prisoners are being moved down on the coast near Florida. That coincides with my own view, and I think it very probable. Will try and go about to-morrow. Hardly think I can go to-day.

Later.—The to-day's batch are going out of the gate. Makes me fairly crazy to wait, fearful I am missing it in not going. This lottery way of living is painful on the nerves. There are all kinds of rumors. Even have the story afloat that now the raid is over that drove us away from Andersonville, we are going back there to stay during the war. That would be a joke.

Nov. 21.—Got up bright and early, went to the creek and had a good wash, came back, after a good walk over the prison, and ate my two large crackers and small piece of bacon left over from yesterday, and again ready for whatever may turn up. Lost my diminutive cake of soap in the water and must again take to sand to scrub with, until fortune again favors me.

Noon.—Five hundred getting ready to go; my turn comes to-morrow, and then we will see what we will see. Decided rumors that Sherman has taken Atlanta and is marching toward Savannah, the heart of the Confederacy. All in good spirits for the first time in a week.

Nov. 22.—And now my turn has come, and I get off with the next load going to-day. My trunk is packed and baggage duly checked; shall try and get a "lay over" ticket, and rusticate on the road. Will see the conductor about it. A nice cool day with sun shining brightly—a fit one for an adventure and I am just the boy to have one.

Later.—On the cars, in vicinity of Savannah en-route for Blackshear, which is pretty well south and not far from the Florida line. Are very crowded in a close box car and fearfully warm. Try to get away to-night.

Escape

In the Woods near Doctortown Station, No. 5, Ga., Nov. 23.—A change has come over the spirit of my dreams. During the night the cars ran very slow, and sometimes stopped for hours on side tracks. A very long, tedious night, and all suffered a great deal with just about standing room only. Impossible to get any sleep. Two guards at each side door, which were open about a foot. Guards were passably decent, although strict. Managed to get near the door, and during the night talked considerable with the two guards on the south side of the car.

At about three o'clock this a. m., and after going over a long bridge which spanned the Altamaha River and in sight of Doctortown, I went through the open door like a flash and rolled down a high embankment. Almost broke my neck, but not quite. Guard fired a shot at me, but as the cars were going, though not very fast, did not hit me. Expected the cars to stop but they did not, and I had the inexpressible joy of seeing them move off out of sight. Then crossed the railroad track going north, went through a large open field and gained the woods, and am now sitting on the ground leaning up against a big pine tree and out from under rebel guard!

Later.—A boy too young to trust has gone by singing and whistling, and carrying a bundle and a tin pail evidently filled with somebody's dinner. In as much as I want to enjoy this out-door Gypsy life, I will not catch and take the dinner away from him. That would be the height of foolishness. Will lay for the next one traveling this way. The next one is a dog and he comes up and looks at me, gives a bark and scuds off. Can't eat a dog.

Thus closes my first day of freedom and it is grand. Only hope they may be many, although I can hardly hope to escape to our lines, not being in a condition to travel.

Nov. 27.—Before daylight came where I now am. Saw alligators—small ones. This out in the woods life is doing me good. Main road three miles away, but there are paths running everywhere. Saw a man an hour ago. Think he was a skulker hiding to keep out of the army, but afraid to hail him. Many of these stay in the woods day-times, and at night go to their homes, getting food.

Nov. 28.—No one has come to me since day before yesterday. Watched and moved until most night of yesterday but could see or hear no one. Afraid I have lost communication. In the distance can see a habitation and will mog along that way. Most noon.

The closing of the fifth day of my escape. Must speak to somebody to-morrow, or starve to death. Good deal of yelling in the woods. Am now in the rear of a hovel, but off quite a ways from it.

Too dark to write more.

Nov. 29.—A woman goes out and in but cannot tell much about her from this distance. No men folks around. Two or three boys playing about. Must approach the house, but hate to.

Noon.—Still right here. Hold my position. More than hungry. Three days since I have eaten anything, with the exception of a small potato and piece of bread eaten two days ago and left from the day before. Chickens running around. Have serious meditations of getting hold of one or two of them after they go to roost, then go farther back into the wilderness, build a fire with my matches and cook them. That would be a royal feast. But if caught at it, it would go harder with me than if caught legitimately.

RECAPTURED

Nov. 30.—Ha! Ha! My boy, you are a prisoner of war again. Once more with a blasted rebel standing guard over me, and it all happened in this wise: Just before dark I went up to that house I spoke of in my writings yesterday. Walked boldly up and rapped at the door; and what was my complete astonishment when a woman answered my rapping. Asked me what I wanted, and I told her something to eat. Told me to come in and set down. Began asking me questions. Told her I was a rebel soldier, had been in the hospital sick and was trying to reach home in the adjoining county. Was very talkative; told how her husband had been killed at Atlanta, &c. She would go out and in from a shanty kitchen in her preparation of my supper.

Well, after a while heard some hounds coming through the woods and towards the house. Looked at the woman and her face pleaded guilty, just as if she had done something very mean. The back door of the house was open and pretty soon half a dozen large blood hounds bounded into the room and began snuffing me over; about this time the woman began to cry. Told her I understood the whole thing and she need not make a scene over it. Said she knew I was a yankee and had sent for some men at Doctortown. Then five horsemen surrounded the house, dismounted and four of them came in with guns cocked prepared for a desperate encounter.

I said: "good evening, gentlemen."

"Good evening," said the foremost, "we are looking for a runaway yankee prowling around here."

"Well," says I, "you needn't look any farther, you have found him."

"Yes, I see," was the answer. They all sat down, and just then the woman said "supper is ready and to draw nigh."

Talked there at the house a full hour on the fortunes of war, &c. Told them of my long imprisonment and escape and all about myself. After a while we got ready to start for this place. One rebel rode in front, one on each side and two in the rear of me. Was informed that if I tried to run they would shoot me. Told them no danger of my running, as I could hardly walk.

And so my adventure has ended and have enjoyed it hugely. Had plenty to eat with the exception of the two days, and at the last had a horseback ride.

My escape has given me confidence in myself, and I shall try it again the first opportunity.

Have seen a Savannah paper which says Sherman and his hosts are marching toward that city, and for the citizens to rally to repel the invader. My swollen ankle is being rubbed to-day with ointment. I tell you there are humane people the world over, who will not see even an enemy suffer if they can help it.

Dec. 5.—Guard said that orders were not to talk with any of the prisoners, and above all not to let us get hold of any newspapers. No citizens are allowed to come near us. That shows which way the wind blows. Half a dozen got away from here last night, and guards more strict to-day, with an increased force. Going to be moved, it is said, in a few days.

Dec. 6.—Thirteen months ago to-day captured—one year and one month. Must be something due me from Uncle Sam in wages, by this time. All come in a lump when it does come. No great loss without small gain, and while I have been suffering the long imprisonment my wages have been accumulating.

Dec. 8.—There are many men of many minds here. That used to be a favorite copy at writing school in Jackson, Mich. "Many men of many minds, many birds of many kinds." How a person's thoughts go back to the old boyhood days in such a place as this. Happiest times of life are those of youth, but we didn't know it. Everybody told us so, but we didn't believe it; but now it is plain. Every one, I think, has that experience.

A Second Escape

In the Woods, Dec 13.—How does that sound for a location to date from? Yesterday long toward night our train started from its abiding place and rolled slowly toward its destination, wherever that might be. When near Savannah, not more than a mile this side, David Buck jumped off the cars and rolled down the bank. I jumped next and Eli Buck came right after me. Hastily got up and joined one another, and hurried off in an easterly direction through the wet, swampy country. A number of shots were fired at us, but we were surprised and glad to find that none hit us, although my cap was knocked off by a bullet hitting the fore-piece.

Finally came near the fort and discovered there were rebels inside and a picket off but a few rods. Major left us and crawled slowly ahead to reconnoitre; returned in a few minutes and told us to follow. We all climbed over the side of the fort, which was very much out of repair. The reserve picket was asleep around a fire which had nearly gone out. Major piloted us through the fort, actually stepping over the sleeping rebels. After getting on the outside there was a wide ditch which we went through. Ditch was partially full of water. We then went way round near the railroad again, and started south.

By near daylight we were five or six miles from Savannah, and then stopped for consultation and rest. Finally went a mile further, where we are now laying low in a swamp, pretty well tired out and muddy beyond recognition.

We got out of a thick settled country safely, and again await developments. Heard drums and bugles playing reveille this morning in many directions, and "We are all surrounded."

David Buck is very confident of getting away to our lines. Eli thinks it is so if Dave says so, and I don't know, or care so very much. The main point with me is to stay out in the woods as long as I can. My old legs have had a hard time of it since last night and ache, and are very lame. It's another beautiful and cold day, this 13th of December. Biting frost nights, but warmer in the day time. Our plan is to work our way to the Ogechee River, and wait for the Stars and Stripes to come to us. Major said Sherman was marching right toward us all the time, driving the rebel army with no trouble at all. Told us to keep our ears open and we would hear cannon one of these days, possibly within a week. The excitement of the last twenty-four hours has worn me out, and I couldn't travel to-day if it was necessary.

Dec. 16.—Another adventure, and a red hot one. Started down the river in our dug-out boat somewhere near midnight. Ran down all right for an hour, frequently seeing rebel pickets and camp fires. Saw we were going right into the lion's mouth, as the farther down the more rebels. All at once our boat gave a lurch and landed in a tree top which was sticking out of the water, and there we were, swaying around in the cold water in the middle or near the middle of the Ogechee.

Were about froze with the cold and wet. A local man warned us that not more than a mile farther down we would have run right into a chain boat, with pickets posted on it. It really seems as if a Divine providence were guiding us. After getting a breakfast of good things started off toward the Big Ogechee River, and have traveled three or four miles.

Dec. 18.—Six days of freedom and what a sight of hardship, sweetened by kind treatment and the satisfaction of being out from under guard. We traveled last night some four miles and now are in a very precarious position. When almost daylight we came to the canal, and found cavalry pickets all along the tow-path; walked along until we came to a lock. A cavalryman was riding his horse up and down by the lock. At the lock there was a smouldering fire. It was absolutely necessary that we get across before daylight.

Dec. 21.—Got up bright and early. Never slept better. Getting rested up. We talk continually. Both Bucks are great talkers, especially David. Cooked and ate our breakfast, and would you believe it the ham is all gone. Incredible, the amount of food we eat. Wonder it don't make us all sick. Sweet potatoes getting low.

Dec. 22.—As Dan Rice used to say in the circus ring: "Here we are again." Sleep so sound that all the battles in America could not wake me up. Are just going for that fresh pork to-day. Have three kinds of meat—fried pig, roast pork and broiled hog. Good any way you can fix it. Won't last us three days at this rate, and if we stay long enough will eat up all the hogs in these woods. Pretty hoggish on our part, and Dave says for gracious sake not to write down how much we eat, but as this diary is to be a record of what takes place, down it goes how much we eat.

SAFE AND SOUND

Dec. 23.—It is not yet daylight in the morning, and are anxiously awaiting the hour to arrive when we may go out to the road. Slept hardly any during the night. More or less fighting all night, and could hear an army go by toward Savannah, also some shouting directly opposite us. Between the hours of about twelve and three all was quiet, and then again more travel. We conjecture that the rebel army has retreated or been driven back, and that the Yankees are now passing along following them up. Shall go out about nine o'clock.

Night.—Safe and sound among our own US Army troops, after an imprisonment of nearly fourteen months. Will not attempt to describe my feelings now. Could not do it. Staying with the 80th Ohio Infantry, and are pretty well tired out from our exertions of the day. At nine o'clock we started out toward the main road. When near it Eli and I stopped, and Dave went ahead to see who was passing. We waited probably fifteen minutes, and then heard Dave yell out: "Come on boys, all right! Hurry up!" Eli and I had a stream to cross on a log. The stream was some fifteen feet wide, and the log about two feet through. I tried to walk that log and fell in my excitement. Verily believe if the water had been a foot deeper I would have drowned. Was up to my arms, and I was so excited that I liked never to have got out. Lost the axe, which Dave had handed to me, and the old stand-by coverlid which had saved my life time and again floated off down the stream, and I went off without securing it—the more shame to me for it. Dave ran out of the woods swinging his arms and yelling like mad, and pretty soon Eli and myself appeared, whooping and yelling.

The 80th Ohio was just going by, or a portion of it, however, and when they saw first one and then another and then the third coming toward them in rebel dress, with clubs which they mistook for guns, they wheeled into line, thinking, perhaps, that a whole regiment would appear next. Dave finally explained by signs, and we approached and satisfied them of our genuineness. Said we were hard looking soldiers, but when we came to tell them where we had been and all the particulars, they did not wonder.

Dec. 24.—The infantry move only a few miles each day, and I believe we stay here all day. Went and saw Mr. Kimball. The officers commanding knew him for a Union man, and none of his belongings were troubled. In fact, he has anything he wants now. Announces his intention of going with the army until the war closes.

Many officers have read portions of my diary, and say such scenes as we have passed through seem incredible. Many inquire if we saw so and so of their friends who went to Andersonville, but of course there were so many there that we cannot remember them.

Evening.—We marched about two or three miles and are again encamped for the night, with pickets out for miles around. Many refugees join the army prepared to go along with them.

Dec. 25.—Christmas day and didn't hang up my stocking. No matter, it wouldn't have held anything. Last Christmas we spent on Belle Island, little thinking long imprisonment awaiting us. Us escaped men are to ride in a forage wagon. The army is getting ready to move. Are now twenty-four miles from Savannah and rebels falling back as we press ahead.

Night.—At about nine o'clock this morning as we sat in the forage wagon top of some corn riding in state, I saw some cavalry coming from the front. Soon recognized Col. Acker at the head of the 9th Michigan Cavalry. Jumped out of the wagon and began dancing and yelling in the middle of the road and in front of the troop. Col. Acker said: "Get out of the road you——lunatic!" Soon made myself known and was like one arisen from the dead. Major Brockway said: "Ransom, you want to start for home. We don't know you, you are dead. No such man as Ransom on the rolls for ten months."

All remember me and are rejoiced to see me back again. Lieut. Col. Way, Surgeon, Adjutant, Sergeant-Major, all shake hands with me. My company "A" was in the rear of the column, and I stood by the road as they moved along, hailing those I recognized. In every case had to tell them who I was and then would go up and shake hands with them at the risk of getting stepped on by the horses. Pretty soon Co. "A" appeared, and wasn't they surprised to see me. The whole company were raised in Jackson, Mich., my home, and I had been regarded as dead for nearly a year.

Could hardly believe it was myself that appeared to them. Every one trying to tell me the news at home all at the same time—how I was reported as having died in Richmond and funeral sermon preached. How so and so had been shot and killed, &c., &c. And then I had to tell them of who of our regiment had died in Andersonville—Dr. Lewis, Tom McGill and others asked me when I escaped, etc. Soon saw I was too tired and out of breath. After resting a few minutes I proceeded to tell him what I knew of Savannah, the line of forts around the city, and of other fortifications between us and the city, the location of the rivers, force of rebels, etc. Asked a great many questions and took down notes, or rather the chief of staff, Estes by name, did. After an extended conversation a dispatch was made up and sent to Gen. Sherman who was a few miles away, with the endorsement that an escaped prisoner had given the information and it was reliable. General Kilpatrick told me I would probably not be called upon to do any more duty as I had done good service as a prisoner of war.

Said he would sign a furlough and recommend that I go home as soon as communication was opened. Thanked me for information and dismissed me with congratulations on my escape.

Fort McAllister was taken to-day, which being the key to Savannah, leaves that city unprotected, hence the evacuation. Communication will now be opened with the gunboats on the coast and I will be sent home to Michigan.

And now this Diary is finished and is full. Shall not write any more, though I hardly know how I shall get along, without a self-imposed task of some kind.

4

Surviving the Jungle

Lt. William Diebold

A GROUP OF EXCITED YOUNG PILOTS CROWDED AROUND THE desk. I tapped one on the arm and asked what all the fuss was about.

"Here!" he said and handed me a sheet of worn, dirty paper. Laboriously written in a scrawling, unsteady hand were words beginning "Somewhere in Hell . . ."

With difficulty I read the remainder of the note: "I am the pilot who crashed. I need a pair of G.I. shoes, quinine, socks, sulfa for boils and infections rotting my limbs off. I would like to borrow a blanket if you could spare one. Cold. Cigarettes would be nice. I'm ashamed for asking for so much. Thanks for whatever you can do."

The note was signed "Lt. G. M. Collins."

I could see why everyone was so excited; the note packed more wallop than anything I'd ever seen. "That was brought into an airstrip in Burma two days ago by a native," a lieutenant explained. "The native said the pilot is in the Naga Hills, in a village we think is called Geda Ga."

It was the mission, I knew vaguely, of the 1352nd Search and Rescue Squadron to which I'd been temporarily assigned to find downed airmen along the Hump route and rescue them. That's all I did know, though, for I was just this morning reporting for duty. Having arrived the night before at this jumping-off place for China supplies, I was supposed to report immediately to the commanding officer, but given the lateness a sergeant at the airfield had directed me to a hut he called a basha and quartered me with fifty other men.

A basha is an American hay mound with doors. The army had gone native: straw roof over a bamboo frame with woven bamboo sides and windows with nothing in them. No glass, no frame, no nothing. They could better be called square holes for ventilation. The one modern touch, cement floors, added little to their attraction. Following a long flight across half of India, I slept well enough that night, though, if I'd known what was in the books for me this morning, there'd have been little sleep.

The inevitable began to kick in when I reported to Major Roland Hedrick, in civilian life a Salt Lake City lawyer.

The major was surrounded by pilots, all talking at once. He was the boss and brains of the outfit, and the pilots were discussing with him—"arguing about" would be more accurate—the note I'd just read. To say I received little attention when I walked into this melee of men puts it mildly; penetrating that circle of gesticulating arms would have been worth a black eye at least.

A pilot near the major made a mountain with one hand, while with the other he imitated an airplane in flight. He was trying to explain how difficult it was to fly around that mountain with the objective of coming low over a native village situated on the mountain's side, near the top. He'd had to come in low over the village, I gathered, to attract the attention of any airman that might be in it. Was the writer of the note in that particular village? Nobody seemed sure.

The major listened patiently enough, but eventually he started chasing off the crowd of officers, moving them gradually toward the door and out into the growing light. One by one they left, each being assured something would be done and that he'd let them know as soon as he knew himself. Figuring he was pretty busy, I turned to leave with them, but, catching my eye, the major indicated I should stay.

"You're Diebold," he said.

So much for a slow and gentle introduction to my new job. I would soon be donning a parachute and standing terrified in an airplane door over a forbidding jungle mountain top, preparing to jump—I hoped—to the downed Lt. G.M. Collins.

Eventually we came to the section of the country where our downed pilot was supposed to be. What a country! If a glacier made these mountains it must have been mad as hell at something. They were the biggest, highest hunks of earth I have ever seen piled in one place. When I thought of climbing around in them, they grew even larger and more formidable.

Anderson found the villages, then flew me from them to the Ledo Road, showing me the way out. It looked simple. There couldn't be more than two mountain ranges towering some two miles up apiece, or more than a hundred miles of solid jungle. Nothing to it! We buzzed the villages a couple of times, and it was some of the best flying I've ever seen done, thank God! First we dived down the side of one mountain, gaining excess air speed, and then shot up the side of an adjacent mountain. It would have been lots of fun if I didn't have to jump out of the ship on one of those shoots up the mountainside.

When I'd talked with the major, he said he hoped this second fly-over would give us an idea of which village the pilot was in, but no matter how close we came to the roofs of the houses—and the pilot came damned close—the only thing we saw were wildly waving natives. No parachute, no panel, no signal of any sort. I began to doubt if our pilot was in either of them, but the only way to find out was still the same as it was before: jump in and look.

Finally, as I knew it must, the time came to go. Pretty much at random we picked one of the villages, and Anderson described how the jump would work. He told me to stand at the rear door, and when the bell rang that was my signal to jump. The walk from the pilot's compartment to the rear of that ship was the longest I've ever made.

Sgt. Stanley Bloom from Boston, Massachusetts, helped me into my chute, showed me how to hook up to my static line, and I took my stand at the door. I could feel my heart thudding against my chest as I looked out. It was so far down to the rushing ground, and it was thick and rough. The village sat in a small clearing—very small from the airplane—but all around it was jungle. I could picture my chute being collapsed by one of the top branches of a tall tree, letting me freefall a hundred feet or so.

It seemed I stood there forever, scared to death! I was afraid even to think about it. I did think of my civilian insurance company and its directors, though. Wouldn't they be the happy lot if they could see me now? Once, back when I was a happy civilian, they insisted I stop flying because it was too great a risk for my insurance. Good God, how would they feel about this? Then the bell rang!

I had been waiting unconsciously for that sound, so it took no planned action on my part to get me out that door. I'd conquered my mind when I stepped up to it, and from then on leaping out was reaction to a sound. I'm sure of this, for I can't remember jumping. The bell rang, and the next thing I knew was the roaring of the slip-stream in my ears, the tumbling of the horizon, the tail of the ship passing overhead . . . and then the almighty jerk.

I'd learned to jump the hard way. Body position in the air was an unknown to me, so mine almost certainly was wrong. Also, my chute harness had been cinched too loose, so I got a terrific jerk. I blacked out for an instant, I guess, for the next thing I knew I was alone in the air, all was quiet and serene, and the airplane was gone.

The feeling of elation and exhilaration that came over me when I looked up and saw that big white canopy is indescribable. The chute had opened. Oh, happy day! I kicked my legs, waved my arms, and wiggled my body to make sure nothing had been broken. Nothing had.

I watched the big plane disappearing over the far mountain with definite misgivings. It made me lonely just to see it go. There I stood in the middle of a group of staring natives . . . and all I could think to do was stare back at them.

The women wore clothes, damn it. Wrapped around their middles were long pieces of varicolored cloth. Around their breasts they wore a plain piece of dirty white cloth or another piece matching the skirt. They all wore necklaces, made of anything from animal teeth on a string to old coins or pieces of metal. The men, most of them, wore nothing but a loincloth, and others had the same wrapping the women wore around their waists.

What surprised me most was their hair. Both men and women alike wore it up, piled on top of their heads. If it weren't for the very definite outline of women's bodies, I would have been bewildered as to which sex was which. As it was, nature provided the curves.

Well, we couldn't stand there staring at one another forever, so I took an important step: I smiled. There was one old geezer the others seemed to treat with respect who I had already guessed was the head man. On top of that, he had some sort of feather in his hair none of the others had. Either the others had lost theirs, or it meant something. I gave him the old try; I smiled directly at him.

He nodded his head a couple of times and gave me what I took to be a tentative smile in return. With that, I felt on more solid ground and decided to try to get things in hand. Scattered all over the clearing were the white para-packs. Some were even in the trees at the edge of the clearing. The kids of the village were beginning to poke experimental noses into their contents, and I could picture the results if they started opening them and spreading their contents all over the area. Best to get them gathered up and at least stacked in a pile where I could keep an eye on them.

I looked at the feather-headed village elder, smiled again, and gave him another cigarette from my last pack—there were more in the dropped supplies, I knew, which was another reason to get them secured. I pointed to the various para-packs and then to one of their houses. He must have understood what I meant because he barked out some orders, and in a flash the packs were being gathered up by the natives. The chief, if that's what he was, led me to one of the houses while this was going on.

What a place those houses were. Built on stilts about ten feet off the ground, they were long, bamboo-woven things with grass roofs. In front, they actually had a porch. Very civilized, I thought, but later I learned the hard way about the porches' uses.

The chief and I wallowed through the mud to his house. I called it mud, with a mental frown, for surrounding the house were two or three water buffalo and a dozen or so animals that slightly resembled pigs. Ah, the beautiful odors of a Naga village I thought as I followed the chief along. We entered his house via a fancy stairway made from a log with notches cut into it for steps. I wondered how my old Naga friend made it up that log on his night out; that is, if his wife gave him a night out.

The inside of the hut resembled a large communal basha, not unlike the one back at the base, though more worn with use. Several rooms ran to the rear of the shack, all connected to each other so that to go to the rearmost room, one had to walk through the sleeping quarters of everyone in the house. The front room looked like the natives' version of a living room or parlor. In the rear of the room a small fire flickered in the center of the floor on sand or something. But what stopped me cold were the decorations on the walls. On every wall hung a heterogeneous collection of dried heads. On some the skin had turned to a brown parchment-like covering. Others were nothing but the grinning, white skull. Though they were almost certainly animal skulls, one look at those and I wanted to move out of there in high gear.

Every kind of head imaginable hung in the shadows. The heads that were simply skulls really frightened me. The open holes that were once eyes, combined with the absence of any lower jaw, gave them a lurid expression. They looked as if they were smiling to me in an open invitation to join them in their vigil.

On one wall were the skulls of huge water buffalo, horns still intact. On another were the skulls of large birds, probably vultures. The long beaks protruded from the skull, and here and there I could see tufts of hairy fuzz.

What really made me gulp and thank Mr. Colt for inventing our .45 automatic were the monkey heads. I've been told since then, by men who should know, that they were monkey heads and not human. But from where I was standing they looked like the largest monkey heads I'd ever seen. They came awfully close to looking like what I thought mine probably looked like under the skin. I began to pick the spot where they'd probably put mine. At least I wanted a good spot, overlooking the porch.

The chief beckoned me over to the fire. I wasn't cold but I thought it a good idea, in view of the heads, to play ball with him. After all, I kept telling myself, I was his guest; morale and good relations, you know, are a lot of little things.

The chief sat cross-legged on the floor and motioned me to join him. He then pulled out a two-foot-long, two-inch-diameter pole made of bamboo, filled it with water, dropped in some brown stuff, put one end in the fire, and propped the other end against a forked stick. We were going to have tea, cooked in bamboo. It was almost too much. The prisoner ate a hearty meal before . . .

Our fire was very smoky, and there was no chimney. I watched the smoke curl up as the chief blew on the fire to make it hot. First the smoke filtered through a series of bamboo layers hanging from vines from the thatched roof. On some layers of bamboo lay meat; on others, nothing. The ones with nothing on them, I later learned, were drying and would be burned in the fire. On the others, the meat looked delicious.

I learned later that when bamboo was used in the fire, the meat was moved out of the smoke. My first lesson in jungle lore: There must be undesirable gases in bamboo smoke. After passing over the meat and helping dry extra bamboo for the fire, the smoke curled on up to the peak of the roof, followed the peak to the end of the house, and there dissipated into the outside air. As the smoke ran along the roof it blackened the straw, or whatever it was that covered the house. Every so often a big hunk of this soot would fall down on my head and the heads of the natives, which they casually brushed off.

The chief had poured water for the tea from fat bamboo logs racked in a row behind him. These were kept constantly full by the women. The nearest water being at the foot of the mountain, they had to make that hike a couple of times a day. Coming up with their backs loaded down with water-filled bamboo gave them a beautiful carriage, and strong legs—and, as I was to learn tomorrow, made them a lot tougher than they looked.

We had our tea from bamboo cups. That tea was so strong it snarled at me as I tried to swallow it. These natives, I decided, had galvanized stomachs. The stuff tasted like boiled tobacco. Nevertheless, I nodded, smiled, and smacked my lips in evident enjoyment. This pleased the chief, I was happy to see, and he, too, smiled, smacked his lips, and said something like "Kajaiee." I treasured the word as my first. It must mean good, although at the taste of the tea, I could hardly believe it.

By this time, the natives outside had piled up all the para-packs. I stood on the porch with the chief and looked at them in dismay. There were so many and all in the wrong village, and I wished Andy hadn't been so hasty in dumping them out of the plane. How I was ever going to get them from where they were over to the far mountain where they should be was beyond me.

It was now late afternoon and too late to try and make the trek to the other village. The jungle looked tough enough in the daytime, and it didn't take a lot of imagination to guess it could be deadly at night. I went down in the mud and lifted all the packs up on the porch. I was amazed to find that one of these native boys could carry one of those packs on his back, as they had done to get them in the pile, but it took three of them to lift one up. My hoisting them onto the porch caused no end of consternation among them. It gave them a mistaken estimate of my strength, which I was to become all too unhappy about the next day on the trail. Up on the porch again, I opened one of the packs and found a couple of cartons of cigarettes. I passed a few cigarettes around to the boys who had brought in the packs. They seemed tickled as hell. It made me think of the number of servants a man could have in that country for a buck a month.

My problem was to get as much of this stuff over to the next mountain as possible. I looked at the chief, pointed to one of the packs, then to the other mountain, and made a couple of motions as if I were carrying one of the packs and walking. Then I pointed to the handful of men below us. It seemed an impossible job. Those few men could never, even if they wanted, carry all this equipment.

Evidently the chief got the idea for he smiled, nodded, said, "Kajaiee," and called one of the older boys up on the porch. They held a lengthy conversation while I stood looking, wondering what the hell was going on. At the end of the conversation, the boy crawled off the porch and, with another companion, started down the trail. Was he being sent for more help? All I could do was to hope for the best.

We went back inside, for more tea I presumed, and sat down by the fire. They did pour more tea and then sat back contentedly smoking their cigarettes. I decided there would just have to be a stop to this tea drinking; I couldn't stand the gaff. Then I remembered what Andy had said about the bottle of medicinal liquor. After what I had been through that day I felt I wouldn't be cheating Uncle Sugar too much if I had a drink or two before dinner, so I found the bottle and did. It was damn good bourbon and was easier to swallow than the native's tea had been, but it also made me realize I was hungry.

I found some rations and started to cook a little dinner over the native's fire. I say dinner, but it consisted mostly of cereal because the rations consisted mostly of cereal. It wasn't what I would usually order for dinner, but, compared to what the Naga chief offered, the cereal looked delicious. His menu, deluxe style, consisted of monkey meat, which was cooked before my eyes. They tossed a dead monkey, whole and entire, into the fire.

The chief, after he had eaten, took out a long bamboo pipe. About a third of the way up the pipe from the bottom, an inch-thick piece of hard vine stuck out. He poured water into the mouth of the pipe, held it upright, and then lay down on the floor. In one hand he had a copper dish with a long handle. In this he put a brown pasty substance. He held this over the fire until the brown stuff came to a sizzle. At the same time he had shredded a green, folded leaf with his knife. He browned the shreds in front of the fire. When they were good and brown, he mixed the sizzling stuff into it. All these elaborate troubles were for what? Was he going to smoke the stuff or eat it?

When the mixture was cooked to his satisfaction, he put it in the vine sticking out of the bamboo. Now I was really puzzled! I've watched a lot of people smoke pipes, but this was the damnedest conglomeration of tobacco or anything else I'd ever seen. I didn't really know that he was smoking opium, but I soon guessed when I saw the beatific look on his face, the utter relaxation of his body, and the "out of this world" look in his eyes. I was surprised, but I wasn't shocked, not after these many years in the Army. Everyone had their own way of getting tight—even if this one was a bit unusual. It certainly seemed to agree with him; he looked so happy, so self-satisfied that I almost envied him. And he wasn't alone, for on all sides of me, the boys were reaching with bamboo tongs for embers out of the fire to light their own pipes. This was going to be quite a party.

I had my choice: either go to bed or have a couple more drinks of medicinal liquor. (The chief had his vice; I had mine.) This opium den held quite a bit of interest, though, so I decided I'd stay up and see how it ended. Anyway, it was darn good liquor. After a few more, the party seemed to be getting dull. Then a song, for no reason I could think of, came out of nowhere into my head, "Old McDonald Had a Farm." It seemed lively enough for the occasion, anyway, so I sang a couple of verses, and it wasn't long until a few natives began chiming in "E-I-E-I-O." Soon they were all doing it, with real gusto, and we had ourselves a chorus.

But after a couple thousand "Old McDonald"s I figured we'd disturbed the jungle enough, and I decided to go to bed. The bourbon had been so good I'd completely forgotten it was at all unusual to be singing in a shack on a mountain in the middle of the Burmese jungle with a bunch of opium-drunk natives. But at the time it all seemed rather natural.

I walked out to the porch and to the para-packs. One of those fool bags had my bed in it, but which one? I tried the one on top, and my luck was good. In it was a jungle hammock, which I'd never used, but it came with directions. The directions went something like this: "Find two trees, ten to fifteen feet apart . . ." etc. In the dark I had little desire to go wandering in the jungle looking for two trees ten to fifteen feet apart, but in the hut there was nothing even remotely resembling two trees. Then I remembered the uprights supporting the porch. Just the spot, I thought. As I fell down the niched log stairway and picked myself out of the mud, I decided Charlie King had been right, there had to be a better way to make a living.

With a flashlight in one hand, directions in the other, and the hammock between my legs, I tried to figure out how it should be put up. Two of these poles under the porch should do it.

The two end ropes I tied to the poles. Then there was the little matter of the mosquito netting that surrounded the hammock and attached to it. At each of the four corners the manufacturers had put a small cord. I tied these to the lattice-work the natives had covering their porch. The whole thing, as I stood back and surveyed my work, made quite a nest.

But when I tried to get into it, it wouldn't stop swinging. A zipper ran the entire height of the mosquito netting with another joining it that ran half the length of the hammock. I tried to crawl through the hole made by the two zippers and somehow made it, but when I was in, I found I'd forgotten to remove my boots. With the type of mud surrounding that hut, removing them was a necessity. I slowly reached down to get them off—a move I shouldn't have tried because I became tangled in the blankets. I guess I was twisting and turning more than the manufacturers of the hammock had foreseen, and I capsized, ending up lying on the part that should have been over my head.

It looked to me like the best thing I could do was get out and start all over, but how? The hammock was swinging furiously back and forth, tossing me around inside like a squirrel in a bag. I'll never know how I got my body out of the torture chamber, but eventually I stood in the mud and looked at the twisted, impossible mess that was supposed to be my bed.

So I started again. I had to sleep somewhere. But how was I to get my boots off and get through the hole without putting my stocking feet in the mud? I tried sitting on the edge and removing them, but it was like sitting on a swing and trying to remove one's shoes. Naturally I ended up standing in the mud in my stocking feet. By this time I was so angry I didn't care how I got into it or where I slept, on the sides, bottom, or top of the hammock. I was sweating, breathing hard, and covered with mud.

The solution turned out to be simple: I dived at the hammock's opening and made it, though it took a second to stop revolving, but eventually the hammock and I ended our struggle right side up. Even so, the blankets were wound around my body so tightly I could hardly move, the mosquito netting was in my mouth, and my feet were wet and muddy. I had also forgotten to take off my web belt so my canteen was jabbing me in the back and my .45 was making a poor impression on my ribs. To top it off, I wanted a cigarette.

Slowly, so as not to upset my precarious equilibrium, I stalked the cigarette pocket with one hand, clutching the side of the hammock with the other. Somehow I got the pack out of my pocket without upsetting the whole works, got the cigarette lit without setting fire to the hammock, and settled back, exhaling a cloud of smoke and listening to the jabbering of the natives in front of their fire. It occurred to me that the bourbon (together with some of the wayward opium smoke) might possibly have contributed to my struggles with the bedding, but I dismissed the idea as unlikely.

It seemed a beautiful night now that I had stability. Surrounding our mountain were other giants of this country, each outlined in cloaks of mist and moonlight. It would have been eerie had it not been for the billion stars surrounding a huge yellow moon. It was so peaceful I almost forgave the man who had invented the jungle hammock.

On a far mountainside, a jackal raised its voice; a nearer one answered. The sound drifted to my ears out of the mist. With the flicker of the fire inside the hut and the voices of the natives, the jackal didn't scare me much. When I became convinced the animal wasn't under my bed, I relaxed again. It was still a beautiful night.

The natives continued to talk, and it wasn't long until I could recognize the different voices. The words were impossible to understand except for one which sounded like they might be trying to say, "American." I didn't care much for that; it seemed to me little good could come out of their becoming too curious about me. One voice rose above the others, and every third word seemed to be "American," and I worried a little more. The less I entered into their conversation, the better I liked it, since I could still close my eyes and picture those heads on their wall. The hair

on the back of my neck crawled at the thought. I grabbed my
.45 and with a trembling hand took a firm grip on it. Of course
the natives were never safer than when I had that gun, but I was
hoping they wouldn't know that.

As the conversation increased almost to shouting, one of the
natives walked out on the porch and looked down at me. With
what I hoped was a forceful voice, but was probably little more
than a squeak, I asked, "Wonderful night for murder, isn't it?"
The character didn't answer. He just stood there in the moonlight
looking at me, the fire lighting up one side of his face.

He stared for what seemed like forever; then to my surprise
came the sound of running water. I couldn't believe it, but in the
moonlight I could see it was true: I was sleeping in the Naga's
bathroom and this guy was using it. After the first Naga, came a
long procession, all relieving themselves over my bed. I thanked
the manufacturer of the jungle hammock for the tarpaulin he had
put over the top; otherwise it would have been a very damp night.

During the night, dozens of natives entered the village. The
two men the chief had sent out earlier evidently had been emis-
saries to other Naga villages, though God knows where they
were in the jungle. The men had done their job well, though.
There seemed to be an ample number to carry our equipment the
next day.

One thing that interested me to no end, and scared me more
than a little when I first saw it down the trail, was their version
of a flashlight. Having decided I was in no danger from the
natives—other than getting peed on—I was lying there relaxed
and smoking. As I looked out into the darkness, I saw a small red
ball bobbing and weaving in the air. The medicinal liquor had been
good, perhaps even better than that, but I hadn't drunk enough to
be seeing things that weren't there. But red balls don't appear for
no reason. All I could do was sit up in the hammock—as much as
I could sit up—and watch them approach. It wasn't really fear that
made me shake, I told myself, it was only nervousness. Then, from

the faint glow of the balls I glimpsed the human forms behind them. I lay back relieved, for the balls were only the glowing tips on the end of bamboo poles.

Finally I went to sleep. It was a fitful, disturbed sleep filled with little brown men looking down at me through their front porch, peeing into the night, and waving red balls in the air. I seemed to be stuck knee-deep in mud and unable to miss the man-made dew that was falling so heavily. It was not a comfortable night.

If the Naga ever went to bed that night I don't know, but at 4:30 in the morning, while it was still dark, the women were up and pounding something I correctly guessed to be rice. The muffled thud, thud, continuous and without rhythm, would wake a hibernating bear. Shortly thereafter I heard the voices of the men and could see the brightening reflection of their fire. Wearily, I swung my feet out of the hammock, wiggled my mud-caked toes, and eased into my boots.

As I climbed the notched ladder, my eyes met a sight I won't easily forget: The big front room of the chief's house was filled to overflowing with brown-skinned Nagas, all of them staring at me. The fire behind them framed their squatting bodies, their piled up hair, with a flickering, weird background. All I could see was the glint of white teeth and the glitter of eyes. The leering, naked skulls on the wall framed them, and the air was heavy with tobacco smoke, sweaty bodies, and effluvium. Standing at the entrance of that room, I tried to smile and said my one Naga word, "Kajaiee." It worked. They actually laughed. The tension was broken. The old chief unfolded himself and came forward, took me by the hand, and led me to the fire.

My God, I thought, not tea, not at this hour! But tea is what the good and venerable chief had in mind. Holding up both hands to him in a negative gesture, I went to the food sack for some good old American coffee. I didn't know how it would taste cooked in a bamboo tube, but it couldn't be worse than their tea.

Taking a bamboo tube from the rack behind the chief, I poured in some coffee and water, stuck the end of it in the fire, and propped up the other end with a forked stick. At first the chief looked puzzled, then slightly annoyed until I poured him a bamboo cupful and he tasted it. His face lit up in evident enjoyment and he passed the cup around the circle of men. A few were missed, so I put another tube-full on to boil. That was a mistake. In the next half-hour, I did nothing but make coffee for the Nagas. They drank it as fast as I could brew it.

Finally calling a halt to the coffee making, I put water on to boil for cereal. The brightly colored box, proclaiming it the finest cereal in the world, was cause in itself for a murmur of assent from my friends. I cooked more than I could possibly eat since I had a feeling this was going to be a repetition of the coffee incident. It was, but I underestimated the food capacity of a Naga.

Batch after batch of cereal went down those hungry gullets. I wondered what they would have done for food if I hadn't been there to cook breakfast for them. When I finally called a halt to this noise, I sat back and contemplated them with a lifted eyebrow. I looked at my burnt fingers and reflected on the peculiarities of life. Once was, I thought, the wife . . . but, hell, that was too long ago to remember.

Still, the Naga were very appreciative and smiled their thanks. In a way, I was rather proud of having pleased and filled them, much like the hostess who has spent hours in the kitchen appreciates guests who enjoy the dinner. I leaned against the wall, lit a cigarette, and gazed with warmth upon the recipients of my labors.

But having finished his cereal and understanding I wasn't going to make any more, the chief moved to the fire and began boiling rice—and in huge quantities. It couldn't be! These people were so small and yet had eaten more per capita than is ordinarily consumed by a food-loving American soldier. The shock, so early in the morning, was almost too much. I sat there and watched with awe as those damn natives ate all that rice—and there wasn't a potbelly in the crowd.

By then the dawn was beginning to lighten up the jungle. Red beams poured down the green mountainsides and probed the interior of our hut. In the valleys, a few trees reached through the mist they'd slept under. In the forest, the animals began to stir and yawn. The strange early morning cries of birds mingled with the dog-like bark of deer. Soon we'll be on our way, I thought, which proved how little I knew yet about the Nagas.

Fooling around with this and that in preparation for the day's hike, I didn't pay much attention to the chief and his men. I presumed, though, that they, too, were getting ready. But when I finally looked over at them, they were all stretched out around the fire smoking their pipes again. I went over to the chief and made signs like walking and hurry-up and pointed to the mountain he'd indicated yesterday as the one where my flyer was. To my gesticulations the old chief just nodded and smiled in a sapient sort of way . . . and continued smoking his pipe. It was most exasperating. Generations of American habit were ahead of me, which included getting a job done when it needed to be done, but like it or not I would have to wait until they were good and ready to go.

Soon, though, my friends began to stir a little. They'd started opening the para-packs, oohing and aahing at each article they uncovered, from cans of beans to a tube of shaving cream, the latter an item I could have done without. Each of the natives had a little basket which would hold, I imagined, about thirty pounds. The baskets were of a peculiar construction. The top of the baskets had two shoulder straps of woven bamboo, with another strap looping from the top of the basket through a wooden yoke. It looked a little puzzling, until they put them on their backs; then it became a sensible arrangement. They put their arms through the two loops attached to the basket and the yoke fitted on the backs of their necks against their shoulders. The end of the other loop went onto their foreheads. It looked so solid and balanced that they probably could have done somersaults without the baskets falling off.

Gradually their work grew efficient: the men formed a circle, baskets in hand, and the chief loaded them. Evidently they had union rules, though, for each man was loaded according to his size. The larger a man was, the larger his load. The chief was the big cheese, and there was little or no argument from the men in the circle.

When all of his men had their baskets full, a considerable number of things remained in the packs. The old chief went out and recruited all the youngsters, male and female, plus a number of young ladies. To all of these he gave lighter loads, but it emptied the para-packs completely.

It was a long and colorful line of porters that started down the trail. Interesting, I thought, that a complete stranger could drop out of the sky with enough equipment to fill a large truck and, merely by asking, get so much help and cooperation. So far there had been no question of payment. Either they didn't expect any or I, somehow, was supposed to know what to give them for their work.

Going downhill was fine as far as I was concerned, no effort at all. The jungle was thick, though, with brush close in on all sides and in many places overhead as well. We went through a field of grass that was at least ten feet high. I gawked so much at everything around me that I kept tripping over rocks and roots in the trail. The chief cut me a bamboo stick and, like a blind child, I felt my way along.

But if downhill was O.K., the jungle nearly smothered me, and I could seldom see more than a few feet off the trail. The jungle was a solid mass of vines, trees, and brush all interlaced, forming a solid, almost impenetrable wall.

Then there were the leeches. As I walked down the trail I could see them sitting up, half their bodies waving around in the air, waiting for me to brush them with my foot or leg. When I did, they attached with such tenacity that pulling them off was a terrific job. In the first place, their bodies are covered with slime; to get a grip with my fingernails was next to impossible. Those fool slugs could crawl through the eye of a shoe or between the belt of my trousers and shirt—which some did. When they hit flesh, they sank in their jaws, excreting a fluid that frees blood of its usual ability to coagulate. Then they grew larger and larger as they drank my blood.

If, after they'd sunk their jaws, I tried to pull them off, their jaws remained, poisoning the wound and causing infection. One leech wouldn't have been hard to deal with, but the jungle was full of them, and they attached themselves by the dozens. They hung from trees, they were on the brush that whipped by bare arms on the trail, they lay in wait in the mud. If a man should lie down on the grass for very long without taking precautions, the leeches would certainly have him.

But I only began to be aware of the leeches gradually and especially after I noticed that after about ten minutes of walking the Naga would stop and pick something off their bodies. Though I couldn't feel anything biting me, I began to look myself over. My God, I thought as I saw them on my legs. I'm establishing a leech-head in Burma. They were all over me. I tried to flick a few of the crowd off, but they'd catch onto my fingers and hang on. It was like trying to throw away chewing gum.

As I struggled, more climbed up my legs from the ground. I was being swamped with leeches. It made me almost panic-stricken; I wanted to run, to do anything to escape these weird, disgusting organisms. They turned what looked like a tropical walk in the woods into a nightmare. From there on, I, too, stopped every few minutes and pulled leeches. The natives in their bare feet and loincloths could see all the leeches that landed on them. Earlier I had thought of the Naga as nearly naked; now I thought of myself as over-clothed. With all my clothing, I was at a disadvantage, and it worried me to think about the ones I couldn't see that were drinking away.

At the foot of the mountain we came to a river, a roaring torrent of water, all the more surprising because the thick growth had muffled its sound until we were almost upon it. The mountainside swept straight down to the stream, and at first it seemed impassable. But the trail had been chosen with care. Behind a huge boulder in the stream was a comparatively quiet pool, and in a second the men had stripped and were in it. The women, too, showed no hesitation as they joined in the swim.

The bath had a two-fold purpose: It was fun, and it washed off the leeches. Slightly abashed, I stripped and joined them. Women or no, the leeches had to go. When I took off my trousers I saw my legs were covered with the fat and blood-swollen creatures. The Nagas stopped their splashing and helped me pick them off my naked body. My crimson face, I guess they thought, must be getting sunburned.

By now the early coolness had passed. The sun was hot, and the cold water tumbling down out of some high place was refreshing. It was fun to stand there and watch these primitive people, unaffected by civilization, relax and enjoy themselves. But it was clear we had to move on. If the poor guy in the village we were making for was in serious shape, minutes might count. This time, though, I took a hint from these "primitives" and started out in nothing more than my shorts and boots. After all, this was their country, and being nearly naked had obvious advantages.

So out of the water and up the mountain we started, and with each step uphill—and each new leech—it became hotter and hotter. The Naga are hill people, and hills are their business, but with me . . . well, hills are wonderful when you're flying over them or walking down them, but the Naga build their trails straight up and down a mountain. The trail went up in front of my face. If I stuck out my tongue, I could have picked up a leech or two on it; and why not? They were everywhere else! I began using both hands and feet to make the grade.

For a while we followed the bed of a small secondary stream tumbling down the hill. The water rushing against my unsteady feet on the slippery rocks made walking not only difficult but hazardous. Where the bank of the stream was steepest was where the Naga, naturally, chose to climb out. We clambered along a slippery mud path for a while, sliding back half a step for every one we moved forward. Then we came to a fallen tree slanted upward across what looked like a shallow depression in the ground. Though the log's surface was covered with slippery moss, the Naga with their bare feet walked along it with ease. Then I tried it. It didn't look too bad: even if I did slide off, the ground below me was covered with foliage, or so I thought. About halfway up the log, my feet started slipping, and off I went, right through the foliage under which I expected to find the ground—but the ground was another ten feet down. The log had covered an over-grown ravine.

I landed stunned and bruised and a little shaken. My friend the chief threw me a vine and hauled me out, a somewhat embarrassed jungle novice. None of the Naga who were watching the performance laughed; I would have felt far better if they had. To the contrary, they seemed upset about the whole thing, which puzzled me. The next log we came to like that one, they all stopped, lay down their packs and built a bamboo railing for me. I felt rather silly but a hell of a lot safer, and I began to realize they were concerned that this big dumb American might hurt himself and ruin the whole trip.

On and on we chugged up the mountain, the hill people keeping up a running conversation as they climbed. I was thankful I was still able to breathe. Every cigarette I ever smoked came back to haunt me. The chief in front of me actually stopped once, lit an old pipe, and continued up the hill. How he did it I'll never know. The odor of that foul tobacco whipping past my nose cut down considerably on my oxygen supply.

It seemed forever, but we finally hit the top. And perched up there was a village, if I may call one house a village. I looked around for the lost pilot, but of course this wasn't the right village; we still had another mountain to climb.

By now it was around noon, and the sun was really pouring it on. The water in my canteen was about to boil—so was my blood, what blood the leeches had left me. All the Nagas jabbered to each other, and I staggered under the shade of the house. When I finally got the sweat out of my eyes enough to see, I lit a cigarette and looked around.

As soon as I did that, though, I had to pass cigarettes out to all the party. There went another pack. The money I could make as a cigarette salesman out here after the war, I thought as I passed them around to eager hands. Everyone quietly sat down for a smoke except one woman who stood in front of me holding a baby in her arms.

The baby was a cute little thing, except where there should have been hair there was nothing but a mass of scabs and running sores. Some of the scabs were dry and puckered and must have hurt the baby like hell. It was almost unimaginable to me, raised in America, that there should be a place where babies were raised without proper medical attention. I felt for the child and, though no doctor, thought there must be something I could do to help.

The mother handed me the baby, and, showing him a small bandage I carried that had a red cross on it, I asked the chief for the medical kit. He got the idea, unpacked a couple of baskets, and found it. First I washed the child's head with warm water and then smoothed the whole thing with boric acid ointment. I remembered that a doc had once used boric acid in my eyes, so I knew it probably wouldn't be too strong for the baby's tender skin. The salve I knew was needed to soften the scabs and relieve the pain, but that's about all I knew. I gave the mother a can of it and, through signs, was able to make her understand to put some on twice a day and to keep the child out of the sun.

All this treatment, though, must have given the Naga the impression I was a medicine man, for they all crowded around, each with a complaint. Here, I guess they thought, was a man who could help them with their aches and pains at last. My presence took on a new meaning for them, and they began clamoring for attention. Being human, I couldn't resist the temptation; also, I figured I could at least help them more than if they had no treatment at all. Naga after Naga came forward, many with the same trouble, infected leech bites. They were rather vicious-looking things in their later stages. Some of the holes looked like volcanoes and bore down to the bone. I opened each one with a sterilized knife, swabbed it clean, applied sulfa powder, and wrapped it with a bandage. I was doubtful about how much good I was doing, but it was at least an effort in the right direction. They all seemed satisfied with my treatment, though, for they went away smiling.

So far, I had been the great white savior, that is until a case appeared that stopped me cold. A woman made her way over to me. She tapped her chest below the breast and grimaced. She was older than some of the girls and rather heavy, and her trouble might have been any number of things. But so as not to lose face with my new crowd of patients, I put on my best professional air: I thumped her chest with one hand tapping the other, put my head down as I had seen doctors do, and listened with an intent expression. Actually I couldn't hear a thing except one hand tapping the other, but I could see the Naga watching in wonderment.

After three or four thumps, I raised my head as if I had found the solution, a smile of assurance playing around my mouth. But the solution I'd found was to my trouble, not hers, for my eye had caught the caption on one of the bottles in the medical kit. It said "bicarbonate of soda, peppermint flavored." I solemnly unscrewed the top, handed her a couple of tablets, and told her to chew them by putting an imaginary pill in my mouth and chewing vigorously. The old gal put the two I'd handed her into her mouth and chewed. The effect was immediate: After rice all her life, the peppermint must have tasted swell. Her face lit up with evident enjoyment. From there on, after she told the rest, I had a dozen cases of chest pains, and my bottle was soon empty.

Other cases came forward as well—various infected cuts, punctures, and sores, and I fixed them all up, one after another. I was making friends by the dozen, and, frankly, I felt sorry for them. And, curiously, I began feeling friendship toward them as well; the fact is, I was learning to like these people. I liked them for their toughness and their willingness to help, for their friendliness and enthusiasm and quickness to smile, and for the way they trusted this oversized American stranger who had entered their lives by dropping out of the sky.

Eventually we started out again. Though I still felt the urgency of getting to the pilot, by now I wasn't in so much of a hurry. My muscles ached, and my head swam. The thought of another grueling climb like that last mountain nauseated me. But off we went.

What goes up must go down, thank the Lord, because for us it was now down, but so steep and muddy that I spent most of my time sliding on what was left of my undershorts. The stones didn't bother my posterior much; it was the sharp roots that did it. Still, we made good time and soon reached another river. This one wasn't as large as the last one, but it was just as welcome. To the natives, who obviously knew this stream was coming, the trip down didn't seem so bad, but to me, who could see another half a day ahead with nothing but leech bites and the sweltering heat, it seemed longer than it was.

We shed our clothing again, and in we went. I took a moment to look at my feet, though, and they seemed like bloody stumps. Blisters everywhere. Then, when I jumped into the pool, damned if I didn't get almost swept downstream with the current. Going under, I grabbed the nearest hand. When I got back onto my feet and blew the water out of my lungs, I was able to mutter a meek "kajaiee." I looked at the person whose hand I had grabbed and who was now holding me up, and my face turned crimson; the big strong hero had been saved by a gal half his size . . . and she wasn't hard on the eyes either. Mumbling at the vagaries of fate, I felt like a country bumpkin, but she smiled at me as if she saved stupid Americans every day. I smiled back . . . and we began to pick leeches off each other. It was fascinating, too, to see where a quick-eyed girl with nimble fingers could think of to look for leeches. I was becoming accustomed to this primitive way of life and began to think it an inviting way to live.

The stream, of course, was at the bottom of the mountain we'd just descended, but to me it had been the top of the day. But from here on it was up, up, forever up. I was so slow that even the women, burdened as they were with packs, pulled away from me. I just couldn't keep up. No longer was I walking: Stumbling and struggling were more the words for it. Climb a hill for an hour, most of us can do, but when it comes to climbing them all day— give me a streetcar. Two hours after we left that stream, I was about finished. I kept thinking of Rudyard Kipling's poem "If." The line kept running through my head—"And so hold on when there is nothing in you . . . you'll be a man, my son!" Hell, I didn't have anything in me now, and I didn't care if I ever was a man. All I wanted at that point was to lie down and die.

I thought I was beginning to imagine things when I heard the sound of airplane motors, but I wasn't. I grabbed the little radio and lay down on the ground and started calling. An opportunity to rest my weary bones is about all it meant to me; I was so exhausted I'd almost forgotten why I was in this hell. I was so hot, so tired, so wet from sweat it had become a battle just to keep moving.

The cool, firm voice that came out of the set brought me around a little. It was Andy. "Where the hell are you, boy?"

"You've got me," I answered. "But where I am is hell sure enough, though I haven't been introduced to Satan yet."

"Well, get on the ball, Diebold. You haven't got all day, you know."

The injustice of it, I thought. He sits up there in a nice cool cockpit in a blue sky I can barely make out through the foliage, turning a wheel and telling me to get to work. I counted to ten and then answered him. "Give us four more hours, and I should be with the body, I think."

"Four hours. O.K., we'll be back then, but hurry up."

I was so mad at the absurdity of it that I beat the hot, steaming jungle floor with my fists while the chief, who had come back down the trail to find out what the fuss was about, clucked his disapproval. Andy had only been riding me, but it was tough to take at that point. It was just as well that I didn't speak the chief's language, for I'm certain if I had I would have been in for a fatherly lecture on temperament.

Wearily we ploughed ahead. My throat was raw from the quick gasps of hot air. Somewhere this God-awful churning of the legs and sweat in the eyes must end, I thought.

It was unexpected when it happened. Around the corner of some heavy brush, they came into view, the most beautiful sight I'd ever seen—two Naga houses. To me, instead of being surrounded by mud and filth, those two huts seemed made of ice cream and peppermint candy. There's no describing reaching the ultimate goal when everything inside you tells you you'll never make it. It's like a gambler raking in an unbelievable pile of winnings. Home never looked better.

I staggered to the nearest log, slumped down on it, and simply stared at those huts. They were only a hundred yards away, but I didn't think I'd make it even that far. Tomorrow, the day after, a thousand days after that, I didn't think I'd be able to move again.

But when I'd regained my breath I thought better of it and made my way up to the largest of the two huts. On the porch stood a wrinkled old man, a welcoming committee of one. My native friends were standing below the porch looking at the old man, and all were talking at once.

As I approached, the jabbering ceased. I stood with the crowd and looked at the old man, too. "We're in the wrong village again," I moaned. "Not that. I simply can't go any farther." The old man spoke a few words to me, none of which, of course, I could understand, and then he motioned me up on the porch. I climbed the notched log and entered the house after him. As tired as I was, I was getting excited. Was he there?

I peered into the dimly lit front room. Over by the fire I could see the outline of a form stretched out on the floor. I walked over to it, afraid of what I might find, but he was there, lying by the fire, the back of his head toward me. But was he alive?

He twisted around, and I saw his face, and tears were running down his cheeks. Neither of us said a word. I knelt beside him, and we gripped hands. It was impossible to say anything; I was too choked with emotion. I tried an experimental smile, but it was forced, for even though he was alive I thought even now we might be too late. He looked to me as if he were on his way out of this lovely world of ours as he lay there softly sobbing.

He was covered with dirty pieces of cloth, so all I could see of him was his face, but that was enough. It told a horrible story of suffering and starvation and exposure. His beard was long and tangled, his hair spread like a woman's on the log he was using as a pillow. The bones of his cheeks stood out in ugly relief below yellowing, bulging eyes. He spoke, through cracked, fever-ridden lips. "Thank the Almighty. You've come."

I spoke with all the unfelt confidence I could muster. "Right you are, lad, and a couple of doctors will be here in a minute. We'll have you running as good as new in no time and out of this fire trap in a jiffy."

He smiled at my slang, and I realized it must have been a long time since he'd heard any language but Naga. He closed his eyes and gave a long sigh. I was afraid this was it, but then he opened them again. "Have you any food?"

"Coming right up," I answered. "Would some nice warm cereal fit the bill?"

"Of course," he said and closed his eyes. I have never made cereal faster. As I cooked, I could see his hands; they were nothing but bones covered with a layer of skin. He was a human skeleton.

When the food was ready, I fed him. All he was able to take were a few spoonfuls and a couple of sips of tea; he was exhausted from the effort. He seemed to go to sleep or he was in a coma, I couldn't tell. I lifted the dirty burlap the natives had covered him with for an examination. He opened his eyes again when I did this. I hoped my face remained normal when I looked, but my stomach turned inside-out. He was all bones, and his legs and body were covered with huge, ulcerous sores. He was looking at me hard, and I had to say something, so I smiled and said, "Prickly heat, eh?" It was a poor attempt at humor, but he managed a feeble grin.

This boy needed a doctor in the worst way. I began praying for the rescue ship to come. This was too much for my first-aid knowledge of medicine. I replaced the sacking and started talking to him, anything to make him feel better. It seemed to help. As I talked, I could see him improve . . . or at least to become more alert. It made him feel safer. Another American was there, he was rescued.

He told me, in a weak voice, that his name was Greenlaw W. Collins (he actually gave his middle initial) and that he was from New Orleans. I took up the conversation and talked about New Orleans since, luckily, I had been there. He liked to hear me talk of his home, it was easy to see. He mumbled in the middle of one of my sentences that it had been his first Hump trip and his last, he hoped. I assured him he was on his way back to New Orleans as of right now.

"I was flying a pea shooter"—a fighter—"and had engine trouble," he said. "The plane went into a spin, so I had to bail out. I landed in a tree and lost my jungle kit, so I had no food. I followed a river I found. How long I don't know, but it was over three weeks."

Out in this country for more than three weeks without a knife, a compass, food, or anything. This boy was tough, and then some.

"The natives found me going down the river and brought me on a litter up here. Don't know how long that was, I lost track of the days. On the way down that river, I slept on rocks in the middle of the water to get away from the leeches and the animals. My shoes wore out, and the rocks cut my feet to ribbons. It was tough going at times. The natives here have been trying to feed me. It's pretty awful stuff, monkey meat and rice and then rice and monkey meat. I just sorta lost my appetite, I guess."

No wonder, I thought, remembering the smell of burning hair before the meal at the other village. A piece of soot fell from the roof onto his face. He raised a shaking hand and brushed it off.

"Did you get my note?" he asked.

"Yep, that's why I'm here."

"Never thought you would. I thought sure I was a goner. You know, it took me a whole day to write it."

Talking was an effort, and he rested a bit. He closed his eyes, but in a moment he spoke again.

"Didja see those sores on my legs?"

"Yes."

"Well, once they got me here I kept 'em open with a native knife. I thought I had better keep them running. That was right, wasn't it?"

"Perfect. You'll be up and running in a week."

"Thanks," he said with a wry smile. I wasn't fooling him, I could see that.

He told me a little more, and I learned other details later, like his eating bamboo shoots, bitter berries, and even leeches!

He talked about the soaking rains, using his socks as gloves and wrapping up his head at night to escape the mosquitoes and crawling pests. In that fetid, humid jungle, his boots rotted and started to fall apart. And most of all he mentioned the cold, how awful cold the nights got, and the terrible, solitary loneliness of that sea of green.

But mostly he seemed to drift in and out of focus. There was no doubt his had been a close thing. What I was worried about was that it was a close thing still, that if we didn't get help there soon, he might not make it.

Then I heard it—the search plane approaching the village. It was faint at first, but in less than a minute it sounded as if the pilot had brought the plane right down in the hut with us. Collins heard it, too, and looked at me.

"Here come your doctors."

I went out on the porch and turned on the radio. Andy's voice came over the ear-phone. "Air rescue calling gravel shuffler. Air rescue calling gravel shuffler."

I was in no mood for jokes right then. "Yeah, this is gravel shuffler, and we need medical help down here as soon as you can get it."

"Stand by Diebold," he answered. "I've got the docs on board, and they'll be right down. How bad is he?"

"He's not too good. Tell them to bring the works as far as equipment goes. And may they be young and strong, for this is no country for the feeble."

"Will do," Andy answered. "And they look pretty big and strong to me."

The plane circled around, and I knew just how those two medicos felt as the big C-47 skimmed down the side of the far mountain. It shot up the side of our mountain and over the village and then a parachute blossomed from the rear. It was exciting to watch from the ground and not a little satisfying. But then the wind caught the falling chute, and it disappeared over the far side of the mountain. I wished the boy luck and then turned to the chief and pointed in the direction the chute had gone. He immediately sent two of his men on the run in that direction.

"Pretty lousy aim," I radioed Andy. "It shouldn't take more than two days to find him out there." He deserved that dig after the gravel shuffler guff he'd been handing me.

Andy didn't answer. Around again came the plane, and the sprawling, tumbling figure of a man flew out of the cargo door of the ship. The figure tumbled and fell straight down, but the chute didn't open. It was free fall, no paratrooper chute! I could see the doctor's arms flailing in the air as his hand grasped for the ripcord and missed. My knees turned to water as I stood there holding my breath. I didn't want to look, but I couldn't tear my eyes away. The sensation of helplessness was awful.

It seemed almost too late when he finally found the ripcord and the chute opened. The canopy streamed out and snapped open above his head, and a split second later he hit the ground. As I ran to where he hit, I hoped and prayed it had opened in time to break his fall. I expected to find him with his hips driven up between his eyebrows. As the natives and I approached on a dead run, he slowly sat up and shook his head.

"My God," he said to no one in particular, "I thought I'd had it."

The doc had landed in soft mud at least six inches deep, the chute slowing his fall and the mud cushioning his landing. That was all that saved him from being seriously injured. He was a big man, over six feet with wide, husky shoulders. After I helped him to his feet, he stuck out his hand, and we shook. His fingers were long and narrow but strong. He had a grip like a vise. This must be the surgeon, and did we need him! "My name's Spruell," he said, "although it was damn near mud." We both laughed in relief. "Bill to my friends. I'll look after the patient. You had better try and find our friend. He's somewhere over in that . . . " He waved his hand in the general direction the other chute had fallen.

"The natives have already gone after him," I said. "Don't worry, they'll get him. They've been a big help. Come on, I'll take you to see Lieutenant Collins. He needs you fast, and I'm not foolin'."

Suddenly I remembered the radio. Andy's voice squawked out at me, "Get on the air, gravel shuffler, get on the air, will ya' before I have to bail out and find out what's goin' on."

"Everything's going to be all right, Andy," I said as the major and I walked toward the hut. As I spoke, I saw the figure of a white man with some natives come limping out of the jungle above the village. "Everything is all right," I corrected. "Everyone accounted for and unhurt as far as I can tell."

"Whew! I'm sure happy as hell about that. They had me plenty worried."

"Don't think for a minute they weren't worried, too."

"Right," he said. "Is there anything else you want?"

"Better stick around for a few minutes until the doc takes a look at Collins. He may need more supplies than we have here, although I can't see what it'd be except a kitchen sink or something."

"If he wants one, tell him we'll drop it."

Around us the natives had gone wild. This was too much for them, a big noisy airplane swooping over the mountain, men dropping from the skies all over the place.

Inside the hut, the major took a quick look at Collins while I laid out the medical supplies dropped to me the day before. The major rummaged through them. "Tell them all I need is some glycerin."

I told Andy who radioed back, "O.K., I'll be back with it in the morning. Good luck, old top."

Up the notched log came the other parachutist. We shook hands, and he introduced himself as Captain "Sandy" Morrissey from Milwaukee, Wisconsin.

The two doctors went immediately to work on Collins. I watched them start to give him blood plasma, and though I wanted to help they didn't seem to need me. Then I thought I'd better be paying off the natives who had helped bring the stuff over from the other village; they might want to go home again. I opened the pack I'd carried and took out my bag of silver rupees. I went down the ladder and tried to hand each of the natives a couple, but they wouldn't take them from me. Instead, they pointed to the chief, so I turned to him and gave him a handful. He took them, went around to each of the natives, and handed them one apiece, then he handed the remainder back to me, keeping one himself.

One rupee, about thirty cents American for all that work. I handed the chief back the extra rupees, enough for another round, and motioned that he give them to the others. Everyone looked highly pleased. Sixty cents for all that mountain climbing burdened down with heavy packs, and they considered it high wages. What a place to retire, I thought.

5

The Loss of the *Indianapolis*

Raymond B. Lech

FIVE MINUTES PAST MIDNIGHT ON JULY 30, 1945, THE FIRST torpedo smashed into the starboard bow of the heavy cruiser USS *Indianapolis*, and an ear-shattering explosion rocked the ship. Three seconds later, the second torpedo found its mark directly under the bridge and blew up. The vessel lifted slightly out of the water, quivered, then promptly settled back down. At the same time, from the bridge to the bow on the starboard side, water was sent soaring into the midnight sky; flame, steam, and smoke belched out of her forward stack, and an enormous ball of fire swept through the entire forward half of the ship. Within seconds, the fire died away. Once again the *Indianapolis* was level and riding high, but now with the bow gone and two huge gaping holes in her right side.

From midships forward, the cruiser was a complete disaster; no light, no power, no communication, no pressure. Although the rear half of the vessel was untouched, the tons of water that gushed into the forward part of the cruiser sealed the fate of the *Indianapolis*.

IN THE WATER THE FIRST DAY: MONDAY, JULY 30, 1945

Quartermaster 3rd Class Vincent Allard found himself with six or seven other men, all desperately hanging onto a coiled floater net. One of them had a bared knife and was busy cutting the tangles in the net so that it would uncoil and spread out. While this was going on, Allard heard a cry for help. He quickly swam toward the sound and in a few seconds found a sailor floating on a pontoon from one of the ship's planes. He guided the man back to the group clustered around the net, but no sooner did he return when again he heard cries for help. Off he went once more and soon spotted two men holding onto a potato crate. One of the boys could swim, but the other could not and was very scared. Telling the swimmer to stick close, Allard began helping the non-swimmer to the safety of the net. On the way toward the group, he heard someone yell that he had a raft. Since it seemed that the raft was closer than the net, Allard changed course and headed for the sound. The voice called again, and Allard thought he recognized it as the *Indianapolis's* skipper, Captain Charles Butler McVay III. Allard called out to ask if it were the captain calling, and Captain McVay replied that it was and to come aboard. They swam a short distance and reached the rafts.

The man who could swim climbed unassisted into the empty second raft, McVay and Allard helped the other sailor in, and then Allard joined McVay in his raft. The two men in the second raft had swallowed an enormous amount of water, and at first Captain McVay thought they were both dying. But after a while, they came around. Just before sunrise, they met up with five men on another raft that had a floater net tied to it. They lashed this raft to theirs, and, at first light Monday morning, the group consisted of three rafts, one net, and nine men. Captain McVay was the only officer.

An inspection of the rafts turned up two canoe paddles, a box of cigarettes, fishing gear, signaling mirrors, and a tin container that held twelve Very (star) shells and a pistol. They also found a canvas bag holding a first-aid kit and matches, but it was soaked and everything inside was useless except for some sealed tubes of ointment. During the day, a water breaker holding three gallons of water floated by. This was given to McVay to be tasted, but salt water had leaked into the archaic wooden container and the water was undrinkable. So as not to create unnecessary fear, the captain didn't pass on the bad news but told everyone it would be rationed out when he thought it was "absolutely necessary that they have a drink."

No food was found on any of the rafts, but fortunately, sometime during the day, an emergency ration can drifted by. Upon opening, they found it was dry inside, and they pulled out a number of cans of Spam and small tins of malted-milk tablets and biscuits. The skipper told the other eight men that one twelve-ounce tin of Spam would be opened daily and divided equally. In addition, everyone would daily receive two biscuits and two malted-milk tablets. Under this quota, he figured they had rations to last ten days.

When the rafts crashed into the sea, their gratings had broken. Nevertheless the men made themselves as comfortable as possible and hung on while they were tossed about by the heavy swells of the unending ocean. At one moment they would be deep in a valley of waves and the next moment on top, looking down into that same valley. While on this unwanted roller-coaster ride, resting momentarily on the crest of a wave, they spotted two other rafts also on the crest of their waves. One raft was about 1,500 yards away and appeared to have one man on it who was calling for help. The other raft was much farther away and looked like it held a group of men who seemed to be in good condition. At this time though, McVay's group was too exhausted to paddle over to the near raft, and any investigation had to be held off until the next day.

During this first day, a monstrous shark decided to investigate the raft and its edible cargo. The shark kept swimming under the raft. The dorsal fin was "almost as white as a sheet of paper," while the body was a darker color. The shark could therefore always be spotted because of the visibility of its white fin in the water. The frightened men attempted to catch the pilot fish by knocking them off with canoe paddles, but this was an exercise in futility. They also tried hitting the shark with paddles, but when they occasionally did manage to do so he swam away and returned a few minutes later. In the days to follow, this unwanted nuisance was to become a real menace.

After spotting the two distant rafts, McVay and the others assumed that they were the only survivors of the ship and, all in all, figured no more than twenty-five or thirty men, including themselves, made it off. What they didn't know at the time was that they had drifted seven to ten miles north of the main groups.

Stranded in the middle of the deep and seemingly never-ending Philippine Sea, the captain understandably became very depressed. He daydreamed about taking a bath, drinking a cocktail, and relaxing in comfort, and in the midst of such thoughts he wished to live, but soon reality broke in upon his fantasies.

He dreaded the idea of seeing again the wives of his now dead officers. While at Mare Island, he and Mrs. McVay had gotten to know these women, and now "I knew there was nothing I could say to them. . . . " His mind drifted back to Guam. He remembered the moment when he was told no escort was needed, and he cursed the people there for not having one available; if there had been an escort, it could have radioed for help and picked up survivors. His final, and unfortunately most nagging, thought was of his personal responsibility: he was the captain, like it or not.

Two hours prior to the close of their first day, a plane flew overhead, its red-and-green running lights clearly visible. McVay fired one of the star shells skyward, but it went unnoticed. The container holding the shells had sixteen fillers but only twelve shells, which was the standard issue for this type of raft. It irked

McVay to see four empty slots. Why couldn't they just fill the entire thing up and be done with it?

As the day drew to an end, however, spirits were high in anticipation of the morrow's rescue. The *Indianapolis* was due in Leyte Gulf in the morning, and when the heavy cruiser didn't show up questions would be asked, a search made, and rescue would be on the way.

After narrowly escaping from his after engine room, Lieutenant Richard Redmayne swam from the starboard side of the *Indianapolis*. Within five minutes, he found a kapok life preserver, which he put on, and for about a half hour he rested in the water alone. Then he spotted a life raft with men on it and joined them. During the remaining dark morning hours, two more rafts and two floater nets joined the group. The three rafts and two nets were lashed together, and they continued to drift, picking up water breakers, floating food containers, and other men.

Surveying the area at first light, they found the hostile sea covered with a heavy oil slick, five-inch powder cans, and an assortment of junk. Many of the men were terribly sick from swallowing sea water and oil, and the ones who had passed out in the water were being held up by their shipmates. A head count was attempted, and they discovered that their group consisted of approximately 150 men, including four officers and five chiefs. Lieutenant Redmayne, as the senior officer, took charge.

In addition to the three rafts and two nets, about 90 percent of the people in the water in this group were wearing life jackets; the ones who didn't have any held onto the side of the rafts or onto men who had jackets, or they hugged empty ammo cans. The rafts themselves were very overcrowded, each one averaging fifteen to twenty men, and the sailors who had been put on the rafts were the ones the officers and others in charge thought to be in the worst condition.

On Monday, nothing much happened. The large group floated, drifted, survived. They spotted the same two afternoon planes McVay had seen and also fired flares at the one plane that evening, with no success.

Certain early signs of insubordination surfaced. One of the men on the floater net was Petty Officer F. Giulio. Because of his particular job aboard ship, he was well known among the crew. On this first day, he kept complaining that he should be put on a raft since the life jacket kept slipping around his legs and he had a hard time keeping afloat. Giulio was the senior ranking man on that net and therefore their natural leader.

Distributed among the rafts and nets were four water casks and about nine or ten emergency tins of food, which contained malted-milk tablets, biscuits, and Spam. During the late afternoon, Giulio and some of his followers broke into the rations and began to eat. A short distance away, Chief Petty Officer Clarence Benton spotted them and immediately ordered them to stop, since all rations were to be divided equally. For the time being, Giulio and his small group obeyed the order.

During the evening Lieutenant Redmayne allowed a small amount of food to be rationed equally to all the men in the group.

At approximately 1:30 a.m., Quartermaster 1st Class Robert Gause spotted a fin. By estimating the distance between the dorsal and tail, he guessed the shark to be about twelve feet long.

Quite a few sailors in his group were critically wounded. There were a large number of severe flash burns of the face, arms, and body, and some men had compound fractures of one sort or another. There were no medical supplies of any kind for the frustrated Doctor Lewis Haynes, and many of the men with fractures and burns died from shock during the first few hours. After removing their life jackets, the dead were allowed to slip away. Before the boiling sun rose over the distant horizon on Monday morning, about fifty of the original four hundred were dead.

By daybreak, this mass of floating humanity had split into three subgroups. The largest group contained about two hundred men, the second one hundred, and the smallest about fifty. These subgroups were separated from each other by a distance of only several hundred yards, at most. Leader of the group of two hundred men was Captain Edward Parke, commanding officer of the Marine Detachment and holder of the Bronze Star for bravery on Guadalcanal. Strong and athletic, he was superb in his energy, leadership, and self-sacrifice. Dr. Haynes remembered him as the typical Marine, one who was very strict with the group and had the situation well in hand.

The main objective was for everyone to stay together. Captain Parke found a cork life ring with about one hundred feet of attached line. To prevent drifting, he strung the line out and each man grabbed a piece of it and took up the slack. In this way, they formed a long line of men which began to curl on itself, as a wagon train would circle against attack. The wounded were brought into the middle and tied to the life ring itself by the strings on their jackets. There was no confusion, and the men stayed well grouped together. If someone did drift off the line, Parke swam over to the man and herded him back in. On several occasions, he gave his jacket to a man without one and swam unsupported until he could find another preserver.

Bravery in this enormous group of "swimmers" was everywhere. Commander Lipski, the ship's gunnery officer, who had been very badly burned, was cheerfully supported all day Monday by Airman 1st Class Anthony Maday. Lieutenant Commander Coleman, who came aboard in Guam, was the leader of a group, and he worked unceasingly to keep them together. Time after time, he swam out to bring in stragglers. Ultimately, Commander Coleman became so weak that he died from exhaustion. And there was Ensign Moynelo, who organized a large group of men. For three days, he kept the group together, rounded up drifters, and took off his own jacket many times and gave it to those without until he could find another. Finally he, too, collapsed and died.

Shortly after dawn on Monday, Lieutenant Commander Moss W. Flannery, commanding officer of VPB-133 based on Tinian, climbed into his Ventura bomber and headed out over the Philippine Sea on routine antisubmarine patrol. Visibility was unlimited and in order to obtain better horizon shots for navigation, instead of flying at his normal 5,000 feet, he dropped down and flew between 1,500 and 2,000 feet. At 9:20 a.m., he flew directly over Dr. Haynes and his group of 350 men. In the water, the men saw this plane coming directly at them, the sun reflecting off its front window, and they began splashing the water with their hands and feet to draw attention. Ensign Park, one of the ship's aviators, had some green marker dye in his jacket and spread it in the water. They all firmly believed that they had been seen and estimated that within five hours seaplanes from Guam would be landing in their midst.

Flannery, however, couldn't see a thing. The best way to spot something as small as a head in the ocean is not to look out at an angle but straight down, and at a height of 500 to 800 feet, not 1,500 feet. Flannery was looking out his side window, and his biggest problem was the glassy sea.

By 10:00 a.m., the sun was reflecting so sharply off the sea that everyone began to suffer from intense photophobia, an intolerance to light. Dr. Haynes was very concerned, since he considered this far worse than snow blindness. It caused severe pain, which was relieved only when the sun went down. Closing the eyelids did not help since the sun burned right through. In order to somewhat ease the discomfort, the men ripped their clothing and blindfolded themselves. Fortunately, their bodies did not burn; they were all covered by fuel oil, which the searing rays of the sun could not penetrate.

For the remainder of the first day, there was constant change among the three subgroups. They would merge for a short time then break apart again. The wounded stayed in fairly good shape, and only a few men died. In order to determine death, Dr. Haynes would place his finger on the pupil of an eye and if there was no reflex it was assumed the man was dead. The jacket would be removed and the body allowed to drift away. In the background, some of the men would recite the Lord's Prayer.

By noontime, the sea became choppy again, with large swells. Practically everyone by this time had swallowed some of the oil-soaked water, and they were all throwing up. Thirst was beginning to get to the men, and Haynes, while trying unsuccessfully to find some first-aid supplies, visited all three groups and cautioned them against drinking salt water. For the moment, all the men agreed not to drink from the sea.

The survivors were beginning to see sharks in the area, but, so far, there were no major attacks. Giles McCoy, of the Marine Detachment, saw a shark attack a dead man. He believed that because of the dead men in the water so much food was available that the sharks were not inclined to bother with those still alive.

That, however, had been in the morning and afternoon. By the time that the merciless sun began to set, large numbers of sharks had arrived on the scene, and the men were scared. Cuts were bleeding. When a shark approached a group, everyone would kick, punch, and create a general racket. This often worked, and the predator would leave. At other times, however, the shark "would have singled out his victim and no amount of shouts or pounding of the water would turn him away. There would be a piercing scream and the water would be churned red as the shark cut his victim to ribbons."

IN THE WATER THE SECOND DAY: TUESDAY, JULY 31, 1945

Yesterday they had been too exhausted to paddle over to the raft holding the one lone man, and this morning he was still calling to them. Thinking him hurt, the McVay group began the tremendous task of pulling nine men on three lashed rafts and a floater net to this isolated and scared soul. Changing the two men paddling once every half hour, it took them four and a half hours to traverse the 1,600 yards separating them and their objective. Upon finally reaching the young man, they saw that, besides being lonely, there was nothing wrong with the new member, and McVay said, "As misery loves company, he wanted somebody to talk to."

There still remained the other group farther away that had been spotted the day before, but the men were now too exhausted to try to reach them. Besides, most of the men had blisters on their hands, and these were creating saltwater ulcers. The new man told the skipper he had seen no one else in the water, and the captain was convinced that his group, plus the small pack of men in the distance, were the sole survivors, even though it seemed incredible that no one else had escaped.

In the morning there was no wind, but the sea could still be described as rough. As the day wore on, the endless water calmed down. There were very long, sweeping swells, but they didn't break and no whitecaps could be seen. Considering the circumstances, the group was comfortable and in fairly good shape.

During the day, Vincent Allard took the large canvas bag that had held the matches, first-aid kits, etc., and fashioned out of the fabric a "cornucopia" cap for everyone. The men pulled the hats over their ears, and this, together with the fuel oil that covered them, saved them from the scorching rays of the sun. To further protect their hands from sunburn, they placed them under the oil-covered water sloshing around in the grating of the rafts.

The fishing kit they found on one of the rafts was a delight to any fisherman's eye, and both McVay and Allard were excellent fishermen. But it didn't help much since there were a number of sharks in the area, and the one big monster of the first day was still performing his merry-go-round act. They did manage to catch some black fish which McVay thought to be in the parrot family; although the meat was very white, he was afraid to let the men eat it. Instead, he used this flesh as bait, hoping to catch nearby schools of bonito and mackerel. However, every time they dropped the line, the shark took what they offered, and, after a while, they gave up the idea of fishing.

During this second twenty-four-hour period, two planes had been spotted; one at 1:00 a.m. and the second at 9:00 p.m. A pair of star shells were fired at both planes, but they weren't seen. The men griped about the shells, for once they reached their maximum height they burst like fireworks and then immediately died. The group wished parachutes were attached, which would float the light back and give the aviator more time to recognize the distress signal.

At dawn on the second day, the isolated Redmayne group had about sixty men on rafts and another sixty to eighty in the water. Meanwhile, during the dark morning hours, some of the more seriously injured men had died.

The water breakers turned out to be a disappointment. Some of the casks were empty while the others contained either salt or cruddy black water. Lieutenant Redmayne said, "It was dirty and tasted as though the salt content was about equal to the salt content of the seawater." These casks were made of wood, and when the rafts crashed into the sea the seams on the casks split, thereby allowing fresh water to escape and salt water to seep in. The casks were large, heavy, and difficult to handle, and in the standard life raft the water would probably become salty after the first use. Once the seal was broken to pour water, it couldn't properly be resealed, thus allowing salt water to seep in. Should the cup become lost, serving fresh water from the cask resulted in great wastage.

First-aid equipment was generally useless, since the containers were not watertight. Anything in tubes remained sealed, but there weren't enough remedies to go around for burns and eye troubles caused by salt water and fuel oil. The food stayed in good condition but, here again, there was a problem since the primary staple was Spam. Not only did this increase thirst because it was salty, but Spam draws sharks. The men discovered this when they opened a can of Spam and sharks gathered all around them.

The policy of the group was to put all men on rafts who were sick, injured, or didn't have life jackets or belts. The problem with this, however, was that men with belts or jackets began taking them off and allowing them to drift away in order to qualify for the relative safety of a raft. This necessitated keeping a close watch on the men. Giulio and his small band were now beginning to start trouble. Giulio, who was still on a floater net, kept insisting that he deserved some time on a raft. This request was not granted, and he continued to complain.

During the early part of this second day, some of the men swam over to Ensign Donald Blum and reported that the food had been broken into. Blum swam back with them to take a look and saw men eating and drinking. This was immediately reported to Redmayne, who then ordered that all food and water be placed on one raft and guarded at all times by the officers and chiefs. Later in the day there were reports that Giulio was again stealing food, but it was not clear whether food was being taken from the guarded raft or all the food had not been handed in. Ensign Harlan Twible, who was on a floater net about forty feet from Giulio, yelled out in a loud, clear voice, "The first man I see eating food not rationed I will report if we ever get in." He further told them that they were acting like a bunch of recruits and not seamen. As far as can be ascertained, there were no deaths in this group during the second day, and everyone appeared to be in fairly good shape. The only problem was Giulio and his gang. The next day would be a different story.

Even though total blackness surrounded them, because of the choppy sea the men were having a very difficult time sleeping. In this inky isolation, some of the weaker members of the crew, who could not face what they thought must be ahead of them, gave up all hope; they silently slipped out of their life jackets and committed suicide by drowning. Numerous deadly fights broke out over life jackets, and about twenty-five men were killed by their shipmates. At dawn, Dr. Haynes saw that the general condition of the men was not good, and the group appeared to be smaller. Haynes later recalled that basically two factors, other than lack of water, contributed greatly to the high mortality: the heat from the tropical sun and the ingestion of salt water. The drinking of salt water in his group was generally not deliberate but occurred during bouts of delirium or from the accidental swallowing of water in the choppy sea.

The constant breaking of waves over the men's heads the first two days, particularly when they tried to rest, caused most of them to develop a mechanical sinusitis. The swallowing of small amounts of seawater and fuel oil could not be avoided, and the sun caused intense headache and photophobia. The combination of these factors resulted in many deaths.

During the latter part of the day, the sea grew calmer. The men's thirst, however, had become overpowering as the placid water became very clear. As the day wore on, the men became more and more exhausted and complained of their thirst. Dr. Haynes noticed that the younger men, largely those without families, started to drink salt water first. As the hot sun continued to beat down on them, an increasing number of survivors were becoming delirious, talking incoherently, and drinking tremendous amounts of salt water.

They started becoming maniacal, thrashing around in the water and exhibiting considerable strength and energy compared to those who were exhausted but still sane. These spells would continue until the man either drowned or went into a coma. Several brave men, wearing rubber life belts, tried to support maniacal men and also drowned, for during the struggles the belts developed punctures or rips and deflated. Haynes kept swimming from one huge huddle of sailors to another, desperately trying to help. All during this time, people were getting discouraged and calling out for help, and he would be there to reassure and calm them down.

There were sharks in the area again. The clear water allowed the men to look down and see them. It seems that during this second day, however, the sharks were going after dead men, especially the bodies that were sinking down into the deeper ocean. They didn't seem to bother the men on the surface.

Things became progressively worse from sundown on the second day. The men's stories become mixed up, and some accounts are totally incoherent, making it difficult to piece together what actually happened. Haynes remembered that shortly after sundown they all experienced severe chills, which lasted for at least an hour. These were followed by high fever, as most of the group became delirious and got out of control. The men fought with one another, thinking there were Japanese in the group, and disorganization and disintegration occurred rapidly. Captain Parke worked until he collapsed. Haynes was so exhausted that he drifted away from the group.

Some of the men attempted to help their shipmates. They swam outside the group, rounding up stragglers and towing them back in. The kapok jackets had a brass ring and also a snap on the back. At night, people who had these jackets on would form a circle and hook them all together. The rest of the men would get in the middle. The corrallers themselves were worried, however, since the jackets had lost so much buoyancy that the feeling of security they provided was rapidly ebbing.

By nightfall, more and more people were removing their preservers and throwing them away. Most of these men died. Haynes swam from one batch of crazed men to another, trying to calm them down. He would locate the groups by the screaming of the delirious men. From this night on, what happened in the water can only be described as a nightmare.

In the Water the Third Day: Wednesday, August 1, 1945

The captain and the men with him were continuing to fare relatively well. McVay still believed that his ship went down with all hands and that, at most, there could only be thirty survivors.

From the opening of this day, the central thought on the minds of the men was to kill the shark; it was big, it kept circling closer and closer, and they were frightened. This monster could easily rip the raft apart with one swift motion of his enormous jaws. But the only weapon they had was a knife from the fishing kit, with a one-inch blade, and there was no way they could tackle this massive creature with a blade that small. So the day passed with the men sitting and staring at the shark, annoyed that a larger weapon was not in the kit and further chafed that not one man had a sheath knife, an implement customarily carried by many of the sailors aboard ship.

Just before first light, a plane flew over, and two star shells were fired. Again at 1:00 p.m., a bomber, heading toward Leyte, passed above. They tried to attract this second plane with mirrors, yellow signal flags, and splashing, but to no avail.

Although the order had been given the day before to bring all food to the command raft, there was still a certain amount of hoarding going on. This morning, however, several more rafts handed their cached rations over to Redmayne. During the day, one cracker, a malted-milk tablet, and a few drops of precious water were allocated to each man. Some survivors tried their luck at fishing but, as with the McVay group, the numerous sharks in the area kept stealing the bait. Not everyone realized there was safety in numbers. Some men swam away. Attempts to stop them failed, and soon after leaving the security of the group these sailors were usually dragged beneath the surface by the sharks.

Toward late afternoon, some of the sailors started becoming delirious again. More and more men were drinking salt water.

Chief Benton (Redmayne's assistant) attempted to talk to these half-crazed men in a calm, reassuring voice, but it wasn't much use. Fights broke out, men started swimming away, and people committed suicide by drowning themselves. A sailor yelled to Redmayne that things were getting very bad on his raft, and Ensign Eames was sent over to investigate. Upon returning, Eames reported that some of the men were making homosexual advances toward one of the other men. Upon hearing these reports, the chief engineer's reaction was to have the people around him recite the Lord's Prayer.

Giulio had been on a net for the previous two days, but this morning the pharmacist's mate decided to transfer him to a raft because Giulio complained that his eyes were bothering him. Shortly thereafter, it was noticed that Giulio and the people with him were eating and drinking. Upon checking the stored rations on the command raft, it was discovered that two of the four water breakers were missing, plus several cans of rations. The officers and chiefs ordered Giulio to return everything immediately, but he ignored them. Some of the senior people then swam over to the mutineers and tried to grab the food and water away, but they were unsuccessful since Giulio and his small band were much stronger than the tired officers. Throughout the day, he and his gang had themselves a veritable Roman feast while others suffered and died.

The early morning hours found Dr. Haynes with a large pack of swimmers headed by Captain Parke of the Marines who, through willpower, strength, and sheer determination, kept the group under control. Before dawn Haynes twice became delirious. At one point, he remembered, "The waves kept hitting me in the face, and I got the impression that people were splashing water in my face as a joke, and I pleaded with them that it wasn't funny and that I was sick. I begged them to stop and kept swimming furiously to make them stop, and then my head cleared."

Most of the men had become hysterical, and some were quickly going mad. A few of the sailors got the idea that people were trying to drown them and that there were Japanese in the group. The cry would circulate, "Get the Jap! Kill him!" Fights broke out, knives were drawn, and several men were brutally stabbed. Mass hysteria reigned.

The doctor did his best to calm them down but was unsuccessful and at one point he himself was held underwater by an insane crewman and had to fight his way back up. Captain Parke desperately tried to regain control but finally became delirious himself and eventually died. Once Parke was gone, the mass madness forced the subgroup to further dissolve, and the men scattered. They wanted to be alone, for no one trusted anyone else.

Under a cloudless sky and full moon, Haynes drifted, isolated but totally alert. A man floated by, and they instinctively backed away from each other. Everyone was crazy. Haynes hated being alone, however, and not very far away he heard the noises that the irrational members of another group were making and began swimming toward the sound. Only a few yards short of this band of men, his strength gave out, and he screamed for help. Breaking off from the pack, his chief pharmacist's mate, John Schmueck, grabbed him and towed him to the safety of their numbers.

Supported by Schmueck, who put his arm through the back of Haynes's jacket and lifted the doctor's body so that it rested on his own hip, Dr. Haynes fell asleep for a few hours. Schmueck himself was not in good shape and was having a difficult time with his rubber life ring. It was defective, and for two days—until he finally got a kapok jacket—he had had to hold his finger over the valve. When the ring would deflate too much, he would have to blow it up again and then hold his finger on it some more.

The new group was well organized and ably led by Ensign Moynelo. Someone in the group suggested using the leg straps on the kapok jackets to snap the men together. This worked very well and prevented them from drifting apart. By daybreak the sea was mirror calm, but the condition of the men was becoming critical. They had difficulty thinking clearly, and most of them talked incoherently and had hallucinations.

By this time, the kapok jackets just kept the men's heads out of the water. There was a great deal of anxiety within Moynelo's group concerning the buoyancy of the preservers since the Navy Manual stated that jackets would remain buoyant for only two days, and they were now well into their third. However, the kapok preservers maintained fair buoyancy, even after one hundred hours, and the mental distress that the men felt on this account turned out to have been uncalled for.

Preservers were, unfortunately, fairly easy to obtain. When a man died (and they were now dying en masse), Haynes would remove his jacket and add it to a pile in the middle of the group. This became their reserve when somebody's jacket went on the "fritz."

Sanity, as we know it, virtually disappeared on this third day. The few men who retained some semblance of sense tried to help their weaker shipmates, but it was a losing battle. Chief Gunner Harrison recalled that "Doctor Haynes's conduct throughout the time he was in the water was, in my opinion, above his normal call of duty. The comfort the men got from just talking to him seemed to quiet them down and relieve some of their worry."

Haynes felt that what kept him going was taking care of the men. They constantly asked him questions about whether the water was salty all the way down and when he thought the planes were coming.

Gunner Harrison remembered, "Early one morning somebody woke me up and wanted to know why we did not stop at an island that we passed. That story caused a great deal of trouble. Several of them believed that those islands were there—three islands. Lieutenant McKissick even dreamed he went to the island and there was a hotel there and they would not let him on the island. The first time I heard the story was, this kid woke me up and wanted to know why we did not stop there." All day long, small numbers of men broke off from the gathering and swam for the "island," never to be seen again.

Noticing a line of men stretching for some distance, Commander Haynes curiously swam to it and asked what was going on. He was told to be quiet for there was a hotel up ahead but it only had one room, and when it was your turn to get in you could sleep for fifteen minutes. Haynes turned and swam away from this procession of patient survivors. Stragglers were continually being rounded up and herded back to the group. Sometimes the job would take up to an hour but Haynes knew that they had to stay together in order to be found.

On this Wednesday afternoon, Ensign Moynelo disappeared with the group who were going to swim to Leyte. It all started out when some quartermaster claimed to have figured out the current and the wind, and how long it would take to swim to Leyte. Approximately twenty-five men joined him. They anticipated that it would take them a day and a half to reach the Philippines, based upon a two-knot current and swimming at one knot per hour. Once this large party disappeared from sight, it was never seen again. This was the largest single group of men lost during the days in the water. All of the strong leaders were now dead, except for Gunner Harrison and Commander Haynes. The doctor recalled that "Gunner Harrison and I were about the only ones left who were well enough to think, and he was just like the Rock of Gibraltar. He always had a smile and kept the group together. He used to say to the fellows, 'If that old broken-down Rickenbacker can stay out on the ocean for a week, we can stay for a month.'" Because of Harrison's leadership, "we managed to keep together. His morale was high, and his cheerful exhortations kept everyone united."

The doctor continued to pronounce men dead. He would remove their jackets, recite the Lord's Prayer, and release the bodies. The water was very clear, and Dr. Haynes remembered the bodies looking like small dolls sinking in the deep sea. He watched them until they faded from sight. A cloud of death hung over everyone, and rescue was no longer discussed. By early evening, all was calm—it was no longer a question of who would die, but when.

IN THE WATER THE FOURTH DAY: THURSDAY, AUGUST 2, 1945

With Lieutenant Redmayne delirious, Ensign Twible tried to command the group until he became totally exhausted and his effectiveness limited. Chief Benton was in a little better shape, however, and issued many orders on his own. During the morning, a man swam over to Twible's raft with cans of crackers and said Giulio sent them. No reason was given, and it is not known whether this was in response to a direct order or a limited act of charity.

More and more people were losing touch with their rational selves. For example, there were plenty of good kapok jackets available, but an insane sailor went up to a man wearing one of the rubber rings, ripped it off his body, and swam away. Unnecessary and foolish acts of this type were taking place throughout the groups. As Freud said, "The primitive stages can always be reestablished; the primitive mind is, in the fullest meaning of the word, imperishable."

The pharmacist's mate in this group, Harold Anthony, worked as hard as humanly possible to aid men in the water and became extremely fatigued. During the night he mentioned to one of his friends that he couldn't keep this pace up much longer and would probably be dead shortly. Twelve hours later, with the relentless Pacific sun beating down on this lonely spot of ocean, the lifeless body of the corpsman was permitted to drift away.

Doctor Haynes's group disbanded again. Small groups were continually forming and breaking up. The night had been particularly difficult, and most of the men suffered from chills, fever, and delirium. These lonely people were now dying in droves, and the helpless physician could only float and watch. By Thursday morning, August 2, the condition of most of the men was critical. Many were in coma and could be aroused only with exceptional effort. The group no longer existed, with the men drifting off and dying one by one. This isolation from the companionship of another human was cataclysmic.

At 9:00 a.m., on Thursday, August 2, securely strapped in the pilot's seat, Lieutenant (jg) Wilbur C. Gwinn pushed the throttles forward, brought the motors of his twin-engine Ventura bomber to an ear-splitting roar, and raced down the Peleliu runway. His mission was a regular day reconnaissance patrol of Sector 19V258. He was to report and attempt to sink any Japanese submarine in his area. The route for the outward leg of his journey just happened to have him flying directly over the heads of the dying men of the *Indianapolis*.

At the very rear of a Ventura is an antenna that trails behind the aircraft. It is used primarily for navigation. In order to keep the antenna from whipping around in the wind, which would make it useless, a weight (known as a "sock") is secured to the end. Once Gwinn gained enough speed to get airborne, he pulled back and the nose of the bomber pointed up toward the blue sky. At the same time, he lost the weight from his navigational antenna. With this "trailing antenna sock" gone, he had two choices: turn around and get it fixed, or continue on patrol and navigate by dead reckoning. Because the weather was excellent, Lieutenant Gwinn decided to go on, took the plane up to 3,000 feet, and over a glassy sea began looking for enemy submarines.

Dead reckoning navigation is not very accurate, and over the Pacific Ocean it is neither a very comfortable nor enviable position to be in. At 11:00 a.m., about an hour and forty-five minutes out of Peleliu, Gwinn figured that since caution is the better part of valor, the whipping antenna being pulled behind the plane should somehow be anchored down. Because the radioman was busy with something else and his co-pilot was concentrating on filling out a weather report, Gwinn resolved to repair it himself. Crawling through the after tunnel of the Ventura, he reached the narrow end and stared at the long, slender, thrashing piece of metal, wondering how to fix it. While attempting to come up with some creative solution to his problem, Gwinn happened to look down from his 3,000-foot perch into the Philippine Sea. At that precise moment, he saw it. The thin line of oil could only have come from a leaking submarine, and the startled pilot rushed back to his left-hand seat and began flying the airplane.

At 11:18 a.m., he changed his course so as to follow the snake-like slick. Not being able to see very well, he brought the bomber down to 900 feet. Mile after mile the slick continued, never seeming to reach an end. Five miles later, he suddenly saw them—thirty heads wrapped in a twenty-five-mile orbit of oil. Many were clinging to the sides of a raft, while others floated and feebly made motions to the plane. Who in the world could these people be? At 11:20 a.m., about two minutes after sighting what had looked like black balls on the water, the pilot dropped down to a wave-skimming 300 feet.

He ordered his radioman to get a message off, and at 11:25 a.m., the following transmission was sent:

SIGHTED 30 SURVIVORS

011-30 NORTH 133-30 EAST

DROPPED TRANSMITTER AND LIFEBOAT EMERGENCY

IFF ON 133-30

Now that he had positioned the thirty survivors, there was nothing more Gwinn could do so he decided to spread out his search. Following the slick on a northerly course, six miles farther on he found forty more men. Continuing on, four miles more had him pass over another fifty-five to seventy-five people—and still farther north, he found scattered groups of twos and threes. After an hour of flying and looking, Lieutenant Gwinn estimated that there were 150 men in the water.

The survivors were dispersed along a line about twenty miles long. He noticed a group so crowded on rafts that he was unable to tell the exact number of rafts they had. He could barely spot a lone oil-covered man, even at his low altitude, unless he was splashing the water.

Gwinn's antenna problem now had to be solved—quickly. The position he sent out in his first message was calculated by dead reckoning and couldn't possibly be accurate. He had to fix the whipping antenna, and once again he crawled through the dark tunnel to reach the end of the bomber. Once there, he put his hand out the tail, grabbed the long rod, and pulled it inside. Taking a rubber hose, he tied it around the tip of the antenna and pushed the length back out, hoping, while crawling back to the pilot's seat, that there would be enough weight to stop the shaking and get a decent fix. They tried, and it worked.

One hour and twenty minutes after sending his first message of thirty survivors, a second dispatch from the bomber was transmitted:

SEND RESCUE SHIP

11-15N 133-47E 150 SURVIVORS

IN LIFE BOAT AND JACKETS

DROPPED RED RAMROD

Gwinn received orders to stick around.

Dr. Haynes saw the thing and prayed it was real. Flying very low, the bomber zoomed over his head and as quickly as it came, it passed and soon was a dot on the opposite horizon. At that moment, Haynes knew he and his fellow survivors were dead men. Their last ounce of strength was giving out, and this plane was like all the others—blind to the living hell beneath it.

After scouting the area, there was no doubt in Gwinn's mind that these were American sailors below him. Turning the plane, he looked for a group which appeared to be alone and without rafts, and began dropping everything in the plane that floated.

When Dr. Haynes saw the distant dot suddenly reverse course and come back toward them, low over the water, he then knew that they had been sighted. Like a sudden tropical squall, things began falling from the sky. Two life rafts were dropped, together with cans of fresh water. The water cans ruptured on landing but the most important thing was that Gwinn saw them, and those fortunate enough to be still alive knew rescue was near.

Once there was nothing left to drop to the splashing, oil-covered men, Gwinn released dye markers and smoke bombs so as not to lose the position.

It would not be until the next day that the Navy finally discovered that these were survivors from the *Indianapolis*. By this time, the entire Pacific was curious as to who these people were. Ashore, many people thought that they had Japanese in the water and weren't in too big a rush to get things moving. A short time before, in this same area, escorts from a convoy had reported they had attacked a Japanese submarine.

However, after the second report citing "150 survivors" came in, all hell broke loose. Because submarines don't carry 150 men, Pacific Fleet knew they had a surface vessel to contend with, and if a Japanese warship had been sunk they would have known about it. It finally dawned on CinCPac that they might have an American ship down, and panic started to set in. Shortly after

Gwinn's second message was received, CinCPac (now in a state of agitation) began radioing ships to report their positions.

For an hour after his second dispatch, Gwinn was all alone, attempting to comfort the dying men beneath him as best he could. Then another plane, on transport duty to the Philippines, appeared. It stayed with the Ventura for about an hour and dropped three of its rafts.

Back at Gwinn's base, the communications officer decoded the first message concerning the thirty survivors and quickly passed it on to his (and Gwinn's) boss, Lieutenant Commander George Atteberry, commanding officer of VPB-152. This was the Peleliu unit of the Search and Reconnaissance Command of Vice Admiral Murray, Commander, Marianas. The unit was under the command of Rear Admiral W. R. Greer.

Atteberry calculated the fuel supply of the lone, circling bomber and estimated that Gwinn would have to leave the scene by 3:30 p.m. in order to land with a small amount of reserve fuel. Not wanting to leave the survivors alone, Commander Atteberry started making some fast decisions.

Not far from the Ventura squadron was a squadron of seaplanes (Dumbos), and Atteberry picked up the phone and told the duty officer of VPB-23 to get a seaplane out to the area by 3:30 p.m. Not having intercepted Gwinn's message, "23" was skeptical about the whole thing and not eager to cooperate. Not liking this attitude, Atteberry drove over to their unit to ascertain the ready status personally. Once there, he decided they couldn't get a plane up in time to relieve Gwinn, so he quickly drove back to his own unit and ordered his plane and crew to get ready for takeoff. At exactly the same moment Gwinn's second message came in, Atteberry, whose call sign was "Gambler Leader," was lifting his bomber off the Peleliu runway.

During the hour-and-a-half flight out, "Leader" was in constant contact with his squadron office and was happy to hear that "23" finally had gotten airborne and on the way. At 2:15 p.m.,

Atteberry spotted Gwinn, together with the PBM, the large seaplane on transport duty, and immediately established voice contact with both. The commander was given a quick tour of the groups in order to size up the situation. Finally, so that the men in the water wouldn't think they were being deserted, the pilot of the PBM was ordered to circle the southwest half of the huge slick while "Gambler Leader" ranged the northeast portion.

Gwinn's fuel supply was running low, and twenty minutes after Atteberry arrived, he sent Gwinn on his way. Lieutenant Gwinn's third and final message read:

RELIEF BY 70V [Atteberry]

RETURNING TO BASE

The PBM also had to go, and for forty-five minutes Commander Atteberry was all alone, circling and comforting those below by his presence. Then out of his cockpit window, he saw the big, lumbering Dumbo waddling toward him from the distant southern horizon.

Patrol Bombing Squadron 23 was told that Atteberry and his planes were going to remain on the scene until "23" got one of their Catalinas out there. Lieutenant R. Adrian Marks happened to be the duty pilot at the time, and 1,400 gallons of gas were loaded into his seaplane. While this was taking place, Marks, together with his air combat intelligence officer, went to group operations to see if they could gather any more information than what Commander Atteberry had given them. Operations had nothing to offer and, unable to believe that there were so many men (i.e., thirty men as per Gwinn's first transmission) in the water, Marks assumed he was going out to pick up a ditched pilot. With a full tank of gas and extra air–sea rescue gear, Lieutenant Marks shoved his mammoth down the Peleliu runway and, once airborne, turned north. The time was 12:45 p.m.

On the way out, "Playmate 2" (Marks's call sign) received word that instead of thirty men in the sea there were now about 150. This was absolutely incomprehensible to Marks, and he assumed that the message must have been garbled in transmission. However, he "thought it would be a good idea to get to the scene as quickly as possible." At 3:03 p.m., he began picking up radio signals from Atteberry, and a little over three hours from takeoff, at 3:50 p.m., "Playmate 2" made visual contact and established communications with the commander.

Marks was dumbfounded—how did all these people get here? "Gambler Leader" instructed "Playmate 2" not to drop a single thing—there was much more than met the eye. For a half hour, Atteberry gave Marks the tour. Then the Dumbo dropped everything it had (saving only one small raft for itself), concentrating on those floaters who had only jackets.

With everything out of the plane, Marks wondered what he could do next. Looking down at the bobbing mass of humanity, he knew they were in horrible shape but also just as important—and maybe more so—he saw the sharks. Therefore, at "about 16:30 I decided a landing would be necessary to gather in the single ones. This decision was based partly on the number of single survivors, and the fact that they were bothered by sharks. We did observe bodies being eaten by sharks." Marks told "Gambler Leader" he was going in, and Atteberry notified his base that the Dumbo was landing and that he himself needed relief.

Preparations were made inside the Catalina for landing, while Marks looked for a spot where he thought the floating plane would do the most good. Never having made a landing at sea before, he was a little nervous. However, "at 17:15 a power stall was made into the wind. The wind was due north, swells about twelve feet high. The plane landed in three bounces, the first bounce being about fifteen feet high." "Playmate 2" was down safe—but not very sound.

The hull was intact, but rivets had sprung loose and seams ripped open from impact. While rivet holes were plugged with pencils and cotton shoved into the seams, the radio compartment was taking on water and was being bailed out at the rate of ten to twelve buckets per hour. In the meantime, the co-pilot went aft and began organizing the rescue effort. Because of the high swells, Marks couldn't see anything from his cockpit seat. Atteberry stayed in direct communication with him, however, and guided the Dumbo toward the survivors. Both pilots made the decision to stay away from men on rafts, since they appeared to be in better shape than those floating alone. There were problems, however, for although every effort was made to pick up the single ones it was necessary to avoid passing near the men on life rafts because they would jump onto the plane.

The side hatch had been opened, and the plane's ladder was hung out. Standing on the rungs was a crewman and, when they passed a swimmer, he would grab him and pull him aboard. This was very unsatisfactory though, because the people in the water were too weak to hang on. Furthermore, when a burned survivor, or one whose arm or leg was broken, was snatched, the pain was excruciating. They tried throwing out their remaining raft with a rope attached for a swimmer to grab (they were too frail to jump in). Then they would reel the raft back in. This proved to be impractical, because Marks continually kept the plane taxiing and anyone hanging on was dragged through the water. Finally, they settled on going up to a man, cutting the engines, bringing him aboard, and then starting up again and going to another swimmer. Once the engines were cut, silence enveloped the area except for the terrifying cries for help heard by the crew of "Playmate 2."

Before night fell, Marks had picked up thirty people and crammed them into the body of his leaking seaplane. All were in bad shape, and they were immediately given water and first aid. Naturally, as soon as the first man was plucked from the sea, Lieutenant Marks learned the *Indianapolis* had gone down. There was no way, however, that he was going to transmit this word in the clear and "I was too busy to code a message of this nature." So it would not be until Friday, August 3, that the U.S. Navy finally learned that one of their heavy cruisers had been sunk just after midnight on July 30.

In the sky above the drifting Dumbo, Atteberry was busy directing Marks and telling other planes coming into the area where to drop their gear in order "to obtain the best possible distribution among them." Between the first sighting and midnight, planes continually flew in, and, at one point, there were eleven aircraft on the scene.

With night upon him, it was impossible for Marks to pick up any more individual swimmers, and he therefore taxied toward a large assembly of men who had had rafts dropped to them earlier in the day. This was Commander Haynes's group. Survivors were packed like sardines inside the hull of the Dumbo, so Marks ordered these men to be laid on top of the wings, covered with parachutes, and given water. This damaged the wing fabric, and it became doubtful whether the Catalina would ever fly again.

In the black of this Pacific night, things began to settle down; the stillness was interrupted only by the occasional pained moans of the *Indianapolis* crew. Marks couldn't move the plane for fear of running people down, so they drifted and waited for rescue. Just before midnight, a searchlight on the far horizon pierced the onyx sky, and at the same time a circling plane dropped a parachute flare over "Playmate 2." The ship changed course and steered toward the beat-up PBY and her precious cargo of fifty-six former *Indianapolis* crewmen.

It was 4:55 p.m. when 1st Lieutenant Richard Alcorn, US Army Air Corps, 4th Emergency Rescue Squadron, forced his Catalina into the air over Palau. Two hours and twenty minutes later, he arrived, and after quickly surveying the situation tossed three of his eleven rafts out the door. He also saw Marks's plane already on the water picking up survivors. Noticing that the swimmers didn't have enough strength to pull themselves into the rubber boats, Alcorn decided not to throw any more out. Instead he landed at 7:30 p.m., bringing his plane down two miles north of Marks.

Within minutes his crew saw the first survivor and pulled him into the aircraft. Then they taxied a few feet, stopped; taxied again, stopped—and kept this up until darkness without seeing another living soul. When Alcorn stopped and searched, they found a tremendous amount of debris in the area, most of it having fallen from the sky during the day.

They also saw bodies, dead bodies everywhere. In the dark, they floated silently with their lone passenger. Soon they heard cries for help from a group of men and sergeants Needham and Higbee volunteered to take one of the rafts, pick them up and bring them back. Alcorn agreed, but with one provision—they could only go as far as the rope attached to raft and plane would take them. Unfortunately, the umbilical cord was not long enough, and the men returned disappointed.

Overhead, planes circled all night. Marks's Dumbo was totally out of commission, but Alcorn continued to signal to the flyers and they reassuringly flashed back to the two. By the end of the day, still no one on shore knew for certain who the people in the water were.

Yet after Gwinn's second frightful message was received, one of the largest rescue operations in U.S. naval history began. The *Cecil J. Doyle* (DE 368) was heading home after an unsuccessful submarine hunt, when she suddenly received orders from the Western Carolines Sub Area to reverse course and steam north to pick up survivors. This was immediately after Gwinn's first transmission. Once the second message came in, the destroyer escort increased speed to 22.5 knots.

At 2:35 p.m., *Doyle's* radio room made voice contact with Commander Atteberry, and they were kept informed of what was going on. The ship was asked to rush but replied that there was no way they could make it to the area until after midnight.

The destroyers *Ralph Talbot* and *Madison*, both on separate patrol off Ulithi, at 4:00 p.m. turned their sleek bows northward and hastened to the scene at thirty-two knots. It was 6:56 p.m. when the *Madison* made contact with the *Doyle* and pointed out that she wouldn't be able to help until 3:00 a.m. the next morning, and the *Talbot* announced that her ETA wasn't until 4:00 a.m.

At 9:49 p.m., *Doyle*'s lookouts spotted their first star shell, and from that moment on flares were always visible. An hour later, the ship's giant twenty-four-inch searchlight was switched on and pointed skyward to give the guarding planes an idea of where she was. Instead of seeking individual people in the water, the destroyer escort headed straight for Marks's Dumbo and, shortly after midnight, the first survivor from the incredibly luckless *Indianapolis* was pulled aboard a rescue ship.

It was noon when they noticed the circling plane far to the south of them. An hour later, there was another, and as the day wore on the planes swarmed over the line separating sky from sea. Frantically the men signaled, but they were too small to be seen. They ripped the kapok out of jackets, threw the silky fiber into an empty 40-mm ammo can, and set it afire, hoping the rising smoke would draw attention to their plight. It didn't work.

Captain McVay was confused and couldn't imagine what was going on. If the men in his group were the only survivors of the ill-fated cruiser, what was going on ten miles to the south of them? They began to feel discouraged, for as darkness blanketed their isolated spot of ocean the search seemed to be moving farther away. McVay was almost certain they were not going to be found and ordered all rations cut in half.

Midnight saw them staring at the tiny pinprick of *Doyle*'s light piercing the black sky, and now they were certain of other survivors. They were also certain, though, that the search area didn't extend north to their position and that it would be a long time, if ever, before they were found. No one slept, and, as the night wore on, this lonely group was very frightened.

The planes had no problem spotting the large Redmayne group and in the afternoon rafts, rations, and other emergency gear showered downward. With the security of sentinels circling above them, the men calmed down and patiently waited for rescue.

After Gwinn dropped the two rafts, they were quickly inflated, and, while the men held onto the side, Haynes was pushed in to investigate. The doctor ordered the sickest men put on the raft. He found an eleven-ounce can of water and doled it out in a plastic cup at the rate of one ounce per man. An enormous amount of equipment was dropped to this "swimmer" group, including a ten-man boat that soon had thirty people in it. But, during the day, it became so hot in the rafts that a great many men jumped back in the water to cool off.

Once the supplies were delivered, the group had almost everything they needed to keep them relatively comfortable until rescue ships arrived. Included in this bonanza were fresh water, rations, emergency medical supplies, and sun helmets. Dr. Haynes greatly appreciated the helmets for, when properly used, not only did they protect the wearer from the roasting sun but they also had a screen which dropped down in front of the face and prevented water from getting in the eyes and up the nose. As for the food, they found it impossible to eat the meat and crackers, but the malted-milk tablets and citrus candies went down easily.

Even though so much was dropped to them, the men's deteriorating physical condition made it essential that they be taken out of the water and given rudimentary first aid and medication; otherwise they wouldn't be alive when the ships came. Commander Haynes decided to swim for the plane. He told the group to stay where they were and explained what he was going to do.

Then he swam toward Marks's plane and, after what seemed like two hours, finally reached it. His group still didn't have enough water, and he asked the crew of the plane to swing closer and give them some. They did so, and an emergency kit containing K-rations and a quart of water. Haynes treated burns and administered morphine to the more seriously wounded.

When nightfall came, they were in much better shape and had enough rafts so that all but four or five were out of the water. Fresh water was still a problem, but at sundown Haynes had found a saltwater converter in one of the rafts. He spent all night trying to make fresh water out of salt water. Because he was so exhausted, the directions didn't help and the effort was a failure. He eventually made two batches of water which tasted horrible, but which the men drank. They even asked for more, but it had taken almost four hours to make the first batch and Haynes had had it. The doctor, who had worked so hard over the last four days, finally surrendered. He took the converter, flung it into the hated sea, and began to cry.

IN THE WATER THE FIFTH DAY: FRIDAY, AUGUST 3, 1945

Ten minutes after midnight, in a rough sea with a north–northwest wind blowing between eight and ten miles per hour, the *Cecil J. Doyle* lowered her heavy-motor whaleboat. It headed directly for the closer of the two Dumbos. Twenty minutes later, it returned with eighteen former crewmen of the *Indianapolis*, taken from Marks's plane. As soon as the first man was lifted aboard, he was asked, "Who are you?" Minutes later, an urgent secret dispatch was sent to the Commander of the Western Carolines:

HAVE ARRIVED AREA X

AM PICKING UP SURVIVORS

FROM U.S.S. INDIANAPOLIS

(CA 35) TORPEODED [*sic*]

AND SUNK LAST SUNDAY NIGHT

Between 12:30 and 4:45 a.m., *Doyle* raised from the brutal sea ninety-three men, which included all survivors aboard Marks's plane and the lone man on Alcorn's. In addition about forty men were retrieved from the water and the rafts. While the whaleboat shuttled back and forth, the mother ship slowly cruised the area, sweeping the watery expanse with her huge searchlight and following the flares dropped from the circling planes. The crew of the whaleboat, meanwhile, had a tough time removing men from the plane and bringing them aboard ship. Transfer was difficult because of the condition of the survivors, some of whom were badly burned from the fires on board the ship, one of whom had a broken leg, and all of whom were terribly weak from thirst and exposure.

At 1:10 a.m., the *Doyle* saw a searchlight to the north and soon discovered it to be the high-speed transport U.S.S. *Bassett*. Two hours later, the destroyer escort U.S.S. *Dufilho* also appeared. Until dawn, the *Doyle*, *Bassett*, and *Dufilho* worked independently, hoisting men to the safety of their steel decks. Sunup brought the two destroyers *Madison* and *Ralph Talbot* on the scene.

First light allowed Marks to inspect his Catalina, and he quickly determined that it would never fly again. At 6:00 a.m., *Doyle* sent her boat over to the Dumbo and transferred the crew and all salvageable gear to the ship.

Lieutenant Alcorn was relieved of his lone survivor by *Doyle* at 4:00 a.m. and, with the sun rising over the eastern horizon, he had to decide whether or not to take off. The sea was very rough and a heavy wind was blowing, but, fortunately, his Catalina was not nearly as beat up as Marks's. He resolved to try it, and at 7:30 a.m., with no trouble at all, he powered his way down the endless runway and lifted off. At almost the same time, *Doyle* poured eighty rounds of 40-mm gunfire into Marks's abandoned plane, and she sank in the same area as the ship whose men she had so valiantly rescued.

After sinking the seaplane, *Doyle* secured from general quarters, and all of her survivors were logged in, treated, and put to bed. The crew of the *Doyle* were extremely helpful to their fellow sailors who had so recently suffered through a living hell. Men moved out of their bunks to make room for the former crewmen of the *Indianapolis* and constantly hovered around them, waiting for the slightest request that they could fill. The men were all given baths, and the oil was removed from their tired bodies. Every thirty minutes, a half glass of water, hot soup, hot coffee, and fruit were served to them, and this continued throughout the night and into the next day. The *Doyle*'s doctor examined everyone and listed them all in medical condition ranging from serious to acute.

As it searched for the living, *Doyle* passed by the bodies of twenty-five to fifty dead sailors floating in life jackets. At 12:20 p.m., *Madison* ordered *Doyle* to take off for Peleliu, and this, the first ship on the scene, was now the first to leave, heading south at 22.5 knots.

All McVay and his isolated band could do was watch the distant searchlights, the falling flares, the circling planes. When the sun rose over the horizon, they were in despair. The entire morning was spent staring at the activity very far away. It did not seem to be coming closer. At 11:30 a.m., they spotted a plane making a box search. It was a very wide pattern, and on each leg it came closer. They found it extremely depressing, for the plane gave no recognition sign. Captain McVay contended that they were never spotted from the air. But they were, for this plane, flown by Marks's squadron leader, Lieutenant Commander M. V. Ricketts, saw them and reported that he sighted two rafts, with five survivors in one and four in the other. By voice radio, he directed the U.S.S. *Ringness* (APD 100) to pick them up. Like *Bassett*, *Ringness* was a high-speed transport sent by Philippine Sea Frontier, and it had just arrived. After receiving Ricketts's message, *Ringness* headed for the spot, and at 4,046 yards she picked McVay up on radar. On the rafts, the spell of isolation and despair was suddenly broken when somebody cried, "My God, look at this! There are two destroyers bearing down on us. Why, they're almost on top of us." The two destroyers were both transports, *Ringness* and the newly arrived *Register*. *Register* turned north to pick up another small group while *Ringness* headed for McVay.

Everyone made it aboard under his own power, and all were immediately given first aid. They had lost about 14 percent of their body weight, and during the afternoon they were given ice cream, coffee, and as much water as they could drink. During the entire four and a half days on the rafts, no one in the group asked for a drink. This was surprising to McVay, since he had assumed people couldn't go that long without water—but they did.

While *Doyle* was taking care of the Haynes group, *Bassett* took care of Lieutenant Redmayne and his men. Lowering her four landing craft at 2:30 a.m., *Bassett's* boats picked up most of Redmayne's people. A head count was taken, and a little over eighty sailors were collected from the original group of 150. *Bassett* next sent a message to Frontier Headquarters:

SURVIVORS ARE FROM USS

INDIANAPOLIS (CA 35) WHICH

WAS TORPEDOED 29 JULY [*sic*] X

CONTINUING TO PICK UP

SURVIVORS X MANY BADLY

INJURED

Ralph Talbot picked up twenty-four survivors and then spent most of the afternoon sinking eight rafts and a small boat with her 20-mm guns. Later she transferred her survivors to *Register*. As soon as *Madison* arrived in the area, *Bassett* reported that she had 150 survivors aboard and desperately needed a doctor. Shortly thereafter, at 5:15 a.m., *Madison*'s physician, Lieutenant (jg) H. A. Stiles, was transferred to the transport. It was at the time the landing craft from *Bassett* came over to pick up Dr. Stiles that *Madison* first learned the survivors were from the *Indianapolis*.

During the day scouting lines were formed with the planes bird-dogging, but nothing was seen except for the dead, and they were generally left where they were. The unpleasant task of recovery and identification was postponed until the next day. The last living man plucked from the Philippine Sea was Captain McVay, who was the last man to enter it.

By the time the blazing Pacific sun reached its zenith on this day, not another living person from *Indianapolis* was to be found in that enormous ocean. She had sailed from San Francisco with 1,196 young men, was torpedoed, and about eight hundred of her crew escaped from the sinking ship. Of these eight hundred, 320 were rescued; two later died in the Philippines, and two on Peleliu. Because of complacency and carelessness, approximately five hundred U.S. sailors (no one will ever know the exact number) died in the waters of the Philippine Sea.

6

Treacherous Passage

Douglas A. Campbell

THE SEA WAS IN A FURIOUS MOOD. PILED ON ITS SURFACE WERE great, gray waves, living monsters who could humble even the greatest warships. Yet, the USS *Flier* was but a submarine, at about 300 feet, one of the smaller vessels in the navy. Even when submerged, it pitched and rolled like a slender twig. But inside *Flier* were no ordinary sailors. They were submariners: men—most of them quite young—selected from the ranks for their virtues of fearlessness and its companion trait, optimism. Their mood was bright. Despite the beastly roar and hiss of the sea above them, none believed that on this day his death was at hand.

The Reaper might come later, when their boat reached the actual battle lines in this, the third year of World War II. And probably not then, either, they thought. The momentum of the conflict had turned in their favor. There was a sense, pervasive on board, that destiny was with the Allies. Everyone expected to be around for the final victory. These were young men—many of them green—led by a handful of sailors creased by the experience of having survived at sea. Death was for someone else, the enemy, even on January 16, 1944, even on the Pacific Ocean, the greatest naval battleground in history, a place where tens of thousands of Americans had already died.

But the men aboard the *Flier* could not ignore the thrashing as she bucked and twisted. For the one young cowboy in the crew, it had to make him think rodeo bull. He and his mates joked uneasily about the sobriety of the welders who had built the submarine back in Groton, Connecticut.

In these angry seas they approached the atoll known as Midway, one of the navy's refueling depots. Once beyond Midway, their first wartime patrol aboard *Flier* would begin, and their record—distinguished or dreadful—would be tallied in tons of enemy shipping sunk. With young hearts and a sense of invincibility, they knew that the slamming of their submarine by the sea was only a tune-up for the coming combat. And they had no fear.

On August 12, the now-battle-tested *Flier* approached Sibutu Passage like a slugger stepping into the batter's box. On the far side of this strait was the Sulu Sea, nearly 90,000 square miles of unbroken blue water shaped roughly like a baseball diamond. Sibutu Passage was home plate. The opposing team—the Japanese soldiers and sailors—had taken all the land around that diamond two years earlier. They were scattered along the first-base line, a string of islands called the Sulu Archipelago that ended in Mindanao, more than 200 miles to the northeast. More Japanese troops were strung along the islands from first base to second—Mindoro, at the top of the diamond, 500 miles due north. The enemy also held third base—the small island of Balabac to the northwest. And the huge island nation of Borneo, due west of Sibutu Passage, was thick with supporting troops, like the bench-dwellers in the dugout. Throughout the more than 7,000 Philippine Islands and their Indonesian and Malaysian neighbors, the Japanese navy and army were arrayed in what until now had been an almost impenetrable defense. Americans entered the Sulu Sea only by submarine, and when they did, they knew it was kill or be killed in this deadly World Series.

Flier's general orders, drafted back in Fremantle, became specific on the evening of August 13 as the submarine approached

Balabac Strait. The word came around dinnertime, the normal hour for submarine headquarters in Australia to broadcast the war news along with any special instructions for the submarines on patrol. On this, the third consecutive day, there was a message for the submarine Robalo, which was scheduled to return from its most recent patrol. The message asked for the boat's location and estimated time of arrival in Fremantle. There was no urgency in the transmission. A returning submarine could easily be a few days late.

There was a message for *Flier*, as well. When the radioman's message was typed into the machine, the officer informed the captain, Commander John Crowley, of the new orders. The submarine *Puffer*, which had been patrolling in the northern Philippines, had encountered a Japanese convoy heading south. *Puffer* had sent torpedoes into several of the ships in the convoy and was now trailing "cripples," the message said. The rest of the convoy, thwarted by *Puffer* from entering Mindoro Strait on the northern end of Palawan, was now traveling southwest, along the western shore of Palawan in the South China Sea. Until now, *Flier*'s assignment had been to patrol the South China Sea, looking particularly for four Japanese submarines making supply runs from Vietnam. The new orders directed *Flier* to go after *Puffer*'s convoy. There was no need for Crowley to change course. *Flier* was already headed for Balabac Strait, and that would take the submarine right into the path of the approaching convoy.

Crowley was energized. The patrol had just begun and already there were targets. The word was passed along by intercom, and the crew knew they were back in the war.

On this evening, Baumgart had lookout duty after dinner, so he donned a pair of red glasses after seven o'clock and wore them for a half hour before he went to the control room. At eight o'clock, he climbed the ladders up through the conning tower. The glasses, filtering the harsh incandescent submarine lighting, prepared his eyes for scanning the darkened ocean. He was wearing his navy denims and boots. The warmth of a night in the tropics required nothing else. And despite his continuing anger over the way he had been assigned this duty, he was beginning to enjoy the hours he spent standing on the A-frame above the deck, cooled by the breeze as *Flier* made eighteen knots across the surface.

The conning tower was crowded with its usual complement of officers and crew. Jim Liddell, the executive and navigation officer, stood at the foot of the ladder leading to the bridge so that he could talk with Crowley, whose stool was on deck beside the hatch. Jim Russo stood beside Liddell, helping him with the charts. Arthur Gibson Howell was at the rear of the compartment, operating the radar. Beside him, Charles Pope, the hero who nearly drowned on the trip between Midway and Hawaii, ran the sonar.

Howell's radar presented him with an image of the nearest shoreline, many miles away. They had traveled on the surface throughout the day and had seen neither Japanese ships nor aircraft, and the radar screen still showed no enemy threats. The night was going as easily as had the day.

Admiral Ralph W. Christie's orders directing *Flier* through Balabac Strait remained unchanged by the message the radioman had transcribed earlier. Crowley was to take the deepest water route through the strait that he could. In deep water, it was assumed, mines could not be anchored. Specifically, the orders directed Crowley to use the Nasubata Channel, one of eight channels between the Sulu and South China seas allowing east and westbound ships to pass through the reef-strewn Balabac Strait. Nasubata Channel was the deepest—more than 500 feet deep in spots—and the broadest, with about five miles' leeway between Roughton Island's reefs to the north and Comiran Island to the south.

As he approached the channel, Crowley had several concerns, as would any skipper. While the ability to navigate safely around natural obstructions such as reefs was always a consideration, in wartime a captain had two more problems to solve. He had to give himself enough room to maneuver if an enemy ship attacked, and he also had to be wary of shallow water where mines could be anchored. Roughton Island's extensive reefs to the north took away maneuvering room and presented a navigation problem. Crowley, talking the matter over with Liddell through the conning-tower hatch, decided he would try a more southerly route through the channel. If he stayed in fifty fathoms—300 feet or more of water—Crowley believed *Flier* would pass through the channel untroubled.

Mines were the only military threat Crowley felt he faced that night. He trusted his radar and its operator, Chief Howell, and felt the device could find a target the size of a surfaced submarine—with the possible exception of a midget submarine—at a range of more than three miles. Unless the Japanese had developed a superior night periscope, he believed that on a night as dark as this one, a submarine could not make a submerged attack. And as Howell reported from below what he was seeing on the radar, Crowley was convinced the only things out there in the dark were islands and mountains, a few of which he knew harbored enemy soldiers. *Flier* could make it through.

Chief Howell relayed a constant stream of radar readings to Liddell, who passed them along to the skipper. And Chief Pope, watching the sonar, gave depth readings. With the radar showing the nearest land about 5,000 yards away, *Flier* was traveling in sixty-five to ninety fathoms of ocean when Pope reported a reading of forty-one fathoms. *Flier* wasn't about to scrape bottom, but the depth was shallow enough to raise Crowley's concern about mines. He asked Liddell, a veteran of a Philippine tour before the war, what he thought.

Crowley was standing in the forward end of the bridge, leaning over the open hatch in the bridge floor to talk with Liddell about taking a new course, when the explosion came. The blast caused the entire submarine to whip to one side and then snap back like an angry stallion trying to throw its rider. Crowley felt the violent motion, but the concussion was without sound, like the thunder from the electrical storms that played their lightning fingers across those distant mountains.

Jim Russo's job had been simply to help handle the conning-tower charts. He was at Liddell's side when the explosion rocked the boat as if it had rammed a wall. Instinctively, he looked down at the hatch to the control room. Something slammed into his cheek below his eye, ripping his flesh like a bullet. A shaft of air was venting straight up from below, blasting out through the hatch to the bridge. Blood was draining down his cheek when Russo felt himself lifted by the column of air, along with Liddell, the 200-pound ex-football-player, straight up to the bridge. Once above deck, Russo—by instinct and without hesitation—followed Liddell, whose shirt had been ripped off by the blast, to the rear of the bridge where, at the railing, they dove into the ocean. When Russo turned around in the water, *Flier* was gone.

Wesley Miller, standing on the A-frame above the bridge, was nearly thrown from his watch but managed to hook his legs over a railing to avoid falling. He was confused. Somehow, he had lost his binoculars, and he was concerned about the discipline that would result. Then there was screaming coming from below and air was blasting out of the hatch in the bridge floor under him. He stood frozen on the A-frame for an instant, although it seemed longer, until he heard someone yell, "Abandon ship!" and saw the bow of the submarine go under. Then the ocean was swelling around him, dragging him down into its darkness. The radio antenna had snagged him. Miller struggled to free himself and then swam and swam, reaching for the surface. Then he was alone in the water, and the submarine was gone.

Al Jacobson, lost in his reverie, watching the lightning and the mountains silhouetted in the darkness, felt the blast of air and, curiously, found Lieutenant Reynolds standing on the deck beside him, complaining that his side hurt. Jacobson told Reynolds to lie down, and then he crouched over the lieutenant, hoping to help him. He assumed that an air bank, used to store compressed air for use in diving and surfacing, had blown, and he told Reynolds to lie still. But as he talked with Reynolds, he saw Ensign Mayer and Ed Casey diving over *Flier*'s side. Just then, water rose around Jacobson and Reynolds, and the submarine sank below them, sucking them down with it. The image in Jacobson's mind was of the two huge propellers at the rear of the boat, still spinning as they passed him, slicing him to bits. He struggled to swim up and away from his death. It took a few seconds before he surfaced in a slick of diesel fuel that floated on warm, calm seas. Baseball-size chunks of cork from inside *Flier* floated around him. He could feel them. But there was no light to see what, or who, else was there.

Crowley, who had been standing to port at the front of the bridge, saw a geyser shoot toward the sky from the forward starboard side of the submarine. The next thing he knew, he was standing against the aft railing of the bridge, near Jacobson. He ran forward to trigger the collision alarm that was mounted on the bulwark just above the conning-tower hatch. When he got there, he smelled diesel fuel. He looked down into the conning tower but it was dark. There was no time!

"Abandon ship!"

The skipper's yell carried across the deck and perhaps a short way down into the submarine, where many in the crew already were being thrown about by the air blast and the flooding that made Crowley's command superfluous. On the bridge, the skipper felt the shaft of air rising from within the submarine, carrying with it the sounds of rushing water and the screams of seventy-one men trapped inside. Some men were climbing the ladder from the conning tower, just in time because the deck was heading under, *Flier*'s engines still driving it like a train entering a tunnel. Crowley found himself in a raging stream of water as the sea poured around the bulwark and into the bridge, and then he was washed out the rear of the bridge, into the sea. In a matter of just twenty seconds after the blast, *Flier* was gone, and after its passing, the ocean was calm. The dead sailors of the Japanese minelayer *Tsugaru* had once again struck from their graves.

A mine had touched the side of *Flier*—just a glancing blow, but enough to trigger its explosives. The geyser had appeared near the rear of the forward torpedo room. The explosion, quiet as it was on the surface, would have been enough to punch a hole through the submarine's superstructure and one or more of its watertight welded-steel compartments.

On this night, Crowley had ordered battle stations for the conning tower, but the rest of the crew was not on alert. If the watertight doors were not dogged in place with their big handles, the blast from the mine—having opened a huge hole in *Flier*'s side—would have flooded the forward torpedo room and the officers' quarters immediately. At the same time, a rupturing of the tanks full of compressed air sent a shockwave through the submarine's ductwork ahead of the flooding water. The seawater raced to the rear, in seconds reaching the control room where Ensign Behr would have been among the first in its path, followed by the bow and stern planesmen and the other sailors handling the various controls.

The flooding would stop the engines as *Flier* sank deeper, and the darkness that Crowley had seen when he looked down the hatch from the bridge would spread throughout the submarine. For the men in the rear, there was but one hope to temper their panic—an escape hatch in the aft torpedo room. If they could get the hatch open, then for the first time since their submarine training in Connecticut, they would strap on their air tanks and take their chances floating to the surface.

But what then?

The darkness was nearly absolute. Al Jacobson could see nothing, but he could taste diesel fuel on his lips. His body felt the warm, wet embrace of the sea as his uniform clung to his arms and legs. All was quiet except for the lapping of small waves. And then there were shouts, the sounds of a human voice, the first indication to the ensign that he was not alone. He began swimming toward the voice, floating easily in the salt water but slowed by the weight of his shirt, trousers, and boots. The strap of his binoculars was still around his neck, and the glasses floated harmlessly by his chest as he did the sidestroke. *Flier*'s sinking had disoriented him, snatching him from the tranquility of a warm ocean night, plunging him into a struggle for survival.

Several of the men had responded to the same yell that had drawn Jacobson. Once they were all together, they shared what they knew and tried to decide what had happened to *Flier*. It could have been an explosion in the batteries, but Crowley discarded that notion. The diesel engines had been running and the batteries were idle, not a situation in which they were likely to explode. The other topic concerned who else from the crew had escaped the boat. With almost no light, they could not expect to see other survivors, so their only choice was to call for them. Soon they had gathered more men into their group. A headcount was taken.

A total of fifteen men responded to the roll call. All fifteen men were already getting a lift. Not only had they escaped the terrifying death of their seventy-one trapped shipmates, but they had also surfaced on a sea that was unusually docile for this time of year. Summer is monsoon season, and storms can whip the Sulu Sea into a froth. Swimming in those waves would have been exhausting, and the chances of all these men finding and communicating with each other would have been slim. With lightning flashing on distant islands, there remained the possibility that a storm could still come, funneling winds between the mountains. But for now, here on the open ocean, the wind was light and the waves were gentle. As long as each man could stay afloat, he could remain with the group. For the next two hours, as they assessed their situation and developed a plan, that is what the men did.

There was a sense shared by most of the men that they were still part of a military unit. Perhaps this was because of their training, to always follow the lead of Crowley and Liddell. It took time for them to realize that there was no longer a formal chain of command, and that neither Crowley nor Liddell was in charge. They needed a plan.

The first thing to consider was their location. The skipper and his executive officer knew where they were. Liddell began explaining the options, most of which everyone already understood. There was land on three sides, Liddell said. To the west was Balabac, the largest chunk of land in the vicinity, roughly ten miles away. Each man was aware that the Japanese occupied that mountainous island. They could swim in that direction and with some certainty, due to the island's long shoreline, land on Balabac's beaches. To the south was Comiran Island, less than two miles away. Every survivor could probably swim that far, despite injuries. But there was a problem with this option: Comiran was tiny—only a few hundred feet across. If, swimming in this opaque darkness, they missed Comiran, they would have another forty miles of ocean before they reached land on one of northern Borneo's islands.

The lightning occasionally lit a mountainside to the northwest, but judging from what they could see, that land was about thirty miles away.

And if they headed toward any eastern quadrant, the Sulu Sea threatened them, with hundreds of miles of ocean, uninterrupted by land of any kind.

These were the options Liddell presented, each one unpromising. And none was worth even attempting right now. There were no stars to guide the men, and no moon, only clouds overhead. And the occasional lightning flash on the horizon, while it gave them something of a beacon, left their eyes blinded for several minutes.

But even the strongest among the survivors could not expect to stay afloat forever, and so they adopted two rules. First, they would turn so that the waves were lapping their left cheeks, and then they would swim in the direction they were facing. The course was randomly chosen, as far as young Jacobson knew. Perhaps Crowley and Liddell had a reason. But the skipper and his second in command did not share their thinking.

The second rule was Crowley's idea—a death sentence for several of the men, and everyone knew it: It would be each man for himself. The cruel reality was that wherever they were going, it was a long way off. Some of the injured men could not swim the distance without help, and if the whole group waited for the injured, the chances were overwhelming that no one would survive.

Crowley was uninjured, but he was the oldest, at thirty-five, and his physique after several years of sedentary submarine service was not particularly athletic. Crowley could be among the first victims of his edict. But like their skipper, all of the men agreed to the pact, and all fifteen began swimming across the waves, which lifted them a few inches and then gently lowered them in a mesmerizing rhythm.

Chief Pope called out in the night for Jim Liddell, asking the distance that lay ahead of them before they reached shore. After two hours in the water, the men still felt little wind. Liddell, pondering Pope's question, knew the entire swim could be fifteen miles or more, but he wanted to be encouraging.

"About nine miles, Chief," Liddell replied.

"Oh, fuck it!" Pope said in disgust. With that, the chief stopped swimming and said no more, his faint image dissolving forever behind the swimmers in the night.

It was not much later that Jacobson, keeping pace with Ed Casey, saw him veer. Instead of calling him back to the course as he had done before, the ensign swam over to his mentor.

"Ed, rest a minute, and then just float on your back and put your feet on my shoulders and I'll push you back," Jacobson offered.

"Remember, we agreed every man for himself?" Casey said, refusing his young friend's gesture. But the two of them swam back toward the group, talking as they went. They were joking about a blowout party they had planned to throw in Perth when the patrol was over, and as they talked, they reached the wake of the others.

Ten minutes later, Casey disappeared in the darkness. When Jacobson and the others called to him, there was no response. The lieutenant had chosen not to burden his shipmates any longer.

Paul Knapp had been struggling like Casey, but was keeping in line with the others. Jacobson saw him swim off to the side without a word. The ensign thought little of it until Knapp did not return. Then he realized the courage it had taken for Knapp to separate himself.

As the night wore on, one after another of the men, when they felt they could swim no more, silently turned to the side and disappeared, each man choosing for himself when his time had come.

If anyone among the survivors were thinking about the beasts that swam below them, none gave voice to the image. But the reefs of the Sulu Sea were habitat for a vast assortment of large animals. Sharks of every description shared the water with barracudas and rays. Some were harmless, like the white and blacktip sharks, and the guitar sharks. But others were legendary, like the hammerheads and bull sharks, predators that would eat another shark as quickly as they would consume a human being.

If the swimmers were ignoring the carnivores beneath them, it may have been because their minds were filled with the death they had just dodged, and, not that far below the sea, their shipmates already dead inside *Flier*. The thing that now would keep these men alive was their determination to keep swimming.

The overcast sky that had kept the stars hidden was overcome at about three o'clock that morning by the moon, rising grudgingly in the east to give the swimmers a navigational beacon. By now, only nine of the original fifteen survivors remained in the group. Wesley Miller straggled far behind the main pack but could hear their voices in the dark, and shouted to them to maintain contact.

At about five o'clock, when the first hint of daybreak was tingeing the sky from black to gray, helmsman Gerald Madeo began to panic. He fell below the surface, and after seven hours in the water, no one had the strength to help him. They simply continued swimming, led away from Madeo by the moon toward an unknown destination.

The trio of Howell, Baumgart, and Jacobson kept pace with each other throughout the morning, cooled under the blazing tropical sun by the same glass-clear sea that had warmed them during the night. Slowly, they drew toward their island, probably helped by a change in the tide or the currents.

It was one o'clock in the afternoon when Jacobson checked his wristwatch. The approaching drone of an airplane came from a distance, and when the men stopped swimming to look, they saw a low-flying Japanese craft, coming directly toward them. A half-dozen heads on the surface of the Sulu Sea were too tiny for the pilot to notice, however, and the plane kept going. The swimmers resumed their strokes, their luck apparently intact.

CHOOSING FREEDOM

The jungle island floated in the distance like a thin, green wafer. Little about its shore could be determined, but it was closer than anything else, and distance was important for the men, who by now had been in the water for nearly seventeen hours. Jacobson, Howell, and Baumgart had managed to stay close to each other since they had first spotted land. If there was anyone else afloat, they were no longer in sight. There were only the three and the island.

And then ahead, almost on a line toward the island, the men noticed something else in the water. It was long, and above it rose some perpendicular objects. Perhaps it was a native fishing boat, they thought, and the objects were the fishermen. They waved, but there was no response, so they decided to avoid the unfriendly thing. Swimming the straight route toward the island, they nevertheless drew closer to it and discovered it was a bamboo tree, its buoyant trunk riding lightly on the surface, its limbs rising toward the afternoon sun. Eager for some rest, they swam to the tree and Jacobson climbed up to have a look at the surrounding area. Howell and Baumgart struggled up beside where he balanced as the ensign scanned the sea. A short way off he saw more swimmers. He began shouting, joined by his mates, their voices carrying across the now-choppy water, their arms waving in excited arcs.

At daylight, when the island was first spotted, Crowley had given the order to anyone within shouting distance: Swim toward land at your own pace. He soon fell behind the rest, alternately swimming and resting when exhaustion overcame him. That he continued to swim is indisputable. What kept him moving is less certain.

Early in the afternoon, Crowley had seen Liddell ahead of him, clinging to another floating tree. The skipper and his executive officer stayed together then until they heard the shouts from Jacobson's group. It took a few minutes for Crowley and Liddell to reach the larger tree and cling to it. For the skipper, the plant had become a lifesaver. Exhausted, he had felt—even with the island in sight—that he could no longer swim. But the shouts from Jacobson and the others gave him new energy.

Breaking branches from the tree for paddles, the five men now straddled its trunk, urging the tree toward the shore. Off to one side, they saw Don Tremaine, swimming alone. He waved back when they shouted and gestured, but he avoided them. Tremaine had seen them but he could not hear them, and had assumed they were natives. If they were too unfriendly to pick him up, he reasoned, he would not chance swimming toward them.

The water changed from dark blue to a pale aqua a few hundred yards from the shore where the coral reef began, and then it was shallow enough for the men to walk. Their feet were wrinkled and white from seventeen hours in the water, and the entire seabed on which they stepped was coral. It was like walking on crushed glass rather than gravel, and the sharp coral edges sliced into the soft soles of their feet. Abandoning their bamboo tree, they stumbled, trying to keep their balance as the hot afternoon sun dried the salt water from their backs. The pain in their feet was numbed by their eagerness to feel dry land. And up on the beach stood Jim Russo, urging them on.

Staggering ashore, the men could, for the first time since *Flier* sank, see each other from head to toe. The sight was shocking. In the ten hours since daylight, the unrelenting rays of the sun had bombarded their water-softened white flesh. Now, where their skin was exposed, they were scalded red. Baumgart alone had long trousers on, saving his legs from the scorching. But like the others, he waded from the ocean with his face and arms as red as if the seawater had been boiling, and his blood drained into the sand from the coral slashes in his feet.

Byan Island, roughly triangular in shape, is just east of Mantangule Island. In 1944, the island was uninhabited by humans. A few hours after the men reached Byan Island, the sun settled beyond sprawling Mantangule and the air grew cool. Crowley and Liddell believed they were on Mantangule Island and that the big land to the west was Balabac, which they knew was occupied by the Japanese. To build a fire, if they could manage it, might attract attention, so they faced a night of cold. Even before sunset had cooled the air, they were swept alternately by fever chills and sweats. In the dusk, they huddled together for warmth, lying directly on the sand and, having successfully outlasted death for a day, sought the peace of sleep.

Neither sleep nor peace was to be theirs, however. Roused by their fevers, they would seek a more comfortable position, only to have the grains of the beach rasp across their sunburned flesh like sandpaper. At times, they were awakened by rats nibbling on their feet. Young Jacobson lay awake, his body shaking, the watch on his wrist slowly ticking off the seconds and minutes. He wanted nothing more than for the hours to pass and the day to come, bringing with it warmth.

They had learned, in their first stumbling hours ashore before nightfall, that the area near the beach offered neither food nor water. So when the sun rose on August 15, 1944, the *Flier* survivors knew they had to begin a search. Crowley directed Tremaine, Russo, and Howell, who had injured his knee when he had jumped off the submarine, to stay on the beach and improve the lean-to shelter. Jacobson and Baumgart were to head east and scout out the island, while Crowley and Liddell would head the other way.

Howell, Russo, and Tremaine started gathering scraps of wood and palm leaves in the hope of creating some real shelter for the coming night. At the same time, Ensign Jacobson and Baumgart hobbled along the shore, Baumgart in trousers and an undershirt, the ensign in his underwear with binoculars dangling from his neck. There were coconuts everywhere along the water's edge. They picked up the ones that looked whole and opened them with their bare hands by smashing them on coral. But each one that broke open left them disappointed, its meat rotten, its milk spoiled.

They trudged for hours without success. And then they rounded a point and ahead they saw a string of islands. Still ankle-deep in the sea and standing on coral beds, they splashed forward until they found a sandy beach where driftwood had gathered. Then they decided it was time to head back. Realizing that if they crossed the island, it should take less time than circling the beach, they tried to climb ashore up the coral cliffs. But the thorns and vines repelled them, and they waded once more into the shallows across the coral, retracing their painful steps toward their shipmates.

They had another reason for leaving together: They wanted to talk about the prospects for the group's ultimate survival. Crowley was familiar with the territory only from having studied nautical charts. Liddell had served on a submarine in the Philippines before the war and had a deeper understanding of the locale. What they had found so far was that they could not stay on this island. It was little more than a coral reef with no food or shelter. The jungle that began at the shore was a tangle of thorns and vines.

Rounding the western tip of the island, they saw their two options: To the northeast, beyond two more small islands, lay a large island. Liddell identified it as Bugsuk Island. And behind them, to the southwest, beyond long, flat Mantangule Island, was the mountainous mass they knew had to be Balabac. Intelligence reports that they had reviewed back in Australia said the Japanese were on Balabac. But from what they remembered, there was less chance of finding the enemy on Bugsuk, which was about five or six miles away. The trip could be made manageable by hopping only to the next island, Gabung, and resting before going on. There were tremendous currents that funneled between islands like these, Crowley and Liddell knew, and in their weakened state, the survivors could easily be swept out to sea if they tried to swim across. They needed another plan, and more information. So Liddell decided to leave Crowley behind and explore a bit further on the northern side of the island. The lieutenant had walked some distance when, coming around a curve in the shore, he saw a man ahead on the beach—a white man, clothed only in underwear.

At daybreak the day before, Wesley Miller had lost contact with the other swimmers. But he saw several islands on the horizon, and, since it was in the direction he had been swimming, he kept going for the closest one. As the afternoon wore on, however, he found that the current was sweeping him to his left, past the nearest island. He would never be able to reach it, he knew, so he began to swim for the next island. But when he was perhaps two miles from his target, the current increased, carrying him fast along the beach. Still he swam toward the shore, cutting the distance in half when, to his left, he saw the end of the island approaching. After that, there was nothing, and Miller believed that his long trek from the Oregon ranch to the middle of the Pacific Ocean was at an end.

It was startling when, letting his feet fall below him, Miller felt his toes touch the bottom. He began walking now, and soon the water was only waist-deep, and to his left the coral actually rose above the surface. Then the sun set over Balabac and Mantangule and the water grew deeper. He no longer could wade, but although he must swim again to survive, his arms and legs were unwilling to move. So he willed himself toward the beach, and when he could touch bottom again, he was too tired to stand. Sand and coral rose beneath him, and he leaned forward in the water so that his knees, not his feet, propelled him ashore while his body and arms floated listlessly. Crawling as an infant might, he worked his way out of the sea and partway up the sand, where his thoughts and his will ceased and he fell asleep. Awakened in the middle of the night by rising water, he dragged himself to higher ground, up against the coral cliff, and slept once more.

In the morning, Miller began to walk along the shore, looking for a way to scale the cliffs. As he stumbled on, he searched for clams in the sand. In a mile of hiking, he had found only solid rock cliffs along the bank, with jungle growth snarling out of their cracks.

Then Liddell found Miller and led him back to Crowley. The skipper, perhaps noticing the sailor for the first time, realized that this crewman was little more than a boy, a child who was pathetically grateful to find that he was not a sole survivor.

Later that afternoon, everyone assembled at the beach and reported on their work. Jacobson and Baumgart had found neither food nor water, but they told of locating a pile of driftwood on the northern beach. Howell, Russo, and Tremaine, when they were not working on the lean-to, had set out seashells to collect water should it rain. And they had found water seeping out of the coral cliffs. They had set some shells below the cliffs and collected some water, one drip at a time—three shells full, in all. Everyone shared it, each person drinking a couple of teaspoons. It was merely seawater that had splashed onto the coral at high tide, but their thirst convinced the men they were getting fresh water.

If they continued to wet their lips with this water for long, they were going to be doomed. The human body, in order to rid itself of excess salt, passes the salt through the kidneys where it is washed away in urine. That means that the body is losing water as well as salt. The more salt in the system, the more water must be expelled. In a short time, the consumption of salt water will actually dehydrate the body, increasing the level of salt in the bloodstream and damaging bodily tissues. Soon, the drinker will die. But first, normal body functions will be damaged. Saliva will dry up, leaving the mouth and tongue without lubrication, exposing them to infection. Drying of the tongue may cause it to swell and split. Death might be preferable.

With the other reports submitted, Crowley told the men of their options. They could head west, eventually reaching Balabac where there was food and shelter—and Japanese soldiers. They would probably be captured and become prisoners of war. (Earlier in the afternoon, another Japanese patrol plane had flown low over the island, the red rising sun insignia on its wings easily seen by the survivors.) Or, they could use the driftwood that Jacobson and Baumgart had found, build a raft, try to reach Bugsuk, and, accepting the uncertainty of finding food and water there, remain free men.

To a man, they chose freedom. They would begin work in the morning.

Sunrise brought all the men back onto their feet. The agony of standing on those festering cuts was not enough to keep them on the beach, and soon the eight were hobbling in the shallow water, where vegetation coated some of the coral, making it less sharp. Splashing up Byan Island's eastern shore, they could see Gabung

Island in the distance. When they reached the place where the two islands were closest together—just under a mile separated them—they began building their raft. Liddell and Russo, both strong men, reached into the jungle from the edge of the beach and tore out vines. As some of the men used the vines to lash the bamboo driftwood logs together, Chief Howell sat on the beach, improvising two paddles by splitting slender bamboo poles partway, inserting small pieces in the split crossway, and then tying them in place with thin vines. Occasionally, he would lick moisture that he found on leaves.

Crowley saw how his men slowed in their work as the day wore on, their movements becoming uncoordinated, their attention wandering. Thirst was on everyone's mind. But even though they scoured the coast looking for edible coconuts, they found none all day.

It was about two-thirty that afternoon, just before slack tide, when the eight men surrounded their little raft and pushed it out toward Gabung. Ahead of them was a crossing of slightly less than one mile. The water was the pale blue of reef water out for several hundred yards off the beach, and the reef resumed on the far side of the channel, where dark blue water indicated a depth that no one would be able to wade. They had brought two long poles with them, and for the first quarter of the voyage, the younger men took turns poling the raft, on which Crowley was the only permanent passenger. The rest of the men leaned on the raft for support as they walked in the shallows across another long bed of razor-sharp coral. Crowley paddled.

Before they had made it halfway across the channel, they saw the daily patrol plane coming in low. Crowley and the man poling slipped into the water, and everyone tried to hide under the raft. The plane kept going, and the men, clinging to the sides, kicked in the deeper water, slowly moving the raft across the channel.

Now on the open water, they found themselves directly in the path of an oncoming squall. Abruptly, they were pelted with large, pure droplets, delicious on their lips, and everyone tipped his head back and opened his mouth. But while the raindrops splattered off their foreheads and cheeks, none of it seemed to find their tongues before the squall passed on into the ocean, leaving the scorching sun in its wake.

They had not yet reached the reef on the far side of the channel when the tide seemed to shift and a new current swept between the islands. With only a quarter of a mile to go, they suddenly seemed unable to make any progress, and the raft appeared to be drifting away from Gabung Island. The men on the sides kicked with all their feeble power and Crowley, feeling like a very elderly thirty-five, paddled, and the raft circled the end of the island and settled in its lee, the current having deposited the men close enough to shore that they could swim the final leg.

It was seven o'clock, more than four hours since they had left Byan Island a mile to the south, and the sun had already set. They found a sandy beach and were content to collapse where they could find room. The little slivers of coconut they had eaten earlier had done little to curb their appetite, and their thirst was only growing. But no one had the energy to forage. More than food and water, right now they wanted sleep.

Sunrise the following morning—August 17—brought with it relief from the tremors of the night and hope that this would be the day the men would eat. Before launching their raft, they gathered to discuss their next steps. It would be another nine or ten hours until the tides allowed them to leave this island for the next one in the chain. Crowley and Liddell took suggestions, and the group decided that their time could be best used by traveling around the island the long way. There would be more chance of finding food if they were covering a longer shoreline. It meant more walking, but now empty stomachs and parched mouths were overpowering the screaming pains from their feet and the swollen and blistered burns on their backs and arms. They pushed the raft into the shallow water and began circling the island to the west. Once more, the coral in the shallow water was softened by plants that grew on it, so wading was less painful than it might have been. But there was a trade-off, because when they were not swimming, their burns were always exposed to the sun as it rose high above the island.

On the eastern side of Byan the day before, the men had walked along the beach with open ocean to their right. Now, walking along Gabung's western coast, they felt surrounded by islands. Mantangule's long, low bulk stretched out to the southwest, and Bugsuk's broad sweep consumed the view to the northeast, only three or so miles across the reef-strewn water. To the north, another large island—Pandanan—was indistinguishable from Bugsuk. And to the northwest, more, smaller islands rose above the reefs to hide the horizon. With their goal of Bugsuk in sight, the men could think of food and water and let those images draw them ahead. But there were distractions. Swarms of stinging insects flew around them, and their thoughts drifted uncontrollably, clouded by the lack of food and water.

Apo Island was on the far side of a strait nearly two miles across, with the dark blue of deep water again in the middle, between the two shores. The men had about two hours to wait for slack tide and the passing of the next enemy patrol plane, and they gathered more coconuts from the beach, but as so often before, none was edible. Surrounded by a sea full of fish and water, they were dying of thirst and starvation.

The airplane arrived on schedule and continued south over the island. Certain the danger had passed, the men pushed their raft back to sea. The water was shallow enough for them to wade and to keep the weight off their feet as they leaned on the raft. Pushing and splashing, they moved their craft into the dark blue of the deeper water.

They were midway between the two islands, with no retreat possible, when someone noticed the fins. Two sharks cruised just beneath the surface, looking for food. The men kept paddling, splashing, and kicking, and the sharks, perhaps sensing the hunger that drove these eight beings, stayed clear.

Aided by the shallow water, the raft crossed between Gabung and Apo islands in only three hours, and the men found a sandy beach just before dark. By now, they knew what to expect. They posted their rat guards and waited in troubled dreams and fitful sleep for the morning.

Sunrise was again their alarm clock, but they lingered until about eight o'clock before gathering around their sole possession, the raft, and heading to the west. Apo is a small, round island, but in all other ways it seemed no different from Byan and Gabung. Again, the men had chosen to take the long way, and each grudging step along the curved shoreline revealed some new aspect of the land ahead. Before noon, they had found the first indication of humans—a dugout canoe abandoned on the beach. The boat was riddled with holes and useless, so they left it and went on. Then they saw a trail leading up over the coral cliff, and Jacobson and Baumgart decided to explore. A trail like this meant human activity. But after a few hundred yards of walking on the coral pavement of the path, the men turned back, leaving the place to the monkeys that chattered and scampered in the trees around them. Joining the other men, they continued north along the shore.

Ancient trees, their trunks varicose and black, their roots writhing like serpents, the weave of their arched branches creating darkened tunnels, grew out from the coral cliffs along the northwestern shore of Apo Island. The men walked under the trees, hidden from observation, until, in the distance, they saw the green shoreline of their destination, Bugsuk Island.

They stood transfixed, for there, under coconut trees that swayed like tall, slender dancers lining the edge of a broad, sandy beach, were houses. There were no Japanese launches on the shore and no sign of activity around the buildings. That did not mean there were no risks. So they would wait and watch.

But not for long.

There were eyes behind the towering coconut trees that swayed in the sea breeze along Bugsuk Island's sparkling beach in a gentle hula. The eyes were watching the *Flier* survivors.

All that Crowley and his men saw when they looked toward the island were the apparently tranquil settlement of houses and, in their imaginations, food and water. But they were cautious. With their raft in tow, they worked their way around the northern edge of Apo Island to a point on the beach where they could no longer see the houses. Their plan was to arrive on Bugsuk just before sunset and to use the half-light of dusk to sneak toward the settlement. By now, their starvation and thirst had robbed the men of whatever athletic ability they had once possessed, so when they swam across the narrow channel between the islands, they would lack the strength to swim against the flow. But if they judged the current correctly, they would land about a mile and a half from the houses. Then they would have enough cover to sneak closer, undetected. There was no more than a half-mile between Apo and the far shore, and all of it was the pale blue of reef water. They expected no problems.

Late that afternoon, they pushed the raft off the sandy beach. Most of the men waded at its side, and when they reached the far shore, they climbed out of the water, not on coral but with another long stretch of white-sand beach under their tender feet. Stowing the raft, they walked west toward the setting sun. They were on a narrow peninsula, on the far side of which was the tidal mouth of a saltwater stream. Crossing the peninsula with a wary eye toward the far shore, they waded into the stream. When they climbed the far bank, they were on the same beach that, to the west, passed in front of the Bugsuk houses. Here a grove of baring trees, a species that, like mangroves, sinks its roots in salt water, blocked their view of the settlement. The men worked their way through the shallow water under the trees, with the low rays of the sun slanting between the tree trunks, and then moved ashore, peering through the grove at what appeared to be a once-thriving but now-abandoned village. The houses that they had seen from Apo Island were surrounded by a coconut grove, and between the survivors and those houses were the remnants of bamboo and palm-leaf native huts.

Jacobson and Baumgart were the last to arrive, their arms filled with coconuts. For the first time in five days, the *Flier* survivors would have unspoiled food to eat, and apparently a place to sleep. The main building in this settlement—well built of bamboo and lumber, with a thatched roof—looked like the home of a person of wealth. But the home had been ransacked, the furniture carted out of its now-barren rooms, and any remnant of the former owners' presence stripped from the now-naked walls.

The house had a good wooden floor for sleeping, probably free from rats and certainly protected from sand crabs. But weary as they were, the men were also excited by their discoveries and were not yet ready for rest. They wanted to explore. Standing in front of the main house and looking south, they could imagine that they were in an exotic resort. A lawn fifty yards deep or more and shaded by the high canopy of coconut trees led to the beach of pure, white, soft sand, framed in this view by drooping coconut palm fronds. Beyond the beach was an island paradise. Stretching out to the left was the chain of islands the men had spent the last four days hopping, and between the last—Byan—and Mantangule, on the right, rose the distant blue mountains of Balabac. A good-size wooden boat—Al Jacobson guessed it was thirty-eight feet long—was beached in front of the house and looked like it had been intentionally destroyed. Nearby was another launch of about the same size that appeared to have been under construction. On either side of the house and inland from it were several clearings, which suggested that the owners had raised vegetables. And farther inland, some of the men reported, there was a stream. In its clear water swam schools of fish, meals for days to come.

Exploring by himself, Earl Baumgart found a curious concrete structure just behind the main house. It stood about five feet high and was another six feet long, and when he climbed atop it he was elated. Someone had built a cistern to collect rainwater, probably from the roof of the house. There was all the water the men would ever need, and more! He called out his discovery to the others, who came running.

Once more, the skipper lived up to his reputation for cautiousness outside of the realm of battle. He told his gathered crew that they should drink sparingly from the cistern. They wanted to guzzle to their thirst's content, he knew. But having gone without water for five days, and with almost no food in the same period, their bodies could not handle much. When he had explained this, each man took a small sip from Baumgart's pool and then went away. Only Chief Howell ignored Crowley's caution. He drank until his belly was full, and then he drank some more.

Now Jacobson and some others set about opening the good coconuts. They found a sharp rock in the ground and smashed each nut against it until they had removed the soft green outer shell. Then they punched out the eye of the inner, hard brown shell, drained the milk, and crushed the nut into pieces that could be chewed.

With these small pleasures, the men began to settle in for the night. Jacobson found a bamboo door that he laid on the floor as his mattress, and he stretched out on it, content. Images filled his head as the palm leaves rustled above him. There were fish and coconuts to eat, a roof over his head, water to drink, and, it appeared, no enemies within miles. There was no more need to walk, so his feet could heal. There was shade from the sun, so his blisters would dry and disappear. This was a place where a man could wait out the war, if he had to.

Not long after Chief Howell drank his fill from the cistern, he began to feel ill. His condition worsened during the night, but there was no help for him. If some of the others showed little sympathy, it may have been because they knew his sickness, self-inflicted as it was, was not lethal. In time, his body would acclimate. The little bit of coconut in their stomachs had satisfied their appetites, and they knew there would be more meals to come. With a home around them to keep away the chilling breezes, they succumbed to their exhaustion, dreaming untroubled dreams.

Once more, they arose with the sun and began planning their day. There was work to be done, and Crowley and Liddell started organizing teams. One group would catch some fish, while another would build a fire for cooking. They had no matches, but Jacobson still had his binoculars, and their lenses would make perfect magnifying glasses for focusing the sun's rays in an incendiary beam on dry tinder. Someone needed to scout the area, and the group would need more coconuts.

Jacobson was the first one up, and he was standing looking out a window toward the rear of the house and the jungle beyond when he saw two small boys—they might have been thirteen or fourteen—emerge from the trees. Jacobson told his shipmates what he saw, and they all were quickly on their feet. It was obvious to them that the boys knew the sailors were there, so they filed out of the house and approached the visitors. The boys were wearing ragged shorts and tattered shirts, and their feet were bare, like the sailors'. Crowley stepped forward.

"Americans or Japanese?" he asked.

"Americanos!" one of the boys, Oros Bogata, said, smiling. "Japanese!" he said, drawing a finger across his throat as if slitting it.

The men felt a collective wave of relief. Then the boy pointed to the cistern by the house.

"Don't drink water," he said.

Perhaps they misunderstood his puzzling words, they thought. But with their *Que sera, sera* attitude, they disregarded that comment and asked whether the boys had any food. Oros patted his small stomach.

"Rice," he said, and he motioned for the men to follow him and his silent friend back into the jungle. Stepping in line behind the boys, they found themselves on a narrow path. The boys, seeing that they were being followed, scampered ahead to a spot where they had left poles with small packs tied at the ends. Each balanced his pole on his shoulder, and then Oros led the file of hobbling, nearly naked men while his friend followed, sweeping the trail behind them to camouflage evidence of the group's passing.

In a short distance, they reached an abandoned sugarcane field. Oros motioned for the men to sit down, and he and his companion cut sections of cane a yard long and offered each man his own piece. The heart of the cane was a sweet and juicy bundle of fibers, and for the next half-hour, Crowley and his men chewed in bliss, until they simply had no more strength left in their jaws.

Back on the path, the boys led the men a short way to a clearing about the size of a football field. In one corner of the field was a raised wooden platform with a thatched roof supported on bamboo poles, but with no walls. Again the boys motioned for the men to sit and rest. Then they dropped their poles and opened their packs. One took a stick, sharpened at one end, and placed the tip in a notched piece of wood that he drew from his pack. He spun the stick between his palms, and in less time than it would have taken to remove a match from a box and strike it, he had some tinder smoldering. Jacobson, the Eagle Scout who had been taught to start fires with a bow and a stick, was impressed.

Then the boys produced a small pot, and one left and got water from a nearby stream. They poured rice from their pack into the pot, and while the fire brought the water to a boil, they cut leaves from a banana tree and made plates for their guests. Now the same boy who had cautioned them against drinking from the cistern gave them a cup of muddy water and, by sign language, told them they should drink it. The men hesitated, so the boy drank some himself. *Que sera, sera!* The men drank, as well.

When the rice was cooked, the boys spread it on the banana leaves. Then they produced three dried fish from the bounty of their packs and divided them among the men. There was enough for everyone.

Four days earlier, Crowley and his men had chosen survival with freedom over survival with food when they had elected to head away from Balabac. Theirs was a decision that prolonged the pain of hunger and thirst, which might easily have been cut short had they allowed themselves instead to come under Japanese control. Now, without hesitation, they had turned themselves over to the authority of two small boys whose friendship they accepted as a stray dog does that of a man with a scrap of food. Led by their stomachs, the sailors had followed the boys into the jungle with only the promise of rice, and now, with the smell of steaming hot rice and fish rising to their nostrils, they attacked their meal.

Their focus changed abruptly when, looking up from his food, one of them saw nine men, bristling with weapons—rifles, blow-guns, and bolos—stepping into the clearing from every point of the compass.

They were surrounded!

The *Flier* survivors had traded their safety for scraps of sustenance. The price of their meal now stared across the clearing at them.

Wesley Miller was ready to bolt like a startled fawn, but these fierce-looking warriors were everywhere. No one budged. The shredded soles of their feet precluded it.

"Hello!" one of the armed men called. His voice was cheerful and a smile lit his face. He dashed across the grass to the platform where the sailors still sat. Crowley struggled to his feet, as did his men at the approach of this stranger. When the man reached them, he grasped the hands of the *Flier* crew, shaking them vigorously.

"Welcome to Bugsuk Island," the man said. "I am Pedro Sarmiento."

Sarmiento said he was the leader of the local bolo battalion, indicating the men who were with him. Sarmiento had instructions from the guerrilla headquarters that if he found any Allied survivors, he was to ship them to a guerrilla outpost on Palawan's southern tip.

Crowley and Liddell were becoming comfortable with Sarmiento, and they were prepared to follow his instructions. At this point someone recalled the earlier direction from the two boys, to not drink the water in the cistern, and asked Sarmiento to explain.

Oh, he replied, earlier in the war, when the Japanese had driven the owner of the home from his property, Sarmiento had poisoned the water with arsenic in hopes that Japanese soldiers would drink it!

Everyone looked at Chief Howell. The man had a cast-iron gut!

A Japanese patrol would reach Bugsuk later in the morning, Sarmiento told the sailors, so they could not remain at the schoolhouse. The Japanese soldiers would inspect the area and then would spend the night in the house where Crowley and his men had slept so peacefully the night before. So the sailors would have to hike at least a mile inland to be safe. The Japanese were afraid to penetrate the center of the island, Sarmiento said.

Sarmiento reported that his instructions from the guerrilla leader, Captain Mayor, were to take any survivors all the way north across the center of Bugsuk and then to bring them by boat to the guerrilla outpost at Cape Buliluyan, the southernmost tip of Palawan. He told Crowley and Liddell that it was important to begin the hike soon. When they said they were ready, he told them to finish their breakfast. Then he sent the two boys back to the beach to make sure the Americans had not left any evidence behind.

A few minutes later, the boys returned with the lens that the sailors had removed from Jacobson's binoculars, with which they had planned to start their fires. Someone offered the lens to Sarmiento, who produced a pipe and tobacco that he lit with the lens. He smiled with gratitude. Then, seeing that they had finished their rice and fish, he invited the men from *Flier* to begin their cross-island trek.

7

An Arduous Challenge

William Pittenger

[EDITOR'S NOTE: TWENTY-TWO UNION SOLDIERS ON A COVERT MISSION to steal a Confederate train running on the Chattanooga Railroad were briefly successful but quickly captured. Eight were executed; eight escaped and eventually made their way to safety in the North. Six, including author William Pettinger, were later exchanged for Confederate prisoners and returned to the Union. Pettinger recounts the adventures of two men from the raiding party those who escaped and made their way to safety.]

No fugitives passed through more romantic adventures than Mark Wood and Alf Wilson. The southward course they took saved them from an energetic pursuit.

The idea that any of our party would seek for the Gulf blockading squadron probably never entered the head of any pursuer. It was well that this route was chosen by Wilson, for in no other way could he possibly have succeeded in carrying his sick comrade with him. The manner in which poor Wood, who had been for months suffering from fever, and was scarcely able to walk about the jail, was taken from "Atlanta to the sea" by a starving comrade, would seem a most improbable invention if met in a work of fiction.

I extract the complete account of the escape, with a few unimportant omissions, from *The Adventures of Alf. Wilson*, written by himself, and first published in book form in Toledo, 1880.

The account begins in the Atlanta jail-yard. The necessity for immediate flight was first seen by Wood, who exclaimed,—

"Alf, come on, quick! the boys are getting over the fence at the back of the jail; hurry up, for there's a company of guards coming double-quick."

This was my old comrade, Mark Wood, and his voice was the first warning I had of the danger that threatened me, or of the necessary change in our programme.

"Then bounce that fence!" I yelled. We both reached the top of the high fence at the same instant, and not a second too soon, for, as I glanced over my shoulder from the fence-top, I saw the guards with gleaming muskets pouring in at the gate, and before I could throw my leg over and spring off a volley was fired, the balls rattling and whizzing all about us. One bullet struck the picket under my thigh, and so close that the splinters lacerated my flesh, and as my feet struck the ground on the outside, I said to Mark, "I am hit."

"Get up and run like——!" exclaimed Mark.

I was on my feet in an instant, not knowing whether my thigh was shattered or not. As I ran I clapped my hand there to see if it bled freely. I pulled away a lot of splinters, and had the satisfaction of finding that I had received only a slight flesh wound made by the picket splinters. Never did I make better use of my legs; there was need of it, too, for the balls were spatting about us in the dirt uncomfortably near. They came so thick and closely at one time that I was almost certain that one or both of us would be hit; but we answered their cries of "Halt! halt!" by springing forward with all the speed we could command.

It was about a mile before we struck the cover of woods, and then the trees were so scattering that they afforded only a doubtful place for concealment. It was now every man for himself, and, like the Duke of Wellington at Waterloo, we longed for darkness or some other friendly interposition in our behalf. Wood had come up with me, and we dodged stealthily from one thicket to another until it began to grow quite dark, when we breathed easier and acted more deliberately, although we well knew we were not out of danger yet.

About this time, we became aware that we were approaching a public road. We soon had warning that it was much better to halt, and not attempt to cross the road. The sound of galloping horsemen in great numbers and the clanking of sabres could be heard near by.

We were so nearly out of breath that we could run no farther for the present, and, on looking hastily about, discovered a low, scrubby pine-bush surrounded with shrubbery. We both darted under its protecting shelter, and lay flat on the ground on our faces, neither having spoken a word to the other for some minutes, on account of our great exhaustion. We were so near the road that we could plainly see all the movements of the rebel cavalry, who were deploying their line something in the manner of skirmishers.

This presented an unexpected difficulty in our way. If we had reached the road two minutes sooner we might have crossed without being seen, but we could not have been there an instant sooner than we were, unless we had had wings, for we had both run until we were ready to fall in our tracks.

We had become separated from the rest of the party, but could still hear the reports of muskets, and knew that the pursuit was still going on, but how many of the escaping party had been killed was beyond our knowledge, though I had seen Captain Fry reeling and stumbling in a manner that led me to fear he was shot. We were thus compelled to lie quietly for some time. While we were waiting here the cavalry was relieved by infantry, and formed into squads to scour the woods.

The place where we lay was not over fifteen steps from where the infantry sentinel was stationed. We could hear every word he spoke to the man on the next post. Their comments on the affair at the jail would have been amusing to us under less serious circumstances, and I wish I could give their words exactly now, for they were ludicrous enough.

Some time late in the evening, while we were still lying under the bush, we became aware that some one was approaching us very quietly. In the dark we could recognize the dim outlines of two men, and we felt certain, as they came so near us that we could have almost touched them, that it was two of our comrades; but we dare not even whisper to them, lest we should cause them to betray themselves, and, perhaps, us too. They were, evidently, from the cautious manner in which they moved, aware that they were very close to the rebel guards. These men, I afterwards learned, were Porter and Wollam.

After waiting a short time to see if they were discovered, and hearing nothing of them, we began to crawl out, concluding that there was no probability of the guards leaving that night. I should judge the sentries were stationed about thirty paces apart, and to get out there was no alternative but to pass between them.

I selected a place and crawled to the other side of the road safely, and then lay perfectly still, while Mark did the same. My hair fairly stood on end as he wriggled along, for it seemed to me once or twice as if one of the sentries would certainly discover him before he would reach me. This was one of our most narrow escapes.

We were no more than safely across the road when a new and unseen obstacle, in the shape of a high fence, presented itself, over which we must climb before we could breathe free. We crawled carefully to the fence, and by great patience and much care, one at a time, managed to get over without attracting the attention of the guards. We felt as if we had accomplished quite an achievement when at last we had escaped beyond the fence a few steps and found ourselves in an open field, where we could push ahead noiselessly, and when, at last, we got away entirely out of hearing, we struck out on a full run.

At the far side of the field we came to a small stream, in which we travelled some distance in the water, to take precaution against pursuit by dogs. Soon after, we struck a thick piece of woods on the slope of a hill-side, which we continued to ascend under the thick foliage for some time. But, at last, exhausted Nature asserted her full sway, and we were compelled to lie down and rest out of sheer inability to go farther.

Up to this time, I think, neither of us had spoken any more than if we had been dumb. As we threw ourselves on the ground, without breath or strength to go farther, we began to realize the weak, helpless condition we were in. It did not appear as if our limbs were strong enough to carry us five miles a day.

When we looked forward to the long journey ahead of us, the hunger and fatigue, it looked a little discouraging. I think, however, a portion of this sense of physical prostration was caused by the sudden relaxation from the great mental strain and excitement which had been upon us from the time of the jail-break and immediately preceding it. This, with the intense exertion in running, in our enfeebled condition, had wellnigh unnerved us. We were wild, too, almost, with joy at our escape.

But we had but little time to rest, rejoice, or feel thankful in. Many contingencies yet stood between us and the goal of our hopes. Many armed enemies; many long, weary miles of travel; many rivers lay across our path, and many days of hunger and many sleepless nights, if we would succeed.

Before we escaped from the prison I studied over the subject of routes very carefully. I had seen enough of night travel in the mountains about Chattanooga and along the Tennessee River, and well knew that the probabilities of our being picked up, should we go in that direction, would be very much greater. I therefore decided in my own mind that I would strike out for the Gulf and try to reach some of the vessels of the Federal blockading squadron. While this would be much the longest route,—the distance, as near as I could calculate, being over three hundred miles,—I thought there would be less vigilance and liability of pursuit in that direction. In this conjecture it turned out that I was correct.

The country was entirely unknown to me, except a slight general idea I had of it from the school geographies. I only knew that the waters of the Chattahoochee River, which flowed west of Atlanta, entered the Gulf.

While we rested on the hill-side I communicated, in a whisper, to Mark my views, and he readily agreed that he would go in any direction I thought best. Accordingly, we rose up and walked to an open place where we could see the stars, and soon determined our course, which was to be slightly south of west, and at once we set out as fast as we could travel. We spoke no words as we walked on, and went as noiselessly as possible, for we were on the lookout for scouting parties of cavalrymen that might be prowling about.

We soon came to the railroad track leading from Atlanta to Columbus, and knew from this that our course was about right. Our march led us through some rough country, and we were compelled to rest quite frequently, so that when it began to grow light in the east we estimated that we were about eight miles from the prison.

We sought out a secluded retreat for the day, and after getting each of us a stout stick, which would answer either as a weapon or a walking-stick, we lay down and slept until late in the afternoon. We woke up much rested, but were so lame and our feet were so sore that we could hardly take a step without excruciating pain. We were hungry, and the scanty morsel of corn-bread we had brought from the prison the previous evening did not go far towards satisfying our sharp appetites. But it was all we had, and we ate it and were thankful, although we did not know where or when we would get our next rations.

I now saw a difficulty in this attempt to get away that we did not encounter in our first attempt to reach the Federal lines. Our clothes had become dirty and ragged, and we had a sort of jail-bird look, that it seemed to me would betray us if we were seen. I was brought to a realization of this fact as I looked at Wood, when we sat together in silence beneath the great tree where we had taken shelter, waiting for the friendly mantle of darkness to shield our movements.

And I suppose my own appearance was no more prepossessing than his. The miserable garments he wore did not cover his nakedness. His face was begrimed with dirt almost set in the skin. He had become thin and emaciated with fever and had a ravenous appetite; his eyes were sunken in his head and seemed to have the wild, unnatural glare of a madman, which at times almost made me shudder.

The poor fellow's pitiable appearance, as he sat there despondently and longingly gazing down on the beautiful valley below, was such as to appeal to a heart of stone. Yet I knew that it was unsafe for us to go to a house, and we agreed not to be seen by a human being if we could avoid it. I felt certain that if we should meet any one, our appearance would at once betray us.

We were in a country where we could not expect to find a friend. We were so weak, and the mental strain and long-continued anxiety, in which we had lived from day to day, had had the effect of making us, I may say, foolishly suspicious and timid of everything. We were startled at every sudden noise, and crouched like sneaking wolves from the sight of man.

While in the midst of unpleasant thoughts, Mark broke the long silence by raising his head and saying, "Alf, it is time for us to go."

Our journey that night took us through a corn-field, where we pulled a few ears of corn and chewed it as we went along. I remember it was hard and made my jaws very tired, but it helped to quiet my gnawing hunger. It was much better than nothing. After a toilsome night's journey, guided by the stars, and over a very rough country, in which we entirely avoided roads, we again secreted ourselves as the streaks of gray began to appear in the east, and, after scraping up a pile of leaves, lay down for the day. When we awoke, late in the afternoon, we found that our feet were so bruised and sore, and that we were otherwise so lame, and withal so weak from hunger, that it taxed our endurance to the utmost to take a single step.

We each took from our pockets an ear of corn, and after crunching and swallowing what we could, we put the rest in our clothes and hobbled off, making but very slow time for the first mile or so. It was in the month of October, and the nights were pretty cool, which, in our poorly-clad condition, compelled us to keep moving all the time to keep comfortably warm.

The next morning came and still we had not reached the river. Again we hid ourselves and slept through the day. When night came and we tried to walk, we found our feet in such a deplorable condition that it did not seem possible for us to go farther. Mark crawled some distance on his hands and knees, and, looking back at me, said in an appealing tone, "Alf, what's a fellow's life but a curse to him when he has to drag it out in this way? I would rather be dead and done with it."

I encouraged him, telling him the worst was over and we would soon reach the river. I suppose we had shaped our course a little too far south, and thus made the distance longer than it would otherwise have been. We struggled on for some time, crawling where the ground was stony, and stopping very often to temporarily quell the pain in our feet. I was a little ahead, and, as the breeze fanned my aching temples, I thought I heard to our right the lull of running water. I told Mark and cheered him up. We forgot our tortures for the time being and scrambled on quite lively, and soon after had the satisfaction of standing on the banks of the Chattahoochee.

De Soto did not feel more joy when he first discovered the Mississippi, the great Father of Waters, nor was the ecstasy of Balboa greater, when, from the cloud-capped summits of Darien, his eyes first beheld the vast expanse of water which he named the Pacific Ocean. Like that great discoverer, we waded out into the water, carrying neither naked sword nor the banner of our country like he, to take possession of our discovery in the name of our rulers, but to bathe our painful feet and cool our parched throats.

We made certain of the direction the river current ran, and started southward in high hopes, although the temptation to go northward to our friends was very strong. We now wanted a boat, and, not long after we started, fortune had another pleasant surprise in store for us, for we came upon a skiff safely moored, with lock and chain, to a tree.

After carefully inspecting the surroundings to see that no
prying eyes were peering on us, we "loosened" the lock with a
stone, and in a few minutes after were smoothly gliding down
the current of the great river, and I doubt if two more joyful
mortals ever navigated a canoe than we two, with that stolen
little craft.

What a happy change! Our weary limbs and painful feet
now had a rest, and yet we were gliding noiselessly on our journey. What wonderful teachers hardship and stern necessity are!
Discontented mortals do not half appreciate the blessings they
have until they have been pupils in the school of adversity. I felt
as if this chilly night's ride, in a little stolen boat, on a strange
river, whose shores were hidden by Plutonian shadows, was the
best and most grateful that I ever had, or ever expected to enjoy.

We pulled off our old boots and bathed our lacerated feet
in the water, and quenched the tormenting thirst caused by the
indigestible hard corn, which was now our only nourishment.
We kept our paddles pretty busy, as we wished to get as far away
as possible from where we took the boat before the dawn of day.

When daylight began to appear, we paddled our craft into
a bayou, safe from view, and secreted ourselves in a thicket for
the day.

Four days and nights had now passed since we had eaten
food, except the morsel of corn-bread we brought out of the
prison. We lay down to sleep the day away, but between our
great hunger and the swarms of mosquitoes we could get but
little rest.

I could, while sleeping, see in my dreams tables spread and
groaning with loads of good things to eat; bread, meat, cheese,
coffee, biscuit, and butter were all within my reach, and were
vanishing before my ravenous appetite, when, in the midst
of the great pleasures of this feast, I would suddenly waken
to a sense of the reality of the case, and what a maddening
disappointment I would feel. With this disturbed sort of rest
we worried through the day, the demands of hunger and our
stomachs getting the better of nature's demand for rest, until
at last we grew desperate, and at early twilight, in the evening,

pulled out of the little bayou, determined on a raid of some sort on a house for food.

We spied a house some distance from the river-bank, which we thought from appearances we could capture with a plausible story or by force.

On approaching, we saw in its immediate vicinity quite a number of cabins, and in the yard surrounding the house about twenty blood-hounds chained to the fence, indicating that these were the premises of an extensive planter. The only occupants of the house were an old man and woman. We apologized for disturbing them, and told them we were soldiers who had been on furlough returning to our regiments at Atlanta, and wished directions to the ferry (we had discovered a ferry as we came down); also, that we were hungry and wanted to get something to eat, provided they felt like feeding hungry soldiers without money, as we had had no pay for some time, and were both moneyless and in bad health, Mark's appearance proving this latter assertion.

It was quite dark, however, and they could not see us very distinctly, but they evidently credited our story, for they told us to be seated and we would soon be made welcome to such food as they had.

They were a couple of quite intelligent but unsophisticated old people, in comfortable circumstances, living, as most Southerners did, away from any highway, and we gained their confidence so far as to feel ourselves assured from suspicion.

I had been in Dixie so long that I had acquired, from the guards and citizens, their vernacular of speech quite perfectly; besides this, we had learned the names of officers and the number of different regiments, such as the Eighth Georgia Cavalry, Fifth Tennessee Infantry, until we were able to tell quite a plausible story, if not too closely questioned.

We asked the old man if there was any late news. He said, "Nothing, except that the Yankee raiders had seized the Atlanta jailer, overpowered the guards, and a number of them escaped and had not yet been caught." We expressed great surprise that such a piece of audacity could be made successful in Atlanta.

The old man said, "They were a desperate, dangerous lot of scoundrels, who ought to have been hung long ago."

He said many of them stood up and fought the soldiers with clubs and bricks, even after the guards had shot them through, and finally they jumped the high fence and ran like deer.

In the mean time we had devoured everything the good woman had set before us on the table. We were ashamed, but our hunger was so much stronger than our sense of shame that we could not leave off, and, if we had not been in a hurry, we would have waited for her to have prepared another meal for us. She said she regretted that she had not more cooked to set before us, but we told her she had been very kind, and thanked them, at the same time bidding them good-night, when we started off, as they supposed, for the ferry.

A short time afterwards we were in our boat pulling down-stream with more vigorous energy than we had before. We kept up a steady stroke of the paddles for some hours, feeling that each stroke placed so much more distance between us and the prison.

While we were thus moving along with steady, cautious stroke, high in the hopes of the future, I suddenly, quicker than a flash, found myself lying flat on my back in the river. What on earth had happened I did not know, the accident had been so sudden. I thought of earthquakes, whales, sharks, torpedoes, and many other things. Luckily, one of my feet caught on the side of the boat, and I drifted with it until Mark came to my assistance and pulled me out.

The cause of my mishap had been a ferry-boat wire, which was stretched across the river, and hung just low enough to catch me fairly as I sat in the stern of the boat. It struck Mark, but he sat in the middle, and fell into the bottom of the boat. We were going at a good speed, and the collision came so suddenly that it is a wonder we did not fare worse. Fortunately, there were no guards at the ferry, so we had no cause to apprehend discovery or molestation. My greatest mishap was a thorough wetting, for the night was frosty and cold, and caused me to chill.

This was followed in the after part of the night by a stupor that I could not shake off, and my continued efforts at the paddle had wellnigh exhausted me. Mark could not manage the boat very well, as he had tried it a number of times. But I felt that I must have rest and sleep, and so gave the boat over into his hands, enjoining him to keep it in the current. I lay down in the bottom of the boat, and soon sank into a state of forgetfulness and sleep. I do not know how long I had slept, but some time in the night Mark aroused me, and told me we could go no farther, as we had come "to the end of the river." It was some time before he could awaken me fully to consciousness, so that I could comprehend our situation.

At last I began to look around, to determine what Mark's "end of the river" meant. I soon discovered that he had run the boat away under a ledge of the mountain, and a dim light could only be seen in one direction. All else around us was impenetrable darkness.

I took the paddle, and worked the boat in the direction of the light, and in a little while we emerged from beneath this overhanging mountain ledge, and again reached the current of the river, down which the boat was soon rapidly gliding. Mark now discovered that the "end of the river" had not yet been reached, but he did not care to take charge of the boat again.

Shortly after this adventure we perceived that we were not to have smooth sailing all the way. The river began to grow rough, and the water ran over benches and ledges of rocks, and, in places, with great velocity, so much so that we narrowly escaped being broken up on several occasions during this night's journey.

We passed over a number of places that we would not have dared to risk in daylight, when we could have seen the danger. It seemed to grow worse and worse as we went on, when daylight warned us that it was time to tie up and hide, which we did, and, the day being warm and pleasant, we had a comfortable rest,—the best since our escape.

On the following night we came to a mill-dam, where the water, judging from the noise, poured over in great volume and force. We manoeuvred around for some time above it, not knowing what to do, but finally discovered what appeared to be an apron near the centre of the dam, and decided to risk running it. Accordingly, we rowed up-stream some distance to get under good headway, then turning the head of the boat down-stream, we bent to our paddles with all our might. We came down with the velocity of an express-train.

What we supposed might have been an apron, was nothing but a break in the dam, and over it we shot like an arrow, shutting our eyes and holding our breath. In an instant after, we landed (luckily right side up) away below in the midst of the angry, foaming torrent, and plying our paddles right vigorously, and keeping the bow of our boat down-stream, we rode out safely, but then and there swore off on running mill-dams in the night.

We continued our journey, though the river was still rough and growing worse. We were constantly among rocks and foaming, headlong torrents of water, while steep rocky walls confined the stream to very narrow limits, and dark, shadowy mountain peaks loomed up in the background, reminding us of the Tennessee about Chattanooga.

We went on from bad to worse, until at last, during the latter part of the night, we were incautiously drawn into a gorge, where it seemed that the destruction of our boat was inevitable. Such was the force and velocity of the water, that we lost all control of the boat, and in one instant would be spinning around in a furious eddy until our heads were fairly dizzy, and in the next we would be dashed against the rocks until it seemed as if our boat would be splintered to pieces.

We regarded our escape here as the narrowest we had made, and as quick as we could do so with safety we landed on the rocks and, with many regrets, abandoned our little craft to begin a tedious, toilsome land journey of three days and nights over rocky hills, bluffs, and mountains along the river.

Just as we landed from the boat Mark started to walk out, and, losing his balance, fell headlong into the river. With considerable difficulty I fished him out, and, the early morning being quite cool, the poor fellow was chilled through and through, and it was with the greatest difficulty that I finally succeeded in getting him up into the mountains, and continued to exercise him by walking, so as to get up a good circulation of his blood.

But he became so benumbed that I finally let him lie down, and gathered a lot of cedar boughs and piled them thickly over him, and then crawled in with him myself, and kept him as warm as possible. Here we slept and rested until late in the afternoon of that day, which became very warm under the bright rays of the sun.

Our progress was very slow, and towards the last extremely painful. The old bruises and blisters on our feet, which were not entirely healed, came back worse than ever, and much of the time we crept along on the rocks on our hands and knees, believing that if once we could get below this range of mountains, we would find navigable waters.

We came in sight of several isolated cabins in these wild, rocky hills, where we managed to beg a little food on two different occasions, which helped us very much. The suffering we endured on our last night's travel I cannot describe. It seemed as if we must give up and die where we were. But at last, when daylight came, to our great delight we saw the spires and smoke-stacks of a town in the distance. We knew this to be Columbus, Georgia, and that when we got below it the river was navigable clear to the Gulf.

We now deemed it prudent to hide ourselves for the day, which we had not done in the mountains, and wait for the friendly cloak of darkness. When night came we made a long, careful detour away out around the suburbs of the town, and at last had the satisfaction of again reaching the river-bank, below the town, where we found good shelter among the dense grapevines and drift-wood. By this time it was nearly morning again, and, like beasts of prey, we betook ourselves to a safe hiding-place.

During all the time we had been in the vicinity of the town we had heard a constant clattering sound, as of a hundred workmen with hammers. This noise came from near the river, where there appeared also to be a great light. When daylight came the noise still continued, and we were near enough so that we could see that it was caused by a large number of workmen engaged on a vessel, which they were covering with iron.

The boat appeared to be very large and of great strength, and evidently was intended for a warlike purpose. On closer inspection the following night I found that she was a powerfully-built gunboat, which they were evidently in great haste to complete, as the hammers of the workmen never ceased on her, night or day, nor for a single moment.

This gunboat was none other than the rebel ram *Chattahoochee*, a formidable iron monster, built as an engine of destruction for the blockading fleet in Appalachicola Bay. The first knowledge the Navy Department had of her was through Wood and myself. The ram, on her first downward trip, blew up near the mouth of Flint River, and never reached the Gulf.

Our great anxiety now was to secure a boat. Wood was so lame he could not walk, and I was not much better. This delayed us here two days and nights. During the nights I was prowling about, up and down, trying to discover some sort of a craft that would float.

In my reconnoitring about the gunboat I had discovered an old skiff chained to a stump quite near and in plain sight of the workmen, to some of whom, no doubt, it belonged. I secured a stout stick for a lever, and crept to the stump to which the boat was chained, when, watching my opportunity, I got a pry in such a manner as to break the lock on the chain. The lights shone so brightly that I could plainly see the men's eyes, and I very much feared they would notice me. However, I worked off with the boat carefully, and half an hour after I had Mark aboard, and we were pulling rapidly down-stream. We found our prize to be a leaky old concern, and one of us was constantly busy keeping her bailed out.

After we had drifted down some miles, we spied three boats tied to the shore on the Alabama side of the river, and as we had been giving our attention entirely to the Georgians all along, we concluded to trade boats on that side of the river, provided we could secure a better boat.

Just as we had loosened the one we selected, three men with a pack of dogs came down the hill towards us, and the head man, evidently the owner, began hallooing to us and calling us slanderous names, such as thieves and the like. We did not stop to bandy words with the fellows, but speedily shoved all the boats into the river, and took a course up the river, as though we were going towards Columbus.

They rent the air with curses upon our heads. In the course of fifteen or twenty minutes they had secured the boats we shoved into the stream, and with the lights they carried we could distinctly see that they were bent on pursuing us.

We took a wide circuit, and then headed downward under cover of the willows, behind several small islands near the Georgia shore, and came out in the main stream far below the islands, while we had the satisfaction of seeing the lights of our pursuers disappearing up the river and prowling about the upper end of the islands, which we were now leaving far behind. We soon lost sight of them, and the strong presumption is that they never succeeded in finding their boat.

We increased our speed, and kept under the shadows of the wooded shores as much as possible, congratulating each other on our lucky boat trade. With a good boat and an open river we felt now that our chances of escape were exceedingly good, and our spirits were buoyant and hopes high, although our stomachs were craving food. But on we swept, hour after hour, down the broad river, happy in the thought that we were fast placing scores of miles between us and the hated prison. The rest given our feet had much allayed the pain we suffered, and when morning came and we had secreted ourselves for the day, we slept well, but awoke in the afternoon ravenously desperate for want of something to eat.

We went out, and, reconnoitring a little, discovered a corn-field. Making sure that there was no one about, we stole into the field and found plenty of corn and pumpkins. The hard corn and river water did not go well together, and proved to be an unpleasant diet to us, so we broke up the pumpkins, ate freely of the seed, and filled our pockets with more for lunch, each of us taking also a few ears of corn.

By the time we got back it was nearly dark, and we pulled out. The pumpkin-seed diet, poor as it was, helped us wonderfully, and we made a big night's journey, passing a steamboat upward bound, which we dodged by pulling under the shadows of the timber and low-hanging bushes.

Thus we progressed, travelling by boat at night and laying by in the daytime. If any reader of this story has ever made a trip on the lower end of the Chattahoochee River, I think he or she will agree with me when I say that the river scenery is peculiarly monotonous and causes a sense of loneliness. It is a vast water-path through dense forests of cypress and other swamp-growing timber. On either side, to the right and left, were endless swamps covered with water, and the river-channel was only observable by its being free from logs and gigantic trees.

Great festoons of gray and sombre moss hung suspended from even the topmost limbs of these trees, reaching clear down to the water, and floated and swung to the music of the sighing winds. Perhaps it was the circumstances in our case that made us feel so, but I remember it as a dismal, lonesome journey. Sometimes we would not see a sign of civilization for forty-eight hours at a stretch.

Besides the torments of hunger, our nights were made almost unendurable by the swarms of blood-thirsty mosquitoes, which came upon us in clouds. I did think that I had learned considerable about mosquitoes in my boyhood days in the Black Swamp of Northwestern Ohio, but for numbers, vocal powers, and ferocity I will trot the Chattahoochee swamp fellows out against any others I have ever met up with.

The ragged clothing, which yet clung to our backs, did not much more than half cover us; especially was this the case with Wood, who was, I may truthfully say, half naked, and was thus doubly annoyed by the omnipresent skeeters.

And my own condition was but little better. To protect ourselves from the pests, we thatched our bodies all over with great skeins of moss, and two more comical-looking beings than we were, thus rigged out, it would be hard to find, but it baffled the bills of our tormentors.

We had two other annoyances,—moccasin-snakes and alligators. The latter, with which the water swarmed as we went farther towards the Gulf, were a terror to me. They were a ferocious, hungry, dangerous-looking beast at best. We knew but little of their habits.

The largest water inhabitant I had ever seen was a Maumee River cat-fish, and the most dangerous, a Black Swamp massasauger. Night or day these gators, like the mosquitoes, were always within sight and hearing. Sometimes during the day, in order to keep out of the water, we would take shelter in a pile of drift-wood.

When we would wake up, after a short nap, every old log and hommock about us would be covered with "gators." They would lie listlessly and lazily, with eyes almost shut, looking hungrily and quizzically out of one corner of their wicked peepers, as if waiting for us to leave, or for a chance to nab one of us by the leg or arm and run.

Mark grew superstitious of these creatures. He said he had read of wolves following a famished buffalo in the same manner, and that sharks would hover around a ship from which a corpse was to be cast overboard, and that, too, even days before death had occurred or was even suspected by the sailors.

But the "gators" were cowardly fellows, and, on the least demonstration on our part, would scramble into the water. Still we feared that they might steal upon and lay hold of us with their powerful jaws while we were asleep. We had learned that they were not apt to attack, except when the object of their voracious appetites lay quiet; but, when once they did lay hold, that they were hard to beat off. They will drag their victim, be it man or beast, instantly under the water, where the struggle soon ends.

After enduring hunger as long as we possibly could, we were finally forced a second time since leaving Columbus to go in search of something to eat. This, I think, was about five or ten miles above Chattahoochee landing. It is not necessary to relate the particulars of our search for a human habitation, and the story of deception we told. It was a little before dark when we struck out on foot so weak, hungry, and faint that we could not walk many steps without resting, in search of something or anything we could devour. We were successful, or partially so, at least, and came back safely, much strengthened, as well as elated over our good luck, when, to our great dismay and chagrin, we found that our boat had been stolen during our absence.

It was evident some one had seen us land and watched until we left, and then taken the boat. I cannot describe our feelings. We scarcely knew what to do. The night was very dark, and it rained incessantly. We waded about in the water, tall grass and cane, and after a while found a little mound or hommock, which projected above the water, and on which we perched ourselves for the night.

Such a dismal, long, rainy night as it was, too! It did seem as if the mosquitoes would carry us away piecemeal towards morning, when the rain had ceased. Had it not been for the food we had eaten, I believe we would have given up in despair. When morning came, we waded up and down in the cane and grass all forenoon, and about the only discovery we made was that another river came in just below us, and we could not go farther without a boat.

During the afternoon I descried something on the far side of the river that looked like a boat partly sunk in the water, one end only of which was out. The next trouble was to get to it, as the river was about three-quarters of a mile wide, as near as we could judge. We found an old piece of plank, which we lashed on three flat rails with a grape-vine, and with a piece of narrow stave for a paddle and to fight off gators, I twined my legs firmly around the centre of the frail craft, while Mark pushed it off into the stream and stood at the edge of the grass watching me.

The raft sunk down until the water came about my waist, but I stuck to it, and after about an hour's hard work I effected a landing on the far side, and not long after found myself rewarded in the possession of a much better boat than the one we had lost the night before. I was not long in bailing out the water and rowing her back to where Mark was, whose gratitude found expression in tears and hearty hand-shaking, as he crept into the boat with me.

We now plied our paddles energetically for a while, until we felt sure we had passed out of reach of the owners of the boat, when we put into the cane and secreted ourselves until night. After this mishap in losing our boat, we resolved that we would not both leave again while our journey lasted, starve or no starve.

During the following day, while we were laid up waiting for night and fighting mosquitoes, I went out, skulking about to see what I could see, and in passing through an old field found some fish-hooks and lines in an old vacant cabin. I appropriated them, and we found them a godsend to us, for they proved the means of keeping us from actual starvation.

We must have had a touch of scurvy, for our mouths and gums had become feverish, and our teeth were loose, and would bleed constantly when we attempted to chew the corn. This was the condition we were in when, providentially, we became possessed of the fish-hooks and lines.

And now for a feast on raw cat-fish, of which we caught a plentiful supply as we journeyed on in the night. I have previously neglected to mention that I had with me an old one-bladed knife without any back, which was our only weapon, defensive or offensive. This old knife I had secreted when we were in the Atlanta prison, and had kept it with me as a precious treasure during all our wanderings.

With this knife and our fingers we managed to skin and dress the fish, which we ate raw with our soaked corn. Matches we had none, nor had we been able to get any, and so we had no fire. I could eat only a mouthful or two of the raw fish at a time. My stomach was weak and feverish, and rebelled against the flesh. Still it tasted palatable.

Mark, poor, hungry fellow, tore it from the bones in great mouthfuls, like a ravenous wolf, until I would beg of him to desist, fearing the results. He would sit and crunch the bloody flesh, and look at me with a wild, strange stare, and never speak a word. His eyes were sunken away in his head, almost out of sight, and as he would seize a fresh piece the pupils of his eyes would dilate with the gloating, ferocious expression of a panther or other carnivorous wild beast.

I had frequently heard of men losing their reason and going mad from the effects of protracted hunger, and I sometimes shuddered as I looked at its telling effects on poor Mark's wasted frame, and the unnatural glare of his eyes. He would mutter and groan in his sleep, and sometimes scream out as if pierced by a knife, when he would suddenly start up and call my name. Towards the last of our journey his condition was much of the time a cause of great anxiety to me. Still, after we began to eat the fish he seemed much better, and I only feared the unnatural quantities of the raw flesh would kill him.

We were now nearing the bay, as was plain to be seen, for on each succeeding morning the river had grown wider. Finally we became well satisfied that we were nearing a large town, which afterwards proved to be Appalachicola, and this made us anxious to learn something of the state of affairs below,— whether there were rebel picket-boats, or obstructions, such as torpedo-boats and the like.

About this time we discovered a cabin some distance from the shore, and, to have a plausible excuse, I took an old pipe Mark had, and filled it with a few crumbs of tobacco which I fished from my old coat-linings, and then taking a piece of rotten wood which would retain fire, I left Mark with the boat and walked over to the house to get a light for my pipe.

The occupants of the cabin proved to be an old Scotchman and his wife. He was very inquisitive, and asked more questions than I cared to answer. But I managed to evade suspicion, and at the same time gained considerable information. I learned that we were about five miles above Appalachicola, and that the Federal blockading squadron was stationed at the mouth of the bay, eighteen miles below the city. I hurried back to the boat, and found Mark rejoicing over a little armful of sweet potatoes he had stolen from a canoe, which he had discovered in my absence.

We got into the boat and at once paddled to the other side of the bay or river, where we entered into an inlet or creek, up which we ran for some distance, when we came to a dense canebrake. Here we secreted ourselves and built a little fire, roasted fish and potatoes, parched corn, and dined in right royal style, although we felt the need of a little salt. Two hungry wolves never ate more ravenously than we did, although we were obliged to restrain ourselves, and leave off while yet hungry.

It was with the utmost difficulty that I absolutely forced Mark to quit. After eating enough for four men, as I thought, he still begged for more. I finally induced him to go to sleep and stored away some of the cooked fish and sweet potatoes for the next day.

The information we had gained was invaluable to us, although I felt I had obtained it at some risk. When night came on we pulled out and passed down on the opposite side of the bay from the city, slowly and cautiously. We had moss in the bottom, on the sides, and in the seats of our boat for our comfort. As soon as we had gone well past the city, whose bright lights we could plainly see, we crossed the bay to the city side below the city, in the hope of finding a more sea-worthy boat.

We were unable to find any other boat, however, and pulled on down the bay as fast as we could. While going down the bay that evening, we ran along in the midst of a large school of huge fish of some description, from which we apprehended danger every instant. These monsters would swim along on all sides of us, with great fins sticking more than a foot out of the water, and extended like a great fan. One of these fish could easily have wrecked our boat with its huge body.

We hoped to reach the blockading fleet before daylight, but the night grew cloudy and we were unable to tell what course we were running, as the bay grew wider and wider as we went out. We decided the best thing we could do was to pull for land, which we reached after midnight, pretty well exhausted with our hard work at the paddles. We tied up our boat and went to a thicket near by and slept soundly.

When we awoke in the morning, we were cheered by the beautiful surroundings,—all just as nature had fashioned them, for the habitation or handiwork of man was nowhere to be seen. Our couch had been a bed of prickly grass, that caused a stinging, itching sensation all over our bodies. We had slept in a wild orange grove.

We made a hasty breakfast on our fish and potatoes left from the night previous, and started for our boat; but imagine our surprise when we found it distant at least two hundred yards from the water. Mark, who had lived in the old country, explained to me that this was the effect of the ocean tide, which had gone out since we landed, and would not come in again until that night. There was no safe course left us but to drag our boat to the water, which we did, after tugging at it for about an hour.

When we were again on the water we could see the spires and high buildings of the city we had passed, but no sight of ships could we see. We took our course as well as we could, and pulled for the open sea. A little boat, which seemed to be a fishing-smack under full sail, passed away to the leeward of us, coming out from the city, and caused us no little concern, but she passed off, and either did not notice us or care to inquire who we were.

We plied our paddles industriously until about the middle of the afternoon, when we spied an island away in the distance. We had been out of sight of land for some time and the view of the island cheered us up a little, for we knew if a rough sea came on that our little boat was liable to get swamped. This island was much farther away than we had supposed. As we neared it we were in some doubt as to whether we should pass to the right or left of it, when our decision was made by the discovery to the left and away in the distance of something that had the appearance of dead trees.

In the same direction, and right in our course, was something that appeared like a bar or gravel-bank. We supposed the old trees stood on another low island or bar beyond. But as we neared this bar, that which at first seemed to be dead trees began to take the shape of ship-masts, and we imagined that we could see something that looked like the dark outlines of black smoke-stacks in the blue, hazy distance. This made us quite nervous, and we pulled away at the paddles with renewed vigor and strength.

Before we were scarcely conscious of it we were close upon the bar, and began to be puzzled how we should get by or around it, for it was longer than it appeared to be when first seen.

Presently we discovered a narrow, shallow channel through it, and we were not long in getting our boat through. As we were going through, Mark gathered in a lot of rough, muddy-looking lumps, which I supposed were boulders, and soon called for my old broken-backed knife, after which I saw him open one of the muddy chunks and eat something from it.

Says I, "Mark! You starving Yank! What in thunder are you at now?"

"Taste this," says he, as he opened another muddy chunk, and I lapped up from the dirty shell the sweetest oyster I had ever tasted.

We were in the midst of a great oyster-bed, the like of which I had never before seen. I had never, in fact, seen an oyster in the shell before. Mark gathered up as many as he could as the boat passed along, and when we reached the still water we made quite a little feast on them as we paddled on. I think I never tasted anything so delicious. We were still very hungry, and the moist, rich, salty flavor of the oysters seemed to suit our weak, famished stomachs to a nicety.

But our little feast was soon cut short by the certain discovery that the dead trees were nothing less then the masts of vessels. We could now plainly see the yards, cross-trees, and great smoke-stacks. We dropped the oysters in the bottom of the boat, and, though quite exhausted, the sight of the vessels so renewed our strength that we made the little boat scud over the still water at a lively rate.

Soon we could see the long, graceful streamers waving from the peaks of the masts, and the outlines of the dark, sombre-looking hulls of the ships.

We were now nearing the ships very fast, and were a little anxious to see their colors, as we had become so suspicious of everybody and everything that we half feared running into the clutches of our enemies. But we were not long in suspense, for suddenly a little breeze sprang up, and I shall never forget my joy on seeing the old flag, the glorious old stars and stripes, as they unfolded to the ocean breeze, and seemed to extend their beneficent protection over us, after nearly eight months of terrible bondage.

We could see the field of blue, studded with its golden stars, and the stripes of white and red! Yes, it was our flag, old *E Pluribus Unum*! We threw down our paddles in the boat, and stood up and yelled and screamed and cried like a couple of foolish boys lost in the woods.

We could not restrain ourselves. Mark wanted to jump overboard and swim to the ships, although we were yet, per-haps, nearly a mile away,—at least too far to swim in his con-dition. After we recovered our senses a little, we picked up the paddles and began rowing again, directing our course towards the largest vessel.

It seems now like a dream to me,—that joyful day,—the most joyful, I was about to say, of my life. I believe there were three vessels in sight. In steering for the largest one, although it was the most distant, we had to pass some distance in front of the bow of a smaller ship or boat. We were now getting so close that we could plainly see the officers and men on the decks in their neat, blue uniforms. We could see the port-holes in the sides of the ships, and the black muzzles of the cannon projecting out.

This gave us much assurance, and we said to ourselves, "Good-by, rebs! We are out of your clutches at last!"

We were rowing our insignificant-looking little boat right along, just as though we intended to capture the biggest vessel in the fleet, when a gruff voice from the ship, whose bow we were passing, commanded us to "Come to, there!"

At the same time we saw a grim-looking old sea-dog, in nice uniform, leaning over the rail, motioning us in with his hand. We turned the bow of our little boat towards him, and, when we came within better speaking distance, he interrogated us, in stentorian voice, about as follows:

"'Who in——are you, and what are you paddling under my guns in this manner for?"

We were half-terrified by the old fellow's angry, stern manner, and did not know what to say to this unexpected, angry interrogation. We paddled on very slowly, while the sailors and officers began to gather in little squads, and look at us with mingled curiosity and merriment.

Presently, the officer hailed us again, with about the same questions. I now stood up in our boat, and answered that we were two men trying to get back to God's country, among friends.

I was now quite uneasy, and suspicious of the situation, and kept my eyes on the officer, for I perceived he was the commander. I shall never forget his stern but puzzled look as we came up under the bow of his vessel.

We had been so overjoyed and excited that we had forgotten to pull the old moss, which covered our nakedness and protected us from the sun, from our backs, and we must have looked like scare-crows or swamp-dragons. I cannot speak so well of my own appearance then, but can see Mark Wood, just as he was on that joyful day, and a more comical, forlorn, starved-looking being cannot well be imagined.

In our boat were a few cat-fish partly skinned, some oysters in the shell, some ears of scorched corn, a lot of moss, and our old boots, for our feet were yet sore, and we went bare-footed when in the boat.

After scrutinizing us in silence for some little time, as we drifted up closer and closer, he again demanded of us some account of our strange conduct and appearance. I told him we were enlisted Federal soldiers, and belonged to the command of General O. M. Mitchel, in Tennessee, to which he growled something about our being "a——long ways from camp."

I then explained to him briefly that we were fugitives, and the causes that led to it; that we were nearly famished with hunger, and that, after skulking through mountains and river by night, we had at last sought protection under the old flag and the guns of his ship.

I could see that his manner towards us had changed. He plainly saw the indications of our distress. He said he had heard of the raiding expedition we spoke of, and commanded us to row up to the ladder and come up the ship's side.

We did so, and Wood went up the steps first. The poor fellow's agitation and joy were so great, and he was so weak, that he could scarcely raise his feet from step to step on the ladder or stairs. The commander, seeing his weak, faltering condition, leaned over the rail, as Wood came up, and, reaching out, took hold to assist him, and, as he did so, the rotten bit of old moss, which covered Mark's shoulder and back, all pulled off, and exposed his emaciated, bony skeleton, which, in truth, was nothing but skin and bones.

The well-fed, sleek-looking sailors seemed to look on in horror, but not more so than the generous-hearted commander, who was moved almost to tears as he was reaching over to help me as I came to the top of the step-ladder. They stared at us in silent wonderment, while the sailors looked down into our little boat with comical curiosity.

8

Pearl Harbor, December 7, 1941

Paul Joseph Travers

HICKAM FIELD: NICHOLAS GAYNOS AND WILLIAM ROLFE

At approximately 7:49 a.m. on 7 December, Lieutenant Commander Kakwichi Takashashi broke away from the first attack wave and steered his group of fighter bombers toward Ford Island and Hickam Field. At 7:55, Japanese bombers made their first appearance over Hickam Field, strafing men and aircraft with machine-gun fire and dive-bombing hangars, barracks, and other buildings.

To prevent sabotage attempts, planes were grouped in parallel rows outside their hangars. Among the fifty-six bombers parked on the runway and concrete aprons were a number of the new B-17 Flying Fortresses.

The planes were so concentrated that the distance between wing tips was ten feet or less.

On this Sunday, Hickam Field was busy with normal work activity. Many officers and enlisted men were present for the arrival of a new group of twelve B-17 bombers, for which Hickam Field was the first stop from the West Coast. The bombers arrived over Pearl Harbor in the middle of the first attack.

Japanese pilots were as surprised as their American counterparts. The American bombers were ignored by Japanese planes and drew fire only when attempting to land. The B-17s, which were unarmed to lighten their load, were low on fuel after a fourteen-hour flight and flew in no recognizable formation.

Japanese Zeros attacked the B-17s when they broke through the light cloud coverage on their approach to Hickam Field. Despite the attack, all the B-17s were able to land: eight at Hickam Field, two at Haleiwa Field, one at Bellows Field, and one on the Kahuku Golf Course.

An ironic set of circumstances led to the arrival of Japanese and American planes over Oahu during the same time span. At 7:02, the radar operators at the army's Opana radar station near Kahuku Point at the northern tip of Oahu detected a large mass of planes heading toward the island.

The message was promptly relayed to the Information Center at Fort Shafter. The officer on duty there believed that the planes were the B-17s.

Due to its strategic importance and convenient location on the southeast side of the harbor entrance halfway between Pearl Harbor and Honolulu, Hickam Field was subject to three attacks.

Although the airfield was neutralized within minutes by the first attack wave, Japanese fighter bombers continued to inflict more damage and casualties while making their sweeping passes over Pearl Harbor. At approximately 8:54, thirty-six Japanese Zeros, under the leadership of Lieutenant Commander Shigekazu Shimazaki, made a final run over Hickam Field. The planes were part of the fighter coverage for the second wave of attack bombers.

When the Zeros encountered little or no air resistance over Oahu, they were free to break formation and attack targets of opportunity. The remaining aircraft on the ground at Hickam Field were easy targets for the Zeros.

The final attack decimated Hickam Field. Barracks were in flames, and the hangars were blown apart by Japanese bombs.

More than eighteen bombers were reduced to burned-out shells or mounds of smoldering metal surrounded by debris.

One curiosity was the excessive strafing of the ball field. Outdated Japanese maps showed the presence of an underground tank farm at the site. Although no underground tanks existed, they had been considered during the late 1930s and had been depicted in a number of maps used for presentations.

The Hickam Field survivors were faced with the grim responsibility of counting their dead and salvaging the few remaining aircraft, but their spirits were lifted by the sight of the bullet-torn American flag still flying near the barracks complex.

The following letter of Private First Class Nicholas Gaynos was typical of the efforts that thousands of servicemen made to notify their families and friends of their well-being. After the attack of 7 December, Oahu was cut off from the outside world by military commanders who readied the island defenses for another Japanese assault. Telephone and telegraph communications between the Hawaiian Islands and the mainland were nonexistent except for priority military transmissions.

Back on the mainland, newspaper stories and radio reports could only supply secondhand accounts of the attack and partial lists of the dead and wounded. Letters sent from Hawaii to the mainland after the attack arrived after a two- to three-week delay. Families anxiously awaited any news about the fate of their loved ones. Mothers and fathers kept a lonely vigil in their homes, dreading an official military visit.

Gaynos's letter is of special interest because it contains an uncensored account of the Pearl Harbor attack. The army censored numerous letters thought to contain sensitive information. Many letters that arrived home resembled cookie cutouts, with more gaps than words.

After more than sixty hours of battle, Gaynos, a battle-worn and bone-weary army radio operator from Fairfield, Connecticut, was able to find temporary reprieve on the wooden floor of a barracks. Using a flashlight to pierce the barracks' darkness, Gaynos wrote a dramatic account of the attack on Hickam Field.

9 December 1941

Dear Folks,

Well, I'm okay and feeling fine. We sure had a hot time here for a while and I thought that my end had come—God, was it hell. I'll give you an eyewitness account of the Japanese air raid on Pearl Harbor and Hickam Field on Sunday, 7 December 1941. This ought to make a good news copy for the *Bridgeport Post*.

Well, Sunday as usual, all of the men were sleeping late because we had no work to do. I was sound asleep, having gone to bed at 4:30 a.m. after being relieved of duty. It was exactly 7:55 when I was almost tossed out of bed by a terrific roar and the ensuing concussion.

Most of the fellows also got up and, on looking out the window, we could see flames about five hundred feet high and huge clouds of smoke coming from Pearl Harbor.

No one thought it was war until we looked out of our eastern windows and saw some of our hangars in flames. Somebody yelled, "They are Japanese planes," but nobody believed it. We all ran out of the barracks and looked skyward. It was plain to see then. They were only from fifty to one hundred feet off the ground, and the huge red circle under their wings proved their identity. Some of them had huge torpedoes under the fuselage almost as long as the ship itself.

The thunder of bombs and the staccato of machine guns made such a deafening roar you had to yell to be heard a few feet away. The splintering of wood as fifty-caliber bullets ripped through the wooden barracks was mixed with screams of men as they ran from one shelter to another. We soon collected our senses and the full realization that war was here.

Some men cried, some laughed, others were terrified, some just couldn't seem to understand what it was all about. I soon had my senses under control and jumped in a car headed for my post. With a hail of bullets and with the planes roaring right over our heads, we raced down the street. I arrived at my transmitters and dove into a hole caused by an exploded bomb. One young fellow was dead, and his legs stuck out of the hole. It reminded me of a book I once read back home. I stayed here until things had quieted down and then scurried for safety in my flimsy office. We all knew they would be back soon so we hurriedly made preparations for their return. It was at 10:20 when the second attack came.

I was busy removing a radio truck to safety. Three men and I kept working as they dived into the big barracks and dropped load after load of bombs. The very ground shook, and my ears were ringing. By this time they spotted my equipment and headed straight for my men and me. I was lying in a small hole about ten feet to the right of my trucks. As the planes dove down at us, I could peek out under the brim of my tin helmet and see them spitting fire at us. The ground in front of me was spraying up and I could see the bombs leave the planes and head straight down at us. One of them was a one-thousand-pound bomb and landed fifty feet on my right. Three kids with a machine gun were shooting at the plane and the bomb landed almost on them. It blew them skyhigh—gun and all.

The dirt and stones fell all over us and I ached all over. I emptied my forty-five pistol time after time into the planes, but it was futile. I thumbed my nose as they roared right over my head. We all swore like hell.

The planes were still roaring around strafing us unmercifully as those of us that were alive got into cars and started to pick up the dead and wounded. One of the kids who was blown up with the machine gun was lying about fifty feet away. I tried to pick him up and he fell apart in my arms. He was covered with dirt and smiling.

We rushed as many as we could to the hospital and gave first aid to those lying near us. Things were now getting quiet and then ambulances, nurses, and trucks came to pick up the men. Some of the things were so ghastly I cannot write of them.

All I can say is that my baptism under fire sure was hell on earth and I saw my Maker on Sunday, 7 December 1941.

Well, after the raid I took about ten men and rounded up a dozen cars and started to gather gasoline, and supplies for my equipment. I kept the best car for myself and kept things moving. Later I found out I was using the general's car and I was wondering why everyone was saluting me. I had everything under control at 2:00 p.m. and sat down and had a good smoke. We had rescued two drums of gas from a blazing yard, and I thought that any moment we would be blown to bits. I worked straight through until Tuesday night.

Boy, was I tired!

I slept on the floor in front of my radio transmitters and fell sound asleep. I was awakened about 2:00 a.m. by rifle shots. Someone said that saboteurs were in the woods. I hunted all night with a cocked forty-five pistol and a thirty-thirty rifle. My hunt wasn't in vain, for I shot about thirty rounds of ammunition and perhaps I did hit some Jap.

Since the war, I have confiscated about $500 worth of radio equipment, soda, beer, cigarettes, and seventeen cars. Some fun! I conked a Jap in the Sears-Roebuck in Honolulu and had him turn over a shortwave receiver. Boy, was he scared.

I hadn't shaved, changed clothes, or washed since Sunday. I had two revolvers, one huge bolo knife—about twenty-six inches long—and a mean look on my face. I was sure having fun scaring hell out of these civilians. Everything is under control now. We will have a good welcome for them next time. I was starting to enjoy this excitement now and I have a twenty-shot Browning automatic rifle now and if I even spot a Japanese I am going to hold that trigger until the magazine is empty. Outside of a few bruises and sore bones, I feel as good as if it had never happened.

So, I shall say good-bye now and don't worry about me as I can see now that if I keep my head I shall be okay. Hope you are all okay back home and wish you all the best of holidays, Merry Christmas to all my friends and say hello to anyone who asks for me and tell them I shall write as soon as I have more time as I am very busy now and I should be sleeping right now. I am writing this by flashlight on the floor and so excuse the pencil and writing.

Aloha,
Son, Brother, Soldier,
Nick

P.S. I won't be a private very long.
P.P.S. I was to have become a corporal on 8 December, only those Japs have disrupted our office and I have to wait now.

In the 1930s, a young man's interest and imagination were easily captured by "those magnificent men in their flying machines." During air battles fought high above the trenches of World War I, the airplane proved a weapon with unlimited potential. The pioneers who operated these frail and flimsy crafts became the first generation of fighter pilots. The "flying aces," who had colorful names, fought legendary battles and became international heroes.

In just a few years, aviation had evolved from a hobby into a science and an industry. Careers were waiting for those willing to join this great adventure.

For Private First Class William Rolfe, who had grown up during the Great Depression, the airplane offered an escape. Aviation meant an opportunity for success:

My mother died in 1937 just after I quit school in the tenth grade. While working as a warehouse manager in Richmond, Virginia, my thoughts were with the future as I was alone in the world with no living relative.

My thought turned to the future in aviation. If I could enlist in the army air corps and get those years of experience as an airplane mechanic, I could then apply for a job with the Federal Aviation Administration as an apprentice airplane mechanic and my future would be assured.

I enlisted in the army air corps on 3 June 1940. The very next day I and a group of other men left the Main Street station bound for Fort Slocum in New York to wait for a ship to Oahu, Hawaii, and Hickam Field. We sailed from New York on the USS *Hunto Ligette*, moving through the sea to Panama, then Panama to San Francisco and then on to Honolulu. It took us about thirty days to make the trip. God, was I seasick. I and others slept above deck for most of the trip. The food smells from the galley were unexplainable. I had thought of falling overboard and I never wanted to set foot on another ship.

The trip from Frisco to Oahu wasn't near as bad as going through the Windward Passage.

On arrival at Hickam Field, I was assigned as a clerk in Headquarters and Headquarter Squadron, Fifth Bombardment Group. After working this area for six months, I requested to attend the Airplane and Engine Mechanic School. Upon graduating from the class, I was given a rating of aircraft and engine mechanic, first class, and assigned to B-18s under the watchful eye of a crew chief.

A few weeks before 7 December 1941, I was assigned to an antisabotage squad. They issued us steel helmets, ammo, 1903 Springfield rifles, and gas masks. On weekends we were taken to strategic points to guard for possible sabotage in downtown Honolulu.

The week before 7 December, we were all restricted to the base. We knew something was up but did not know just what. On 7 December, the restriction was lifted, so most of us were going to leave the base and a lot had already gone.

The time was 7:15 a.m., 7 December. While sitting on the side of my bunk getting dressed in my civilian clothes, I heard a bomb go off, another, another, and another. I pulled on my pants, ran to the windows just as a Jap Zero came flying low over my barracks with machine gun going. I could see his fixed landing gear and the big red circle under each wing. I yelled "Great God! The Japs are here!"

The other guys at the time laughed at me. Looking over at Pearl Harbor, I could see our ships at anchor with smoke pouring from them and Jap planes over them like hornets. Airmen, running out of the barracks onto the parade ground to get a better look, most of them in their underwear, were machine-gunned by the Jap planes winging over Hickam after dropping their bombs on the navy ships that couldn't seem to get out of their way.

I grabbed my rifle, helmet, and ammo after changing into blue denim dungarees and went down to the first floor of the barracks. The only person I could see in charge was a corporal, who was telling everyone to go to their station.

I went to the hangar line. Crews were trying to start the B-18s as the ordnance men were trying to load bombs in the bomb-bay doors. A lot of these brave men, like many others, died on the spot without the planes getting off the ground. I fired several times at Jap planes, but I'll never know if I hit any. Antiaircraft were shooting with their coast artillery. We saw a couple of B-17s trying to land with Japs on their tail, and they couldn't. High-flying planes came over the hangar line dropping bombs; how I didn't get killed, I'll never know.

Orders were passed around that the Japs were wearing blue coveralls and that if any of us had on blue denim to change immediately because any person wearing blue would probably be shot on sight, with no questions asked. I changed into my other uniform quickly and never knew what happened to my blues from that date on.

That Sunday night on 7 December, most of us had an idea that the Japs would try to land on the island. At some time I can't remember, all hell broke loose. It seems that a pilot was coming in for a landing at Pearl Harbor after having been out on a search mission, but he used the wrong required approach. Every gun in the area let loose on him; the tracer bullets lit up the sky. I heard later that he had been shot down but made it to shore safely.

Monday, 8 December, was spent trying to piece together airplanes so they would fly, and getting organized.

In January 1942, William Rolfe was transferred to the 72nd Bomb Squadron at Bellows Field as a B-17 mechanic. In June 1942, the squadron participated in the Battle of Midway. In 1943, his commission as a second lieutenant resulted in a billet at Patterson Field in Dayton, Ohio. His aviation career ended in 1945 with a discharge from active service and a promotion in the army reserves.

THE PUNCHBOWL: W. J. WALKER

Commonly known as the Punchbowl, the extinct volcanic crater overlooking the heart of downtown Honolulu was named Puowaina (Hill of Sacrifice) by ancient Hawaiians. Centuries before the arrival of the white explorers, Polynesian priests made human sacrifices during pagan ceremonies to appease the gods. The flat-topped crater had a panoramic view of Oahu's southern portion. Because of its strategic location, the crater was utilized as a defensive position for the island's defense. By the early 1940s, the military importance of the crater had diminished, and it was used primarily as an observation post. The crater also became a popular day spot for tourists, picnickers, and hikers, as well as a popular nightspot for enchanted couples seeking a romantic refuge overlooking the lights of Honolulu.

For Corporal W. J. Walker, the Punchbowl provided a bird's-eye view of the Japanese attack on Pearl Harbor on the morning of 7 December 1941.

My military career began in 1937, when I enlisted in the army. At that time I figured that life in the service had to be better than life on a small farm in Mississippi. For a number of years, my family had operated a sawmill, cutting to size trees brought in by the loggers and those families clearing the land for wood to build their farms.

After all the timber in the area had been cut, the sawmill business slowly grinded to a stop. The family then took to a farm so poor that the welfare people wouldn't even help us. In 1937, I realized it was time to see some of the rest of the world and what it had to offer. In November 1941, after being in Hawaii for over a year, I was assigned to guard detachment responsible for the security of the Punchbowl. Our hours of patrol ran from the early evening to the early morning.

On the evening of 6 December, I had been ordered to take three men to the Punchbowl and set up an observation security post. We arrived at the crater at approximately 9:00 p.m. and within no time were taking verbal abuse from the civilians and military personnel who came to the crater with their lovers to enjoy their outdoor open-air parties. It was not hard to see why they were attracted to this spot. The view from our observation post was breathtaking.

Directly in front of us was the city of Honolulu. To our left were Waikiki Beach and Diamond Head, which was farther down the coastline. To our right were Pearl Harbor and Hickam Field. With such a view, it was not too hard to miss having weekend liberty and being out on the town ourselves.

Hawaiians said that the crater was named Puowaina for the custom of sacrificing human lives to the gods. The men often joked that the only things sacrificed today were virgins under the moon over Hawaii.

Things for the rest of the night were pretty much quiet. At 2:00 a.m. on 7 December, I received a call from a private first class on duty, who was next in command at the post. At the time, I was trying to get a few much-needed winks of sleep while still in uniform. When I heard the call for "corporal of the guard," I immediately grabbed my rifle and ran down to the private first class's post. At this time of the morning, I had no idea what the commotion was all about. By this time, most of civilian and military personnel on the island were calling it a night and making their way home, wherever that was for the night. When I got to the checkpoint, there was an admiral seated in a large touring sedan with about six cars and maybe ten motorcycles lined up behind his sedan waiting to get through the checkpoint.

As the admiral got out of the sedan, I saluted him and explained our purpose for being there and stated my orders as they were given to me by a commander. The admiral replied in a sarcastic tone as he pointed toward Pearl Harbor, "Corporal, what in the hell do you foot soldiers think the navy is doing down there?"

Without waiting for me to reply, he answered his own question, "We are here to take care of anything the Nips want to start and to protect the army."

After some quick deliberation in my own mind, I told the admiral he could pass, but the rest of the party would have to have their credentials checked. The admiral muttered something under his breath about the army, returned to his sedan, and turned around at the checkpoint, leading his entourage back down the crater. It appeared that the admiral wanted to impress his friends and end his Saturday-night party at sunrise in the Punchbowl.

Of course, at the time, the admiral and I didn't know that three-quarters of his mighty navy would be sunk or crippled less than six hours later.

The rest of the early Sunday passed without any further incidents. We stayed up on the crater the rest of the morning, enjoying the sunrise out over the ocean and looking forward to coming down off the hill and getting a good hot meal. As with any Sunday morning, things over Honolulu were very quiet. The only people who stirred were the early churchgoers or the late-Saturday-night partiers.

It was around 7:50 a.m. that we noticed the sounds of airplanes buzzing over the city and Pearl Harbor. The only thing unusual about this was the fact that it was Sunday morning. Usually, most flying and training exercises were done during the week. We thought it unusual that the army or navy pilots would put in flight time on Sunday morning. We didn't think about the planes again, until we heard explosions coming from the direction of Pearl Harbor. At first I thought that there was an explosion aboard one of the ships, but after repeated explosions and the sight of more airplanes over Pearl, it hit me that we were being attacked. I couldn't believe what my eyes were seeing. I thought I was in some kind of crazy dream.

As the attack increased in force, I called my officer of the day at Fort Ruger and tried to report a picture in his mind of what I was seeing from up on the crater. As I reported what I was seeing, the captain listened for a few moments and then burst out laughing over the phone. I heard him say to someone in his office, "Pour me another cup of coffee; a drunk is trying to tell me something crazy."

The captain then said he wanted to speak to the private first class. I heard him ask the private first class, "Private, be honest. Isn't Corporal Walker drunk?" The private first class replied, "Captain, if Corporal Walker is drunk, I'm drunk, too, because I'm seeing the same things he is." I think the captain finally gave up on the conversation. He told us to remain at our post until further word. From the Punchbowl, we watched the attack over the next two hours. We were helpless to do anything. The whole attack was taking place before our very eyes, yet there wasn't a thing we could do to help. It was like sitting in the top row of a ballpark and watching the action taking place far below on the field.

With field glasses, we were able to see what was going on at a closer range, but, when the fires and bombs started to form large smoke clouds over the harbor, our line of vision was partially blocked. By early afternoon of that day, we were able to see that a number of ships had been sunk or capsized.

From where we stood, the damage to the fleet looked great, but we had no way of knowing the losses. Later that morning, I received a call from our captain, who told us not to let any civilians or unauthorized military personnel in our area. We started to worry that Japanese snipers or foreign agents would try to take our position to direct another attack on the harbor or try to pinpoint our losses after the attack. We remained at our position in the Punchbowl for about a week until after the attack. We received a number of reinforcements, but for the most part things were quiet after the attack. With martial law in effect, along with a curfew and a blackout, attempted visits to the Punchbowl were few. Every time we heard a vehicle or something move outside our position, we tightened the grips we had on our rifles and swallowed hard, because we didn't know what to expect next. The days following the attack, we were able to watch the efforts to put the fleet back together.

Pearl Harbor seemed to be in a race with the clock to get the ships floating once again. The harbor was always alive with a beehive of activity. Although we were doing our part guarding the Punchbowl, we all felt we could be more useful if we were down in the harbor helping in some other way. After a few days had passed and it was unlikely the Japanese would attack again, we were able to relax a little and start thinking where in the war we would be going.

After the second week in December had passed, I was still waiting for that hot home-cooked meal and wondering how the admiral had fared with his party.

For W. J. Walker, the attack on Pearl Harbor was the beginning of a forty-four-month tour of duty in the Pacific campaign. World War II was one of the highlights of his thirty-year career, which ended with retirement in 1967.

In 1949, the Punchbowl did indeed become the Hill of Sacrifice. In that year, the 114-acre floor of the Punchbowl became officially known as the National Memorial Cemetery of the Pacific. Today, beneath simple flagstone markers lie more than twenty-six thousand dead from World War I, World War II, the Korean War, and the Vietnam War. Among the servicemen, servicewomen, and dependents are twenty-two recipients of the Medal of Honor. The famous war correspondent Ernie Pyle is buried with the soldiers he immortalized in print. Also located in the Punchbowl is the Garden of the Missing, a marble monument inscribed with thousands of names of servicemen and servicewomen missing in action. Since 1979, the Punchbowl has become Hawaii's leading visitor attraction. Every day, thousands of islanders and visitors bring leis and flowers to honor and remember those who sacrificed their lives for their country. The schedule of ceremonies is highlighted each year with a sunrise Easter service. On this day, thousands of visitors participate in a moving ceremony to honor these and other fallen warriors.

COASTAL ARTILLERY: ROY BLICK AND ALEX COBB

Like the other defensive installations and fortifications that dotted the coastline of Oahu at strategic points, Fort Kamehameha was ineffective in defending Pearl Harbor from Japanese bombers. Named after Kamehameha I, the legendary king who united the islands of Hawaii under his rule with a victory at the Battle of Nuuanu Pali in April 1795, the fort was the largest coastal artillery fortification guarding the entrance to Pearl Harbor. Many military analysts considered the fort the pillar of inland defense. Although the fort, located on the southeast peninsula at the harbor entrance just below Hickam Field, appeared a formidable sentinel guarding the "gates to the harbor," it contained outdated weaponry and represented military tactics and thinking of a past era.

Military brass could boast of the island's fortifications and claim to the world that they had made Oahu an impenetrable fortress. This claim was justifiable for military preparations in the early 1900s, when battle plans for an invasion centered on an amphibious assault force. However, the utilization of the airplane as a weapon of war revolutionized military tactics after World War I. The airplane was the constant element of surprise, which could link continents in a matter of hours and deliver a payload of death and destruction greater than any assault force. Although large invasion forces supported by offshore naval fleets were not obsolete, military brass were gradually turning their attention to the use of large strike forces employing a number of aircraft carriers.

While it was not impossible that the Japanese would anchor their armada off the coast of Oahu and attempt to seize the island by establishing a number of strategic beachheads, it was unlikely when all the circumstances were considered and studied. If such an offensive was undertaken, the sixteen-inch guns of Fort Kamehameha and other coastal artillery installations would prove insurmountable barriers.

Despite their drawbacks, coastal fortifications for military bases such as Pearl Harbor were a necessity in the early 1940s. However, on 7 December these concrete sentinels and their personnel could only bear eyewitness to the attack on the fleet. Private Roy Blick was guarding the sentinel at Fort Kamehameha during the attack.

I had a southern heritage with both grandparents serving in the Civil War with the Confederacy, an uncle who volunteered and lost his life in the Spanish-American War in Cuba, and other relatives who served in World War I. I was proud of those who had served and realized that we were drawing closer to another war every day.

I had joined the Civil Conservation Corps in 1940 and was stationed at Camp William Tell at Tell City, Indiana. On 3 February 1941, I left camp to go home to Lyon County, Kentucky, for the weekend. I had an hour wait for another bus in Evansville, so while I was waiting, I took a walk that delayed my trip to Kentucky and home for almost four years. My walk took me past the post office, where I saw a recruiting sign. I went in to talk with the recruiting sergeant and enlisted for two years of overseas service as a replacement and was to get credit for a three-year enlistment. By 11:00 p.m., I was in Fort Benjamin Harrison in Indianapolis, Indiana. By 6 February, I was in Fort Slocum, New York, to await overseas shipment.

On 2 April, I left Fort Slocum for the Brooklyn Army and Navy Overseas Replacement Depot. On 8 April, I sailed on the USS *Washington* for Pearl Harbor, by way of the Panama Canal and San Francisco. On board we had twenty-five-hundred troops and a cargo of war bandages for the Chinese.

On 26 April, I arrived in Hawaii and went into training camp for six weeks. When the training was completed, I was assigned to A Battery, Fifteenth Coast Artillery, Fort Kamehameha, Territory of Hawaii, Pearl Harbor Defense. For a time, I was assigned to Fort Weaver, across the Pearl Harbor channel from Fort Kamehameha.

By late summer, I had made the rating of first and fourth and was gun mechanic on the number-one sixteen-inch gun. I lived in the gun emplacement, with bunks in the toolshed.

On 7 December 1941, I awoke about 7:30 a.m. and was alone that morning at the sixteen-inch gun battery, except for the guards in the gun emplacement. One off-duty guard was asleep on an army cot under a tree, and the guard on duty was walking post and waiting for his relief, who had gone to chow. I told the guard that I would take his post if he wanted to go to chow before they threw everything out. He took me up on the offer, and I took his post to wait for his relief.

It was a beautiful Sunday morning with a good breeze. I was on the post only a few minutes when I heard a flight of planes coming in from the seaward side of our gun position. When the planes came over our position and flew over the Japanese salt beds into the harbor, they were very low and I could plainly see the Japanese pilots. The large red circles under the wings were easy to identify. I called to Private Parsons, who was sleeping on the cot, that the Japanese were bombing the harbor. By this time, the guard had come back from chow, so I locked the gates to the gun position and divided the hundred rounds of ammo for the 1903 Springfields that we were armed with.

By now, the woods in Fort Weaver were full of smoke with shrapnel from the antiaircraft fire and strafing planes. The gun crew was trying to make it to the gun position from the A Battery campsite near the marine barracks. The crew was using the woods for cover and yelling for me to open the gates. As I was moving toward the gate, a large object hit the sand nearby and sent a shower of sand and dust in the air. I hit the ground and waited, but whatever it was it didn't explode. I never went back to dig in the sand and find out what exactly it was.

When the gun crew made it to the gun emplacement, we took our battle stations. After someone shot the lock off of the magazine entrance, we were able to get out ammo by the case. We had plenty of targets and fired a lot of rounds, but we never knew if we hit anything. Being gun mechanic, I had to check the pressure on the recoil cylinders and the recuperators on the sixteen-inch gun. We had by that time gotten orders to be ready to fire, if we could get a target for the sixteen-inch gun. We never did get a target for the big gun, and we never fired a round from it during the attack. After checking the sixteen-inch gun, I took my position again, firing my Springfield at passing Japanese planes.

When a Japanese strafer ripped the sand within five feet of me, I took a position under the sixteen-inch gun that was depressed to about three feet off the ground. The gun finally found some use.

After the attack, we had no way of knowing what was next. From our position, we could see the smoke and fire in the harbor and hear explosions as they echoed across the water. We remained at our gun position for the day, and weeks and months following that. We dug trenches and built pillboxes by day and waited for the invasion by night. We had orders to defend the battery to the last man. The invasion never came, and in time the war moved across the Pacific.

Most of us remained with the sixteen-inch guns, A Battery Fifteenth Coast Artillery, for the defense of Pearl Harbor. We always remarked how fortunate we were that we never had to fire the sixteen-inch guns in actual defense of the harbor. If it ever did come to that, we knew we were in deep trouble and would most likely be fighting for our lives until the last man fell.

Roy Blick remained at the sixteen-inch gun at Fort Weaver for the duration of the war and was promoted to sergeant and gun commander. In August 1945, he departed for the mainland and on 9 September 1945 was discharged at Camp Atterbury, Indiana. He then returned home to Kentucky.

Another vital link in the chain of coastal artillery units was Fort Ruger. Built behind Diamond Head crater, Hawaii's most famous and distinguishable natural landmark, the installation provided air and sea defense for Oahu's southeast portion.

Any attackers traveling to the southern portions of Oahu by way of its eastern coast placed themselves in jeopardy. Just east of Waikiki Beach, the crater was also the strategic piece of high terrain that dominated the southeast portions of the coast as far west as Pearl Harbor. Whoever had control of this position could easily control Oahu.

In a ground war resulting from an invasion of Oahu, Fort Ruger and Diamond Head crater most likely could have been the site of one of the bloodiest and most bitterly contested battles in American history. With each passing hour after the attack on Pearl Harbor, the possibilities for such a battle diminished. Although Fort Ruger was bypassed by Japanese bombers, it did participate in the defense of Oahu.

Alex Cobb was one serviceman who witnessed the attack from the fringes of the target area and felt its devastating effects radiate across the island.

I was born 1 December 1917 in Richmond, Indiana, but at age one moved to the East. I was really brought up in Newark, Delaware, where I attended public schools and graduated from the University of Delaware in 1940, with a Reserve Officers' Training Corps commission as a second lieutenant in the Coast Artillery Corps.

In April 1941, I was called on active duty at Fort DuPont, Delaware, where I was assigned as plotting-room officer in a submarine mine battery. Several months later, I responded to an officers' call asking for volunteers in the first and second lieutenant grade (Coast Artillery Corps) for the Hawaiian Department. Several of my close buddies joined me, and by July 1941 we had arrived in Honolulu by the President Line from San Francisco.

I was assigned to Fort Ruger, up behind Diamond Head crater, and became junior officer in an eighty-man antiaircraft detachment. The unit was part of C Battery, Sixteenth Coast Artillery, with gun emplacements at Black Point, on the east side of Diamond Head. My battery commander was First Lieutenant Elvin T. Wayment, from Utah. There were just two of us running the battery. He was battery commander and I was everything else (executive officer, range officer, mess officer, motor pool officer, chemical officer, and, after radar arrived in 1942, I became radar officer).

Elvin Wayment was an excellent officer to train under, although at the time I probably didn't appreciate it. Being a Mormon, he was a real taskmaster. He took his job very seriously and wanted the officers to work twice as hard as the enlisted men. He had attended Utah State on a basketball scholarship and ended up playing varsity football, earning all-conference honors at center for his last two years. We nicknamed him "Tarzan." He was very athletic and had a most competitive spirit about everything we did, whether it was training the battery, running the obstacle course, or playing volleyball.

When I reported for duty, First Lieutenant Wayment immediately had me jump down in a crater and learn how to run a jackhammer, which he had scrounged up from somewhere along with some dynamite and blasting caps. We were making ammunition and personnel shelters alongside the three three-inch fixed-mount antiaircraft guns. They had to be blasted out of lava rock. Later, we covered them with wooden beams and several layers of sandbags. I would say we were well ahead of most of the other fixed-mount antiaircraft batteries on Oahu in this respect when the attack came.

On 6 December, we had a morning parade at Fort Ruger, and in the afternoon I attended the Shrine football game between University of Hawaii and Willamette University (Washington). That evening I put in a brief appearance at a reception at the officers' club, then picked up my girlfriend and took her out to a party given by some mutual friends in the Hickam housing area. We didn't leave until the wee hours of the morning, and I was just lucky we didn't decide to spend the night, or otherwise I would have had a terrible time trying to get back across town to the battery.

I was rooming with three other officers in a bachelor officers' quarters overlooking the parade ground at Fort Ruger, Territory of Hawaii. Shortly after 8:00 a.m., one of the officers, Lieutenant Francis Pallister, who had been at the officers' mess for breakfast, came running up the stairs urging us to wake up and get to our duty stations immediately. He said we were in condition three (battle stations), but he didn't know exactly what was going on. Most of us thought at that point it was just another practice alert.

I stepped onto an upstairs screened porch on the way to the bathroom and, looking out over Honolulu Harbor with Pearl Harbor in the distance, could see strange black (navy) antiaircraft bursts over the island. There was also a large plume of black smoke rising in the distance from the direction of Pearl Harbor. I decided to speed things up!

I dressed rapidly, grabbed my canteen and leggings (you always needed these for alerts), and followed my battery commander, First Lieutenant Elvin T. Wayment, in my car down to our gun site at Black Point, just to the east of Diamond Head. We had three three-inch fixed-mount antiaircraft guns, which were protecting a seacoast battery consisting of two eight-inch fixed-mount railway guns. This gun emplacement served as the easternmost defense from the sea for Honolulu Harbor.

At the time of the attack, approximately half of our eighty-man antiaircraft detachment was eating breakfast at the permanent battery's mess hall at Fort Ruger. Some of our men were also on pass, although the number of passes had been limited since we went into condition two (man the close-in defense) in early November.

We commenced setting up our fire director and stereo-scopic height finder. Normally these units required a crew of eight men to carry them from the storage area, but on this particular morning we made the trip with as few as four or five men, the balance having been assigned to bring ammunition from the seacoast battery's casemate to the antiaircraft gun emplacements.

As I was battery-range officer, we set up the B.C. Scope and began orienting the battery. We tracked several planes bearing large Japanese "meatballs," but they were out of the range of our guns. We were manned and ready to fire, as I recall, about 8:45 to 9:00 a.m. Finally the post executive officer came down from Fort Ruger and officially informed First Lieutenant Wayment that we were "at war with Japan" and that we should undertake firing on any "enemy places" that came within range of our battery. This must have been about 9:15 to 9:30, and we only spotted one or two planes in our sector after that.

There were some fires set in the Kaimuki section of Hono-lulu to the north of Fort Ruger, and several spent navy antiair-craft shells landed in Diamond Head crater. A steady stream of confusing, conflicting, and, as it later turned out, false messages from higher echelons flowed into our command-post message center. Diamond Head blocked our view of the chaotic situa-tion at Pearl Harbor. It was a confusing time.

We spent the rest of the day "liberating" tools and build-ing materials from nearby construction projects in order to commence construction of a permanent mess hall, a latrine, and, eventually, permanent living quarters adjacent to our gun emplacements. It looked like it was going to be a long war!

Several weeks later our antiaircraft battery received a written commendation from the commanding general for the advanced state of our gun emplacement camouflage and the construction of safe ammunition storage pits at the three guns, which we had excavated from the lavarock foundation which forms Black Point. All of this resulted in an advanced state of readiness on 7 December 1941.

Alex Cobb gained his silver bars midway through the war and in 1944 made captain. After attending Advanced Gunnery School at Camp Davis, North Carolina, he returned to the Pacific theater as operations commander of the aircraft warning system for the 53rd Antiaircraft Brigade on Okinawa. In August 1945, Cobb was discharged with the rank of major.

9

Outlasting a Typhoon

Buckner Melton Jr.

CAL CALHOUN, FRESH FROM DESTROYER-MINESWEEPER DUTY AT Pearl, had stood on the bridge of his new command, putting her through her paces as she steamed out of Puget Sound, and he wasn't entirely pleased.

She was USS *Dewey*, Destroyer Squadron 1's flagship, a *Farragut*-class destroyer named for the renowned admiral of Manila Bay fame. At ten years of age she was in excellent shape. Her turbines thrummed as she knifed through the water, and the faint haze that streamed from her twin stacks told Calhoun that the boilers were both well crewed and efficient. For the most part he was satisfied; yet she still worried him.

First sketched out by Bethlehem Steel, she had been built in Maine by Bath Iron Works and launched just over a decade before. She was quite top heavy.

Calhoun could tell from the way *Dewey* was handling that something was wrong. She had done well as she steamed through Juan de Fuca Strait at flank speed, just out of refit at Bremerton and in need of a shakedown, and Calhoun, who had been aboard less than a week, wanted to see how she handled.

As she moved into open sea, he barked a helm command from where he stood on the port bridge wing. "Right, ten degrees rudder!"

As the destroyer swept into the moderate turn, she heeled over to fifteen degrees with an awkward lurch, hanging there far too long. That was the first thing that told Calhoun, with his five years of destroyer experience, that *Dewey* had some kind of problem. Finishing up with his full-power trial, he began to put *Dewey* through a series of moderate and more daring turns at various speeds.

His instinct had been right; a pattern soon became clear. On turns the ship heeled considerably and then hung there, returning to even keel very slowly. It was a sign of poor stability.

Calhoun next conferred with his exec, a seasoned lieutenant commander named Frank Bampton, who had served aboard *Dewey* for nearly the whole of the war in the Pacific. *Dewey*, Bampton observed, had "always had a lazy roll," but this behavior was new.

Calhoun didn't like it.

The sluggish, lazy behavior of *Dewey* was a nuisance, but he didn't consider it actually dangerous, as long as he knew about it. Certainly, he wasn't worried about capsizing.

The squadron put to sea, shaping course for Pearl Harbor, and ultimately Ulithi.

Destroyers faced the biggest threats from weather and sea, and in the open ocean these threats, which every ship in the fleet faced, were of two major types. The first was that heavy pounding from, for instance, a typhoon, would compromise the ship's structural soundness. Certainly men on larger ships had moments during the typhoon of December 18 when they wondered if their vessels were going to hold together, though in the end all of them did.

The other threat was that the high winds, the towering seas, or some other conditions would degrade a destroyer's stability, making her prone to plunging or capsizing. These behaviors, in turn, would cause flooding, which would reduce the ship's buoyancy.

One of the variables that went into the stability factor on December 18 was the amount of fuel left in the destroyers. With bunkers nearly dry, a ship bobs on the water, with more freeboard at which the seas and winds could batter. Thus, the same condition that caused the empty *Fletcher*s to remain in the typhoon's path, desperately trying to replenish, also made them supremely vulnerable to the effects of that storm.

The *Farragut*-class ships, on the other hand, while sharing the same limitations that small size imposed, were fat with Navy Special on December 18.

They steamed in the company of the fleet oilers, and they had left Ulithi more recently. Unlike the flush-decked *Fletcher*s, they had raised forecastles, which reduced the water they took over the bow. In general terms, then, they seemed better off than their modern sisters as the gales swept upon them.

But still, there was that odd heeling that *Dewey* had experienced a couple of months earlier during her sea trials.

Lieutenant Commander Bill Rogers, *Aylwin*'s skipper, had smelled a typhoon as early as noon on the seventeenth, just about the time that the replenishment effort was coming apart. Like others, he had noted a sharply falling glass in the hours that followed. That evening, when his radio messenger gave him the news about the refueling rendezvous change and a report of a weather disturbance, even before giving his OOD the general order to rig for heavy weather, he'd told Erwin Jackson to strike her ready service ammunition below. This would lower the ship's center of gravity and make her more stable. It would also make her temporarily impotent in the face of a submarine attack, but, as Rogers had pointed out at the time, the whole fleet was with *Aylwin*, and anyway the worsening conditions strongly suggested that nobody was going to do any attacking in the near future.

Soon after midnight, *Aylwin* and the replenishment task group were steaming through on-again, off-again squalls, with freshening gales blowing from north to northeast. The seas had been rougher than usual for twelve hours, and heavier still since around sunset. With the increasing pounding and the corrosive salt spray that mixed with the squalls' freshwater, the ship's electrical system was in jeopardy.

At 0245 it went out.

The interruption lasted only ten minutes, but that is a long time on a black and heaving sea on which other warships are moving. By the time the power came back on, *Aylwin* had dropped out of formation, and she didn't regain her place for another half hour.

The event was a harbinger.

By daybreak, some destroyer officers were already reporting hurricane conditions, even though fleet commander Admiral William F. "Bull" Halsey, on massive *New Jersey*, didn't cancel refueling attempts until two hours later. By then, the small boys already knew they were in trouble. Aboard *Aylwin*, Rogers put together repair parties and stationed his electricians around the ship to handle any new damage to the electrical system. On other vessels, skippers took similar steps.

Around 0800, the wind's force leapt up, and it became a roaring giant trying to throw *Aylwin* and the other ships off balance. Sometimes the winds and waves synchronized, swatting the ships around as if they were matchsticks; at other moments, the elements fought each other, with the vessels caught in the middle, maneuvering only with the greatest of difficulty.

Slowly the task group formations began coming apart.

Aboard the *Fletcher*-class *Cushing*, Captain L. F. Volk had decided to ballast soon after the forenoon watch began, a bit after 0800. *Cushing*, like most of the *Fletcher*s, was low on fuel and riding high. To make her more stable, Volk ordered some of her fuel tanks to be flooded with salt water.

An hour and fifteen minutes later, *Cushing* secured ballasting, having pumped fifteen tons of water aboard. She was riding more easily but still not well, and other ships were also having trouble staying on course. The spray and driving rain, on top of the high walls of seawater, had reduced visibility to a half mile or less, an uncomfortably small margin for ships trying to hold formation.

Suddenly, shortly before 1000, the lookouts sighted a jeep carrier—perhaps the out-of-control *Cape Esperance*, perhaps another—cutting across *Cushing*'s bow only eight hundred yards away. Backing down emergency full, Volk sounded three blasts of the ship's horn and threw his helm over hard, skirting the carrier.

Cushing then labored to rejoin the formation.

Dewey, too, was in trouble. The weird rolling that Captain Calhoun had noticed off Bremerton now reasserted itself; by mid-morning, the destroyer was regularly rolling ten degrees farther to starboard than she did to port, and the typhoon was still getting worse. Her visibility was down to three hundred yards when a carrier came looming at her out of the storm on a collision course, the wind gusting past at nearly a hundred knots.

"Hard left rudder," ordered Calhoun. "Come to course 130 degrees."

Dewey swung round under the stern of the flattop, and through the spray Calhoun read her name: *Monterey*.

The carrier safely behind, Calhoun now prepared to resume his proper place in his formation. "Right full rudder, return to course 180 degrees," he said. The helmsman spun the wheel over, but *Dewey* swung her head sluggishly.

"She's not answering, Cap'n," the quartermaster observed.

Calhoun decided to give the rudder some help with the engines. "Port ahead full," he ordered.

It didn't do any good. *Dewey* continued to disobey helm and engine commands.

Calhoun was beginning to run out of options. "Left full rudder," he snapped. "Port stop. Starboard ahead full!" He was now trying to turn *Dewey* in the other direction, around to port, in a vast circle of nearly three hundred degrees to get her back on the task unit's course.

The destroyer swung her head twenty degrees and then stopped. The sea had her, and she was helpless.

Quickly, Calhoun got onto the TBS, giving *Dewey*'s voice call sign. "This is Achilles," he reported. "I am out of control, crossing through the formation from starboard to port. Keep clear!"

Dewey was totally blind. The men on the bridge could not even see their own jackstaff on the stem of the ship, and the radar screen was fouled with sea return. They could only hope that the other ships in the unit could somehow see *Dewey*.

Then a huge black hull was coming at *Dewey* out of the typhoon directly ahead of her. As the destroyer hurtled down a mountainous wave at the oiler, the other ship was lifted out of her way by the next wave. It had been close. "I could have thrown a spud at her," Calhoun said to his assistant gunnery officer.

At last *Dewey* steamed clear of the formation. Calhoun, worried about the ship's ominous rolling and at the prompting of his squadron commander, began ballasting his port tanks. As he did, he heard over his TBS before it went out that *Monaghan*, too, was out of control.

Aboard *Monaghan*, the roar and shriek of the typhoon was enormous, as it was on every ship in the fleet. As the waves grew steeper and higher, *Monaghan* began the long, heavy rolling that some of the lighter carriers were experiencing, except that the destroyer's rolling was worse. This wasn't because *Monaghan* was running low on fuel. Her oil king, Water Tender Second Class Joe McCrane, had sounded her tanks around daybreak and found plenty of Navy Special aboard.

The ship was simply unstable.

Around 1100, while trying to fight down his concern that on one of these long, hard rolls *Monaghan* would stay on her side without righting, McCrane got word to start ballasting some of the tanks with salt water. He quickly made his way to the shaft alley and opened the appropriate valves, but by then it was too late. The seas had grown rougher than ever before; the wind was smashing at the ship from the port beam, and *Monaghan* crept slowly, at almost a standstill, her forty-thousand-horsepower engines seemingly impotent.

It was impossible to survive on the ship's open decks, wind and wave swept. McCrane, along with a few dozen others, took refuge in the after head on the main deck as the ship kept heeling crazily. In the tight compartment, fear was beginning to spread. "Dear Lord, bring it back. Oh God! Bring it back!" a sailor sang out whenever the ship heeled over. "Don't let us drown now!"

Then, when *Monaghan* righted, he would yell, "Thank you, dear Lord! Thank you!"

Beyond the sealed hatch, life rafts and other weather deck gear had long since been beaten to pieces or torn away from the ship; now the elements started to break *Monaghan* herself. Down in the guts of the ship, the engine and fire room overhead began to separate from the bulkheads as the typhoon's insensate fury increased. *Monaghan* was starting to come apart. Water was forcing its way in, probably through the vent shafts, perhaps even down the stacks on the most extreme rolls, and the fire and bilge pumps struggled to get it back out.

Then came the death blow. As *Monaghan* heeled far over, farther than she had yet gone, her generators and steering engine went out. The lights failed; radio, radar, telephones, everything electrical was suddenly dead.

Monaghan's crew grimly endeavored to cope. Deprived of communications, the steering engine room crew sent a runner up to the bridge to tell the captain, Lieutenant Commander Bruce Garrett, that the sailors would try to steer manually if he could give them a course.

The engines still labored; but the odds were now heavily against the destroyer. A few minutes later came another series of long, hard rolls, and then it finally happened. On the last one, *Monaghan* simply stayed on her beam ends, refusing to right herself. Water poured down the stacks, into the superstructure, and through every opening in the hull it could find. *Monaghan* was downflooding, massive amounts of seawater stealing her buoyancy.

In the after head, the sailors knew she was done for. McCrane and dozens of others now wrestled open the port hatches—*Monaghan* lay on her starboard side—and climbed out onto the vertical after deck. The waves, in concert with a hundred-knot wind, clawed at them, grabbing them and hurling them off the foundering ship. Gunner's Mate Joseph Guio, who hailed from Holliday's Cove, West Virginia, stood outside the hatch, refusing to leave, helping to pull his shipmates out of the compartment; others at the hatch helped him as long as they could. One minute Fireman First Class William Kramer was helping pull a friend through the hatch; the next he was spinning wildly through the water, tumbling away from the wreck. Popping to the surface, he spotted a life raft nearby. He seized it and held on.

McCrane, too, had been washed loose, and he went skittering along the superstructure, grabbing hold of a depth charge rack. He boosted himself up and walked along the torpedo tubes amidships; he was afraid to jump into the water, having seen others who'd tried that smashed to bits against the ship's hull. But then another wave hit him and washed him overboard, and he, too, was being pounded against the hull. Choking and splashing as if he were a puppy in the froth of oily sea, McCrane at last got a grip on himself and began to strike out away from the ship more calmly.

"Hey, Joe!" he suddenly heard from behind him. "Grab that raft back of you!" It was Joe Guio, now naked and bleeding. McCrane spotted the raft and dragged himself aboard; it was the same one that Kramer managed to find.

Before long more than a dozen sailors were there. The wind kept catching at the flimsy life raft; as Kramer, McCrane, and the others tried to lock the bottom into position, it flipped over nearly a half dozen times, scattering the men as if they were ninepins. At last they accomplished their task and dragged themselves aboard, hauling the injured Guio in after them.

Nearby, the iron hull of their foundering vessel slowly turned turtle, trapping scores of their shipmates inside it, and began to sink toward the bottom of the Philippine Sea.

Monaghan's battle had ended.

Dewey's mad gallop through the formation, meanwhile, hadn't ended her troubles. On the contrary, it seemed a ride into even worse danger. She was taking on water with every roll and intermittently losing steering control. By noon the crew had at least two bucket brigades going to try to deal with the flooding, one in the mess hall and another aft. In the steering control room, sailors were reduced to stuffing rags in the ventilators to try to squelch the deluge.

Dewey had a major problem with her port engine. Something was wrong with the lubricating oil suction. *Dewey* was wracked with the same insane rolling that was plaguing her sisters, and every time she went over to starboard past forty degrees, the oil supply to the engine just vanished.

Cal Calhoun tried to keep the engine in play, but his engineers had to stop the port screw every time the suction went out; if they didn't, the turbines would seize. Calhoun shifted his fuel to port to try to counteract the starboard rolling, but still the wild motion continued.

As *Dewey's* rolls approached and then passed sixty degrees, Calhoun recalled that her stability tests had established her maximum roll at around seventy degrees. He also knew that since those tests, she'd had a lot of top weight added. As *Dewey's* rolls began to edge even closer to the seventy-degree mark, Calhoun began praying.

"Dear God," he said silently each time she went over, "please make her come back!"

All over the ship watertight doors were leaking, and the force of the waves during the rolling sprang at least two of them. One was the steering control room door, and as the sea came in, it blew out the steering motors.

The half dozen sailors there were reduced to heaving the massive rudder to and fro by their raw muscle power. Water poured down into the engine spaces, clouding the deadly hot regions in steam; here, too, the blowers were dead and the temperature was around 160 degrees. Water rained onto the main electrical switchboard, located just below a hatch that now leaked like a sieve, and sparks leapt as circuits shorted out. Electrical fires were popping up all over the ship when, around 1130, the main board finally gave out.

Dewey was suddenly without any electrical power.

In the bridge, the cacophony was monstrous, a combination of roaring seas, chaotic gales, and a horrid screeching from the ship's rigging, something Calhoun later described as "hell's chorus." When Calhoun's lookouts and signalmen turned out of the wind and looked toward him, he saw that their faces were bleeding from the wind and salt spray abrasion. Men were staggering and falling all over the ship, and on one roll Calhoun lost his own grip on a stanchion. Instantly he was airborne, flying toward a far bulkhead.

His face hit, and he went out.

A minute or two later he came to, down on his hands and knees. "Call the doctor," he heard over the voice of the storm. "The captain's broken his nose!"

His nose, in fact, wasn't broken, and he was soon functioning once more, though there was little he could do at this point; *Dewey* was without electricity and one engine, in irons, out of control, and out of contact with the rest of the fleet.

Things were now desperate, as if they had not been before. The starboard rolls, each one now lasting for up to a minute, were so steep that the starboard bridge wing torpedo director was fully submerged each time. Calhoun watched, incredulous, as his executive officer, Lieutenant Frank Bampton, used his helmet to bail water off the bridge. "Hell, Frank," he yelled, "you're going to have to bail the whole damned Pacific Ocean!"

Bampton kept bailing. "I've got to do something!" he screamed back.

The task group's screen commander, Captain Mercer, riding out the storm on the bridge with Calhoun, tried to keep up his own spirits, but he doubted his flagship would come through the typhoon. By now the rolls were beyond the range of the bridge inclinometer, which stopped at seventy-three degrees, and even that of the engine room instrument, which maxed at seventy-five. During one of them, while Calhoun and Mercer hung from a stanchion facing each other, the starboard pilothouse window directly below them, they had a remarkably calm conversation.

"If we go over and end up in this sea," asked Mercer, "do you think you can make it?"

Calhoun, in his early thirties, was fit, and he had a wife and son to live for.

"Yes," he replied. "I think I can."

Mercer disclosed that he himself was a poor swimmer. "I don't feel too badly about it," he said nevertheless. "I've had a good life and my insurance is all paid up," he continued with a smile.

"But I feel sorry for all of these youngsters," he went on, "many of them married and with families. Their lives have hardly begun and a lot of them wouldn't make it."

"Well, Commodore," Calhoun responded, "I'm betting on the *Dewey*. I think she'll get us through."

"Skipper, I agree with you," Mercer said over the howling voice of the wind.

At the height of the storm Calhoun considered cutting away the ship's mast to try to get her center of gravity down. But he feared that, instead of breaking away cleanly, the mast would pendulum down; if it did, the crosstree might hull the ship at the fire room. Then, not too long afterward, he saw that one of the guy wires that held the forward stack in place had slackened, and the wind was jerking it heavily. Quickly, he warned the signal gang to watch out; then the guy wire snapped with a deafening crack, slashing against the port wing of the bridge.

With that, the forward stack tore loose, collapsing like a huge, heavy sock onto the ship's starboard side and knocking overboard the ship's whaleboat, which had miraculously stayed in place until now. The steam line to the ship's siren, now broken, added an ear-splitting shriek to the howl of the storm.

But if it was a harbinger, it was a good one. Freed of the stack's sail area and of the topside weight of the whaleboat, the ship began to ride somewhat more easily.

The ship was in a bit better condition, then, around 1300, when her barometer dropped off the scale and the winds fell well below the 125 knots of before.

Dewey had reached the eye wall.

Then, in the dying light, *Dewey* suddenly burst out of the storm. One moment she was in a typhoon, with wind and spume lashing out at her; the next she was in a patch of clear ocean, her lookouts now able to see, though dense clouds still hung overhead and the mountainous swell continued to surge hard against her. A few thousand yards astern of her, *Tabberer* broke into the clearing.

By December 22, the battered fleet was on its way to Ulithi. Behind it, the remains of the typhoon, embraced by a cold front north of Luzon, swirled, sputtered, and died.

10

Escaping the Chicago Massacre

Lieutenant Linai T. Helm

FLEMINGTON, NEW JERSEY,
6th June, 1814.
Dear Sir:—

I hope you will excuse the length of time I have taken to communicate the history of the unfortunate massacre of Chicago. It is now nearly finished, and in two weeks you may expect it. As the history cannot possibly be written with truth without eternally disgracing Major Heald, I wish you could find out whether I shall be cashiered or censured for bringing to light the conduct of so great a man as many think him.

You know I am the only officer that has escaped to tell the news. Some of the men have got off, but where they are I know not; they would be able to testify to some of the principal facts. I have waited a long time expecting a court of inquiry on his conduct but see plainly it is to be overlooked. I am resolved now to do myself justice even if I have to leave the service to publish the history. I shall be happy to hear from you immediately on the receipt of this.

I have the honor to be sir,
with great respect,
Your obedient servant,

L. T. HELM.

THE MASSACRE AT CHICAGO

It was the evening of April 7, 1812. The children were dancing before the fire to the music of their father's violin. The tea table was spread, and they were awaiting the return of their mother, who had gone to visit a sick neighbor about a quarter of a mile up the river.

Suddenly their sports were interrupted. The door was thrown open, and Mrs. Kinzie rushed in, pale with terror, and scarcely able to speak. "The Indians! the Indians!" she gasped.

"The Indians? What? Where?" they all demanded in alarm.

"Up at Lee's Place, killing and scalping!"

With difficulty Mrs. Kinzie composed herself sufficiently to say that, while she was at Burns', a man and a boy had been seen running down with all speed on the opposite side of the river. They had called across to the Burns family to save themselves, for the Indians were at Lee's Place, from which the two had just made their escape. Having given this terrifying news, they had made all speed for the fort, which was on the same side of the river.

All was now consternation and dismay in the Kinzie household. The family were hurried into two old pirogues that lay moored near the house, and paddled with all possible haste across the river to take refuge in the fort.

All that the man and boy who had made their escape were able to tell was soon known; but, in order to render their story more intelligible, it is necessary to describe the situation.

Lee's Place, since known as Hardscrabble, was a farm intersected by the Chicago River, about four miles from its mouth. The farmhouse stood on the west bank of the south branch of this river. On the north side of the main stream, but near its junction with Lake Michigan, stood the dwelling house and trading establishment of Mr. Kinzie.

The fort was situated on the southern bank, directly opposite this mansion, the river and a few rods of sloping green turf on either side being all that intervened between them.

The fort was differently constructed from the one erected on the same site in 1816. It had two blockhouses on the southern side, and on the northern a sally port, or subterranean passage from the parade ground to the river. This was designed to facilitate escape in case of an emergency or as a means of supplying the garrison with water during a siege.

In the fort at this period were three officers, Captain Heald, who was in command, Lieutenant Helm, the son-in-law of Mr. Kinzie, and Ensign Ronan—the last two very young men—and the surgeon, Dr. Van Voorhees.

The garrison numbered about seventy-five men, very few of whom were effective.

A constant and friendly intercourse had been maintained between these troops and the Indians. It is true that the principal men of the Potowatomi nation, like those of most other tribes, went yearly to Fort Malden, in Canada, to receive the large number of presents with which the British Government, for many years, had been in the habit of purchasing their alliance; and it was well known that many of the Potowatomi, as well as Winnebago, had been engaged with the Ottawa and Shawnee at the battle of Tippecanoe, the preceding autumn; yet, as the principal chiefs of all the bands in the neighborhood appeared to be on the most amicable terms with the Americans, no interruption of their harmony was at any time anticipated.

After August 15, however, many circumstances were recalled that might have opened the eyes of the whites had they not been blinded by a false security.

One incident in particular may be mentioned.

In the spring preceding the destruction of the fort, two Indians of the Calumet band came to the fort on a visit to the commanding officer. As they passed through the quarters, they saw Mrs. Heald and Mrs. Helm playing at battledoor.

Turning to the interpreter, one of them, Nau-non-gee, remarked, "The white chiefs' wives are amusing themselves very much; it will not be long before they are hoeing in our cornfields!"

At the time this was considered an idle threat, or, at most, an ebullition of jealous feeling at the contrast between the situation of their own women and that of the "white chiefs' wives." Some months after, how bitterly was it remembered!

The farm at Lee's Place was occupied by a Mr. White and three persons employed by him.

In the afternoon of the day on which our narrative commences, a party of ten or twelve Indians, dressed and painted, arrived at the house. According to the custom among savages, they entered and seated themselves without ceremony.

Something in their appearance and manner excited the suspicion of one of the household, a Frenchman, who remarked, "I do not like the looks of these Indians—they are none of our folks. I know by their dress and paint that they are not Potowatomi."

Another of the men, a discharged soldier, then said to a boy who was present, "If that is the case, we'd better get away from them if we can. Say nothing; but do as you see me do."

There were two canoes tied near the bank, and the soldier walked leisurely towards them. Some of the Indians inquired where he was going. He pointed to the cattle standing among the haystacks on the opposite bank, making signs that they must go and fodder them, and that they would then return and get their supper.

As the afternoon was far advanced, this explanation was accepted without question.

The soldier got into one canoe, and the boy into the other. The stream was narrow, and they were soon across. Having gained the opposite side, they pulled some hay for the cattle, made a show of herding them, and when they had gradually made a circuit, so that their movements were concealed by the haystacks, took to the woods, close at hand, and then started for the fort.

They had run about a quarter of a mile when they heard two guns discharged in succession. These guns they supposed to have been leveled at the companions they had left.

They ran without stopping until they arrived opposite Burns' where, as before related, they called across to warn the family of their danger, and then hastened on to the fort.

It now occurred to those who had secured their own safety that the Burns family was still exposed to imminent peril. The question was, who would hazard his life to bring them to a place of security? The gallant young officer, Ensign Ronan, with a party of five or six soldiers, volunteered to go to their rescue.

They ascended the river in a scow, took the mother, with her infant, scarcely a day old, upon her bed to the boat, and carefully conveyed her with the other members of the family to the fort.

The same afternoon a party of soldiers, consisting of a corporal and six men, had obtained leave to go fishing up the river. They had not returned when the fugitives from Lee's Place arrived at the fort. It was now night and, fearing they might encounter the Indians, the commanding officer ordered a cannon fired, warning them of their danger.

It will be remembered that the unsettled state of the country after the battle of Tippecanoe, the preceding November, had rendered every man vigilant, and the slightest alarm was an admonition to "beware of the Indians."

At the time the cannon was fired the fishing party were about two miles above Lee's Place. Hearing the signal, they put out their torches and dropped down the river towards the garrison, as silently as possible.

When they reached Lee's Place, it was proposed to stop and warn the inmates to be on their guard, as the signal from the fort indicated some kind of danger. All was still as death around the house. The soldiers groped their way along, and as the corporal jumped over the small inclosure he placed his hand upon the dead body of a man. He soon ascertained that the head was without a scalp, and otherwise mutilated. The faithful dog of the murdered man stood guarding the lifeless remains of his master.

The tale was told. The men retreated to their canoes, and reached the fort unmolested about eleven o'clock at night.

The next morning a party of citizens and soldiers volunteered to go to Lee's Place to learn further the fate of its occupants. The body of Mr. White was found pierced by two balls, with eleven stabs in the breast. The Frenchman also lay dead, his dog still beside him. The bodies were brought to the fort and buried in its immediate vicinity.

Later it was learned from traders out in the Indian country that the perpetrators of the deed were a party of Winnebago who had come into the neighborhood to "take some white scalps." Their plan had been to proceed down the river from Lee's Place and kill every white man outside the walls of the fort. However, hearing the report of the cannon, and not knowing what it portended, they thought it best to retreat to their homes on Rock River.

The settlers outside the fort and a few discharged soldiers now intrenched themselves in the Agency House. This building stood west of the fort, between the pickets and the river, and distant about twenty rods from the former.

It was an old-fashioned log house, with a hall running through the center, and one large room on each side. Piazzas extended the whole length of the building, in front and rear. These were now planked up, for greater security; portholes were cut, and sentinels posted at night.

As the enemy were believed to be still lurking in the neighborhood, or, emboldened by former success, were likely to return at any moment, an order was issued prohibiting any soldier or citizen from leaving the vicinity of the garrison without a guard.

One night a sergeant and a private, who were out on patrol, came suddenly upon a party of Indians in the pasture adjoining the esplanade. The sergeant fired his piece, and both retreated towards the fort. Before they could reach it, an Indian threw his tomahawk, which missed the sergeant and struck a wagon standing near. The sentinel from the blockhouse immediately fired while the men got safely in. The next morning traces of blood were found for a considerable distance into the prairie, and from this and the appearance of the long grass, where it was evident a body had lain, it was certain some execution had been done.

On another occasion Indians entered the esplanade to steal horses. Not finding any in the stable, as they had expected to, they relieved their disappointment by stabbing all the sheep in the stable and then letting them loose. The poor animals flocked towards the fort. This gave the alarm. The garrison was aroused, and parties were sent out; but the marauders escaped unmolested. The inmates of the fort experienced no further alarm for many weeks.

On the afternoon of August 7, Winnemeg, or Catfish, a Potowatomi chief, arrived at the post, bringing dispatches from General Hull. These announced that war had been declared between the United States and Great Britain, and that General Hull, at the head of the Northwestern army, had arrived at Detroit; also, that the Island of Mackinac had fallen into the hands of the British.

The orders to Captain Heald were to "evacuate the fort, if practicable, and, in that event, to distribute all the United States property contained in the fort, and in the United States factory or agency, among the Indians in the neighborhood."

After having delivered his dispatches, Winnemeg requested a private interview with Mr. Kinzie, who had taken up his residence in the fort. He told Mr. Kinzie he was acquainted with the purport of the communications he had brought, and begged him to ascertain if it were the intention of Captain Heald to evacuate the post. He advised strongly against such a step, inasmuch as the garrison was well supplied with ammunition, and with provisions for six months.

It would, therefore, be far better, he thought, to remain until reinforcements could be sent. If, however, Captain Heald should decide to leave the post, it should by all means be done immediately. The Potowatomi, through whose country they must pass, being ignorant of the object of Winnemeg's mission, a forced march might be made before the hostile Indians were prepared to interrupt them.

Of this advice, so earnestly given, Captain Heald was immediately informed. He replied that it was his intention to evacuate the post, but that, inasmuch as he had received orders to distribute the United States property, he should not feel justified in leaving until he had collected the Indians of the neighborhood and made an equitable division among them.

Winnemeg then suggested the expediency of marching out, and leaving all things standing; possibly while the Indians were engaged in the partition of the spoils the troops might effect their retreat unmolested. This advice, strongly seconded by Mr. Kinzie, did not meet the approbation of the commanding officer.

The order to evacuate the post was read next morning upon parade. It is difficult to understand why, in such an emergency, Captain Heald omitted the usual form of holding a council of war with his officers. It can be accounted for only by the fact of a want of harmonious feeling between him and one of his junior officers, Ensign Ronan, a high-spirited and somewhat overbearing, but brave and generous, young man.

In the course of the day, no council having been called, the officers waited on Captain Heald, seeking information regarding the course he intended to pursue. When they learned his intentions, they remonstrated with him, on the following grounds:

First, it was highly improbable that the command would be permitted to pass through the country in safety to Fort Wayne. For although it had been said that some of the chiefs had opposed an attack upon the fort, planned the preceding autumn, yet it was well known that they had been actuated in that matter by motives of personal regard for one family, that of Mr. Kinzie, and not by any general friendly feeling towards the Americans; and that, in any event, it was hardly to be expected that these few individuals would be able to control the whole tribe, who were thirsting for blood.

In the next place, their march must necessarily be slow, as their movements must be accommodated to the helplessness of the women and children, of whom there were a number with the detachment. Of their small force some of the soldiers were super-annuated, others invalid.

Therefore, since the course to be pursued was left discretional, their unanimous advice was to remain where they were, and fortify themselves as strongly as possible. Succor from the other side of the peninsula might arrive before they could be attacked by the British from Mackinac; and even should help not come, it were far better to fall into the hands of the British than to become the victims of the savages.

Captain Heald argued in reply that "a special order had been issued by the War Department that no post should be surrendered without battle having been given, and his force was totally inadequate to an engagement with the Indians; that he should unquestionably be censured for remaining when there appeared a prospect of a safe march through; and that, upon the whole, he deemed it expedient to assemble the Indians, distribute the property among them, and then ask them for an escort to Fort Wayne, with the promise of a considerable reward upon their safe arrival, adding that he had full confidence in the friendly professions of the Indians, from whom, as well as from the soldiers, the capture of Mackinac had been kept a profound secret."

From this time the officers held themselves aloof, and spoke but little upon the subject, though they considered Captain Heald's project little short of madness. The dissatisfaction among the soldiers increased hourly, until it reached a high pitch of insubordination.

On one occasion, when conversing with Mr. Kinzie upon the parade, Captain Heald remarked, "I could not remain, even if I thought it best, for I have but a small store of provisions."

"Why, captain," said a soldier who stood near, forgetting all etiquette in the excitement of the moment, "you have cattle enough to last the troops six months."

"But," replied Captain Heald, "I have no salt to preserve it with."

"Then jerk it," said the man, "as the Indians do their venison."

The Indians now became daily more unruly. Entering the fort in defiance of the sentinels, they made their way without ceremony into the officers' quarters. One day an Indian took up a rifle and fired it in the parlor of the commanding officer, as an expression of defiance. Some believed that this was intended among the young men as a signal for an attack.

The old chiefs passed backwards and forwards among the assembled groups with the appearance of the most lively agitation, while the squaws rushed to and fro in great excitement, evidently prepared for some fearful scene.

Any further manifestation of ill feeling was, however, suppressed for the time and, strange as it may seem, Captain Heald continued to entertain a conviction of having created so amicable a disposition among the Indians as to insure the safety of the command on their march to Fort Wayne.

Thus passed the time until August 12. The feelings of the inmates of the fort during this time may be better imagined than described. Each morning that dawned seemed to bring them nearer to that most appalling fate—butchery by a savage foe; and at night they scarcely dared yield to slumber, lest they should be aroused by the war whoop and tomahawk. Gloom and mistrust prevailed, and the want of unanimity among the officers prevented the consolation they might have found in mutual sympathy and encouragement.

The Indians being assembled from the neighboring villages, a council was held with them on the afternoon of August 12. Captain Heald alone attended on the part of the military. He had requested his officers to accompany him, but they had declined. They had been secretly informed that the young chiefs intended to fall upon the officers and massacre them while in council, but they could not persuade Captain Heald of the truth of their information.

They waited therefore only until, accompanied by Mr. Kinzie, he had left the garrison, when they took command of the block-houses overlooking the esplanade on which the council was held, opened the portholes, and pointed the cannon so as to command the whole assembly. By this means, probably, the lives of the whites who were present in council were preserved.

In council, the commanding officer informed the Indians that it was his intention to distribute among them, the next day, not only the goods lodged in the United States factory, but also the ammunition and provisions, with which the garrison was well supplied. He then requested the Potowatomi to furnish him an escort to Fort Wayne, promising them, in addition to the presents they were now about to receive, a liberal reward on arriving there. With many professions of friendship and good will, the savages assented to all he proposed, and promised all he required.

After the council, Mr. Kinzie, who well understood not only the Indian character but the present tone of feeling among them, had a long interview with Captain Heald, in hopes of opening his eyes to the real state of affairs.

He reminded him that since the trouble with the Indians along the Wabash and in the vicinity, there had appeared to be a settled plan of hostilities towards the whites, in consequence of which it had been the policy of the Americans to withhold from the Indians whatever would enable them to carry on their warfare upon the defenseless inhabitants of the frontier.

Mr. Kinzie also recalled to Captain Heald how, having left home for Detroit, the preceding autumn, on receiving news at De Charme's of the battle of Tippecanoe, he had immediately returned to Chicago, that he might dispatch orders to his traders to furnish no ammunition to the Indians. As a result, all the ammunition the traders had on hand was secreted, and those traders who had not already started for their wintering grounds took neither powder nor shot with them.

Captain Heald was struck with the inadvisability of furnishing the enemy (for such they must now consider their old neighbors) with arms against himself, and determined to destroy all the ammunition except what should be necessary for the use of his own troops.

On August 13 the goods, consisting of blankets, broadcloths, calicoes, paints, and miscellaneous supplies were distributed, as stipulated. The same evening part of the ammunition and liquor was carried into the sally port, and there thrown into a well which had been dug to supply the garrison with water in case of emergency. The remainder was transported, as secretly as possible, through the northern gate; the heads of the barrels were knocked in, and the contents poured into the river.

The same fate was shared by a large quantity of alcohol belonging to Mr. Kinzie, which had been deposited in a warehouse near his residence opposite the fort.

The Indians suspected what was going on, and crept, serpent-like, as near the scene of action as possible; but a vigilant watch was kept up, and no one was suffered to approach but those engaged in the affair. All the muskets not necessary for the command on the march were broken up and thrown into the well, together with bags of shot, flints, gunscrews; in short, everything relating to weapons of defense.

Some relief to the general feeling of despondency was afforded by the arrival, on August 14, of Captain Wells with fifteen friendly Miami.

Of this brave man, who forms so conspicuous a figure in our frontier annals, it is unnecessary here to say more than that he had resided from boyhood among the Indians, and hence possessed a perfect knowledge of their character and habits.

At Fort Wayne he had heard of the order to evacuate the fort at Chicago, and, knowing the hostile determination of the Potowatomi, had made a rapid march across the country to prevent the exposure of his relative, Captain Heald, and his troops to certain destruction.

But he came "all too late." When he reached the post he found that the ammunition had been destroyed, and the provisions given to the Indians. There was, therefore, no alternative, and every preparation was made for the march of the troops on the following morning.

On the afternoon of the same day a second council was held with the Indians. They expressed great indignation at the destruction of the ammunition and liquor. Notwithstanding the precautions that had been taken to preserve secrecy, the noise of knocking in the heads of the barrels had betrayed the operations of the preceding night; indeed, so great was the quantity of liquor thrown into the river that next morning the water was, as one expressed it, "strong grog."

Murmurs and threats were everywhere heard among the savages. It was evident that the first moment of exposure would subject the troops to some manifestation of their disappointment and resentment.

Among the chiefs were several who, although they shared the general hostile feeling of their tribe towards the Americans, yet retained a personal regard for the troops at this post and for the few white citizens of the place. These chiefs exerted their utmost influence to allay the revengeful feelings of the young men, and to avert their sanguinary designs, but without effect.

On the evening succeeding the council Black Partridge, a conspicuous chief, entered the quarters of the commanding officer.

"Father," said he, "I come to deliver up to you the medal I wear. It was given me by the Americans, and I have long worn it in token of our mutual friendship. But our young men are resolved to imbrue their hands in the blood of the whites. I cannot restrain them, and I will not wear a token of peace while I am compelled to act as an enemy."

Had further evidence been wanting, this circumstance would have sufficiently justified the devoted band in their melancholy anticipations. Nevertheless, they went steadily on with the necessary preparations; and, amid the horrors of the situation there were not wanting gallant hearts who strove to encourage in their desponding companions the hopes of escape they themselves were far from indulging.

Of the ammunition there had been reserved but twenty-five rounds, besides one box of cartridges, contained in the baggage wagons. This must, under any circumstances of danger, have proved an inadequate supply; but the prospect of a fatiguing march, in their present ineffective state, forbade the troops embarrassing themselves with a larger quantity.

The morning of August 15 arrived. Nine o'clock was the hour named for starting and all things were in readiness.

Mr. Kinzie, having volunteered to accompany the troops in their march, had intrusted his family to the care of some friendly Indians, who promised to convey them in a boat around the head of Lake Michigan to a point on the St. Joseph River, there to be joined by the troops, should their march be permitted.

Early in the morning Mr. Kinzie received a message from To-pee-nee-bee, a chief of the St. Joseph band, informing him that mischief was intended by the Potowatomi who had engaged to escort the detachment, and urging him to relinquish his plan of accompanying the troops by land, promising him that the boat containing his family should be permitted to pass in safety to St. Joseph.

Mr. Kinzie declined this proposal, as he believed his presence might restrain the fury of the savages, so warmly were the greater number of them attached to him and his family.

Seldom does one find a man who, like John Kinzie, refuses safety for himself in order to stand or fall with his countrymen, and who, as stern as any Spartan, bids farewell to his dear ones to go forward to almost certain destruction.

The party in the boat consisted of Mrs. Kinzie and her four younger children, their nurse Josette, a clerk of Mr. Kinzie's, two servants, and the boatmen, besides the two Indians who were to act as their protectors. The boat started, but had scarcely reached the mouth of the river, which, it will be recalled, was here half a mile below the fort, when another messenger from To-pee-nee-bee arrived to detain it. There was no mistaking the meaning of this detention.

In breathless anxiety sat the wife and mother. She was a woman of unusual energy and strength of character, yet her heart died within her as she folded her arms about her helpless infants and gazed upon the march of her husband and eldest child to what seemed certain death.

As the troops left the fort, the band struck up the Dead March. On they came, in military array, but with solemn mien, Captain Wells in the lead at the head of his little band of Miami. He had blackened his face before leaving the garrison, in token of his impending fate. The troops took their route along the lake shore; but when they reached the point where the range of sand hills intervening between the prairie and the beach commenced, the escort of Potowatomi, in number about five hundred, took the level of the prairie, instead of continuing along the shore with the Americans and Miami.

They had marched perhaps a mile and a half when Captain Wells, who had kept somewhat in advance with his Miami, came riding furiously back.

"They are about to attack us," shouted he; "form instantly, and charge upon them."

Scarcely were the words uttered, when a volley was showered from among the sand hills. The troops, brought hastily into line, charged up the bank. One man, a veteran of seventy winters, fell as they ascended. The remainder of the scene is best described in the words of an eyewitness and participator in the tragedy, Mrs. Helm, the wife of Captain (then Lieutenant) Helm, and stepdaughter of Mr. Kinzie.

After we had left the bank the firing became general. The Miami fled at the outset. Their chief rode up to the Potowatomi, and said: "You have deceived us and the Americans. You have done a bad action, and (brandishing his tomahawk) I will be the first to head a party of Americans to return and punish your treachery."

So saying, he galloped after his companions, who were now scurrying across the prairies.

The troops behaved most gallantly. They were but a handful, but they seemed resolved to sell their lives as dearly as possible. Our horses pranced and bounded, and could hardly be restrained as the balls whistled among them. I drew off a little, and gazed upon my husband and father, who were yet unharmed. I felt that my hour was come, and endeavored to forget those I loved, and prepare myself for my approaching fate.

While I was thus engaged, the surgeon, Dr. Van Voorhees, came up. He was badly wounded. His horse had been shot under him, and he had received a ball in his leg. Every muscle of his face was quivering with the agony of terror. He said to me, "Do you think they will take our lives? I am badly wounded, but I think not mortally. Perhaps we might purchase our lives by promising them a large reward. Do you think there is any chance?"

"Dr. Van Voorhees," said I, "do not let us waste the moments that yet remain to us in such vain hopes. Our fate is inevitable. In a few moments we must appear before the bar of God. Let us make what preparation is yet in our power."

"Oh, I cannot die!" exclaimed he, "I am not fit to die—if I had but a short time to prepare—death is awful!"

I pointed to Ensign Ronan, who, though mortally wounded and nearly down, was still fighting with desperation on one knee.

"Look at that man!" said I. "At least he dies like a soldier."

"Yes," replied the unfortunate surgeon, with a convulsive gasp, "but he has no terrors of the future—he is an atheist."

At this moment a young Indian raised his tomahawk over me. Springing aside, I partially avoided the blow, which, intended for my skull, fell on my shoulder. I seized the Indian around the neck, and while exerting my utmost strength to get possession of his scalping-knife, hanging in a scabbard over his breast, I was dragged from his grasp by another and older Indian.

The latter bore me struggling and resisting towards the lake. Despite the rapidity with which I was hurried along, I recognized, as I passed, the lifeless remains of the unfortunate surgeon. Some murderous tomahawk had stretched him upon the very spot where I had last seen him.

I was immediately plunged into the water and held there with a forcible hand, notwithstanding my resistance. I soon perceived, however, that the object of my captor was not to drown me, for he held me firmly in such a position as to keep my head above water. This reassured me, and, regarding him attentively, I soon recognized, in spite of the paint with which he was disguised, the Black Partridge.

When the firing had nearly subsided, my preserver bore me from the water and conducted me up the sand banks. It was a burning August morning, and walking through the sand in my drenched condition was inexpressibly painful and fatiguing.

I stooped and took off my shoes to free them from the sand with which they were nearly filled, when a squaw seized and carried them off, and I was obliged to proceed without them.

When we had gained the prairie, I was met by my father, who told me that my husband was safe and but slightly wounded. I was led gently back towards the Chicago River, along the southern bank of which was the Potowatomi encampment. Once I was placed upon a horse without a saddle, but, finding the motion insupportable, I sprang off. Assisted partly by my kind conductor, Black Partridge, and partly by another Indian, Pee-so-tum, who held dangling in his hand a scalp which by the black ribbon around the queue I recognized as that of Captain Wells, I dragged my fainting steps to one of the wigwams.

The wife of Wau-bee-nee-mah, a chief from the Illinois River, was standing near. Seeing my exhausted condition, she seized a kettle, dipped up some water from a stream that flowed near, threw into it some maple sugar, and, stirring it with her hand, gave it to me to drink. This act of kindness, in the midst of so many horrors, touched me deeply. But my attention was soon diverted to other things.

The fort, since the troops marched out, had become a scene of plunder. The cattle had been shot as they ran at large, and lay about, dead or dying. This work of butchery had commenced just as we were leaving the fort. I vividly recalled a remark of Ensign Ronan, as the firing went on. "Such," turning to me, "is to be our fate—to be shot down like brutes!"

"Well, sir," said the commanding officer, who overheard him, "are you afraid?"

"No," replied the high-spirited young man, "I can march up to the enemy where you dare not show your face." And his subsequent gallant behavior showed this was no idle boast.

As the noise of the firing grew gradually fainter and the stragglers from the victorious party came dropping in, I received confirmation of what my father had hurriedly communicated in our meeting on the lake shore: the whites had surrendered, after the loss of about two thirds of their number.

They had stipulated, through the interpreter, Peresh Leclerc, that their lives and those of the remaining women and children be spared, and that they be delivered in safety at certain of the British posts, unless ransomed by traders in the Indian country. It appears that the wounded prisoners were not considered as included in the stipulation, and upon their being brought into camp an awful scene ensued.

An old squaw, infuriated by the loss of friends, or perhaps excited by the sanguinary scenes around her, seemed possessed by a demoniac ferocity. Seizing a stable fork she assaulted one miserable victim, already groaning and writhing in the agony of wounds aggravated by the scorching beams of the sun. With a delicacy of feeling scarcely to have been expected under such circumstances, Wau-bee-nee-mah stretched a mat across two poles, between me and this dreadful scene. I was thus in some degree shielded from its horrors, though I could not close my ears to the cries of the sufferer. The following night five more of the wounded prisoners were tomahawked.

After the first attack, it appears the Americans charged upon a band of Indians concealed in a sort of ravine between the sand banks and the prairie. The Indians gathered together, and after hard fighting, in which the number of whites was reduced to twenty-eight, their band succeeded in breaking through the enemy and gaining a rise of ground not far from Oak Woods. Further contest now seeming hopeless, Lieutenant Helm sent Peresh Leclerc, the boy in the service of Mr. Kinzie, who had accompanied the troops and fought manfully on their side, to propose terms of capitulation. It was stipulated, as told in Mrs. Helm's narrative, that the lives of all the survivors should be spared, and a ransom permitted as soon as practicable.

But in the meantime horrible scenes had indeed been enacted. During the engagement near the sand hills one young savage climbed into the baggage wagon which sheltered the twelve children of the white families, and tomahawked the entire group.

Captain Wells, who was fighting near, beheld the deed, and exclaimed:

"Is that their game, butchering the women and children? Then I will kill, too!"

So saying, he turned his horse's head and started for the Indian camp, near the fort, where the braves had left their squaws and children.

Several Indians followed him as he galloped along. Lying flat on the neck of his horse, and loading and firing in that position, he turned occasionally on his pursuers. But at length their balls took effect, killing his horse, and severely wounding the Captain. At this moment he was met by Winnemeg and Wau-ban-see, who endeavored to save him from the men who had now overtaken him. As they helped him along, after having disengaged him from his horse, he received his deathblow from Pee-so-tum, who stabbed him in the back.

The heroic resolution shown during the fight by the wife of one of the soldiers, a Mrs. Corbin, deserves to be recorded. She had from the first expressed the determination never to fall into the hands of the savages, believing that their prisoners were invariably subjected to tortures worse than death.

When, therefore, a party came upon her to make her prisoner, she fought with desperation, refusing to surrender, although assured, by signs, of safety and kind treatment. Literally, she suffered herself to be cut to pieces, rather than become their captive.

There was a Sergeant Holt, who early in the engagement received a ball in the neck. Finding himself badly wounded, he gave his sword to his wife, who was on horseback near him, telling her to defend herself. He then made for the lake, to keep out of the way of the balls.

Mrs. Holt rode a very fine horse, which the Indians were desirous of possessing, and they therefore attacked her in the hope of dismounting her. They fought only with the butt ends of their guns, for their object was not to kill her. She hacked and hewed at their pieces as they were thrust against her, now on this side, now that. Finally, she broke loose and dashed out into the prairie, where the Indians pursued her, shouting and laughing, and now and then calling out, "The brave woman! do not hurt her!"

At length they overtook her, and while she was engaged with two or three in front, one succeeded in seizing her by the neck from behind, and in dragging her from her horse, large and powerful woman though she was. Notwithstanding their guns had been so hacked and injured, and they themselves severely cut, her captors seemed to regard her only with admiration. They took her to a trader on the Illinois River, who showed her every kindness during her captivity, and later restored her to her friends.

Meanwhile those of Mr. Kinzie's family who had remained in the boat, near the mouth of the river, were carefully guarded by Kee-po-tah and another Indian. They had seen the smoke, then the blaze, and immediately after, the report of the first tremendous discharge had sounded in their ears. Then all was confusion. They knew nothing of the events of the battle until they saw an Indian coming towards them from the battle ground, leading a horse on which sat a lady, apparently wounded.

"That is Mrs. Heald," cried Mrs. Kinzie. "That Indian will kill her. Run, Chandonnai," to one of Mr. Kinzie's clerks, "take the mule that is tied there, and offer it to him to release her."

Mrs. Heald's captor, by this time, was in the act of disengaging her bonnet from her head, in order to scalp her. Chandonnai ran up and offered the mule as a ransom, with the promise of ten bottles of whisky as soon as they should reach his village. The whisky was a strong temptation.

"But," said the Indian, "she is badly wounded—she will die. Will you give me the whisky at all events?"

Chandonnai promised that he would, and the bargain was concluded. The savage placed the lady's bonnet on his own head, and, after an ineffectual effort on the part of some squaws to rob her of her shoes and stockings, she was brought on board the boat, where she lay moaning with pain from the many bullet wounds in her arms.

Having wished to possess themselves of her horse uninjured, the Indians had aimed their shots so as to disable the rider, without in any way harming her steed.

Mrs. Heald had not lain long in the boat when a young Indian of savage aspect was seen approaching. A buffalo robe was hastily drawn over her, and she was admonished to suppress all sound of complaint, as she valued her life.

The heroic woman remained perfectly silent while the savage drew near. He had a pistol in his hand, which he rested on the side of the boat, while, with a fearful scowl, he looked pryingly around. One of the servants, who stood in the bow of the boat, seized an ax that lay near and signed to him that if he shot he would cleave his skull, telling him that the boat contained only the family of Shaw-nee-aw-kee. Upon this, the Indian retired. It afterwards appeared that the object of his search was Mr. Burnett, a trader from St. Joseph with whom he had some account to settle.

When the boat was at length permitted to return to the house of Mr. Kinzie, and Mrs. Heald was removed there, it became necessary to dress her wounds.

Mr. Kinzie applied to an old chief who stood by, and who, like most of his tribe, possessed some skill in surgery, to extract a ball from the arm of the sufferer.

"No, father," replied the Indian. "I cannot do it—it makes me sick here," placing his hand on his heart.

Mr. Kinzie himself then performed the operation with his penknife.

At their own house, the family of Mr. Kinzie were closely guarded by their Indian friends, whose intention it was to carry them to Detroit for security. The rest of the prisoners remained at the wigwams of their captors.

On the following morning, the work of plunder being completed, the Indians set fire to the fort. A very equitable distribution of the finery appeared to have been made, and shawls, ribbons, and feathers fluttered about in all directions. The ludicrous appearance of one young fellow arrayed in a muslin gown and a lady's bonnet would, under other circumstances, have been a matter of great amusement.

Black Partridge, Wau-ban-see, and Kee-po-tah, with two other Indians, established themselves in the porch of the Kinzie house as sentinels, to protect the family from any evil that the young men might be incited to commit, and all remained tranquil for a short space after the conflagration.

Very soon, however, a party of Indians from the Wabash made their appearance. These were, decidedly, the most hostile and implacable of all the tribes of the Potowatomi.

Being more remote, they had shared less than some of their brethren in the kindness of Mr. Kinzie and his family, and consequently their friendly regard was not so strong.

Runners had been sent to the villages to apprise these Indians of the intended evacuation of the post, as well as of the plan to attack the troops.

Thirsting to participate in such an event, they had hurried to the scene, and great was their mortification, on arriving at the river Aux Plaines, to meet a party of their friends with their chief, Nee-scot-nee-meg, badly wounded, and learn that the battle was over, the spoils divided, and the scalps all taken. Arriving at Chicago they blackened their faces, and proceeded toward the dwelling of Mr. Kinzie.

From his station on the piazza Black Partridge had watched their approach, and his fears were particularly awakened for the safety of Mrs. Helm, Mr. Kinzie's stepdaughter, who had recently come to the post, and was personally unknown to the more remote Indians.

By his advice she was made to assume the ordinary dress of a Frenchwoman of the country—a short gown and petticoat with a blue cotton handkerchief wrapped around her head. In this disguise she was conducted by Black Partridge himself to the house of Ouilmette, a Frenchman who formed a part of the establishment of Mr. Kinzie and whose dwelling was close at hand.

It so happened that the Indians came first to this house in their search for prisoners. As they approached, the inmates, fearful that the fair complexion and general appearance of Mrs. Helm might betray her as an American, raised a large feather bed and placed her under the edge of it upon the bedstead, with her face to the wall. Mrs. Bisson, a half-breed sister of Ouilmette's wife, then seated herself with her sewing upon the front of the bed.

It was a hot day in August, and the feverish excitement of fear and agitation, together with her position, which was nearly suffocating, became so intolerable that Mrs. Helm at length entreated to be released and given up to the Indians.

"I can but die," said she; "let them put an end to my misery at once."

Mrs. Bisson replied, "Your death would be the destruction of us all, for Black Partridge has resolved that if one drop of the blood of your family is spilled, he will take the lives of all concerned in it, even his nearest friends; and if once the work of murder commences, there will be no end of it, so long as there remains one white person or half-breed in the country."

This expostulation nerved Mrs. Helm with fresh courage.

The Indians entered, and from her hiding place she could occasionally see them gliding about and stealthily inspecting every part of the room, though without making any ostensible search, until, apparently satisfied that there was no one concealed, they left the house.

All this time Mrs. Bisson had kept her seat upon the side of the bed, calmly sorting and arranging the patchwork of the quilt on which she was engaged, and preserving an appearance of the utmost tranquillity, although she knew not but that the next moment she might receive a tomahawk in her brain. Her self-command unquestionably saved the lives of all who were present.

From Ouilmette's house the party of Indians proceeded to the dwelling of Mr. Kinzie. They entered the parlor in which the family were assembled with their faithful protectors, and seated themselves upon the floor, in silence.

Black Partridge perceived from their moody and revengeful looks what was passing in their minds, but he dared not remonstrate with them. He only observed in a low tone to Wau-ban-see, "We have endeavored to save our friends, but it is in vain—nothing will save them now."

At this moment a friendly whoop was heard from a party of newcomers on the opposite bank of the river. As the canoes in which they had hastily embarked touched the bank near the house, Black Partridge sprang to meet their leader.

"Who are you?" demanded he.

"A man. Who are you?"

"A man like yourself. But tell me who you are,"—meaning, Tell me your disposition, and which side you are for.

"I am a Sau-ga-nash!"

"Then make all speed to the house—your friend is in danger, and you alone can save him."

Billy Caldwell, for it was he, entered the parlor with a calm step, and without a trace of agitation in his manner. He deliberately took off his accouterments and placed them with his rifle behind the door, then saluted the hostile savages.

"How now, my friends! A good day to you. I was told there were enemies here, but I am glad to find only friends. Why have you blackened your faces? Is it that you are mourning for the friends you have lost in battle?" purposely misunderstanding this token of evil designs. "Or is it that you are fasting? If so, ask our friend, here, and he will give you to eat. He is the Indian's friend, and never yet refused them what they had need of."

Thus taken by surprise, the savages were ashamed to acknowledge their bloody purpose. They, therefore, said modestly that they had come to beg of their friends some white cotton in which to wrap their dead before interring them. This was given to them, with some other presents, and they peaceably took their departure from the premises.

With Mr. Kinzie's party was a non-commissioned officer who had made his escape in a singular manner. As the troops had been about to leave the fort, it was found that the baggage horses of the surgeon had strayed off. The quartermaster sergeant, Griffith, was sent to find and bring them on, it being absolutely necessary to recover them, since their packs contained part of the surgeon's apparatus and the medicines for the march.

For a long time Griffith had been on the sick report and for this reason was given charge of the baggage, instead of being placed with the troops. His efforts to recover the horses proved unsuccessful, and, alarmed at certain appearances of disorder and hostile intention among the Indians, he was hastening to rejoin his party when he was met and made prisoner by To-pee-nee-bee.

Having taken his arms and accouterments from him, the chief put him into a canoe and paddled him across the river, bidding him make for the woods and secrete himself. This Griffith did; and in the afternoon of the following day, seeing from his lurking place that all appeared quiet, he ventured to steal cautiously into Ouilmette's garden, where he concealed himself for a time behind some currant bushes.

At length he determined to enter the house, and accordingly climbed up through a small back window into the room where the family were, entering just as the Wabash Indians had left the house of Ouilmette for that of Mr. Kinzie. The danger of the sergeant was now imminent. The family stripped him of his uniform and arrayed him in a suit of deerskin, with belt, moccasins, and pipe, like a French *engagé*. His dark complexion and heavy black whiskers favored the disguise. The family were all ordered to address him in French, and, although utterly ignorant of this language, he continued to pass for a *Weem-tee-gosh*, and as such remained with Mr. Kinzie and his family, undetected by his enemies, until they reached a place of safety.

On the third day after the battle, Mr. Kinzie and his family, with the clerks of the establishment, were put into a boat, under the care of François, an interpreter, and conveyed to St. Joseph, where they remained until the following November, under the protection of To-pee-nee-bee's band. With the exception of Mr. Kinzie they were then conducted to Detroit, under the escort of Chandonnai and their trusty Indian friend, Kee-po-tah, and delivered as prisoners of war to Colonel McKee, the British Indian Agent.

Mr. Kinzie himself was held at St. Joseph and did not succeed in rejoining his family until some months later. On his arrival at Detroit he was paroled by General Proctor.

Lieutenant Helm, who was likewise wounded, was carried by some friendly Indians to their village on the Au Sable and thence to Peoria, where he was liberated through the intervention of Mr. Thomas Forsyth, the half brother of Mr. Kinzie. Mrs. Helm accompanied her parents to St. Joseph, where they resided for several months in the family of Alexander Robinson, receiving from them all possible kindness and hospitality.

Later Mrs. Helm was joined by her husband in Detroit, where they both were arrested by order of the British commander, and sent on horseback, in the dead of winter, through Canada to Fort George on the Niagara frontier.

When they arrived at that post, there had been no official appointed to receive them, and, notwithstanding their long and fatiguing journey in the coldest, most inclement weather, Mrs. Helm, a delicate woman of seventeen years, was permitted to sit waiting in her saddle, outside the gate, for more than an hour, before the refreshment of fire or food, or even the shelter of a roof, was offered her. When Colonel Sheaffe, who was absent at the time, was informed of this brutal inhospitality, he expressed the greatest indignation. He waited on Mrs. Helm immediately, apologized in the most courteous manner, and treated both her and Lieutenant Helm with the greatest consideration and kindness, until, by an exchange of prisoners, they were liberated and found means of reaching their friends in Steuben County, N. Y.

Captain and Mrs. Heald were sent across the lake to St. Joseph the day after the battle. The Captain had received two wounds in the engagement, his wife seven.

Captain Heald had been taken prisoner by an Indian from the Kankakee, who had a strong personal regard for him, and who, when he saw Mrs. Heald's wounded and enfeebled state, released her husband that he might accompany her to St. Joseph. To the latter place they were accordingly carried by Chandonnai and his party. In the meantime, the Indian who had so nobly released his prisoner returned to his village on the Kankakee, where he had the mortification of finding that his conduct had excited great dissatisfaction among his band. So great was the displeasure manifested that he resolved to make a journey to St. Joseph and reclaim his prisoner.

News of his intention being brought to To-pee-nee-bee and Kee-po-tah, under whose care the prisoners were, they held a private council with Chandonnai, Mr. Kinzie, and the principal men of the village, the result of which was a determination to send Captain and Mrs. Heald to the Island of Mackinac and deliver them up to the British.

They were accordingly put in a bark canoe, and paddled by Robinson and his wife a distance of three hundred miles along the coast of Michigan, and surrendered as prisoners of war to the commanding officer at Mackinac.

As an instance of Captain Heald's procrastinating spirit it may be mentioned that, even after he had received positive word that his Indian captor was on the way from the Kankakee to St. Joseph to retake him, he would still have delayed at that place another day, to make preparation for a more comfortable journey to Mackinac.

The soldiers from Fort Dearborn, with their wives and surviving children, were dispersed among the different villages of the Potowatomi upon the Illinois, Wabash, and Rock rivers, and at Milwaukee, until the following spring, when the greater number of them were carried to Detroit and ransomed.

Mrs. Burns, with her infant, became the prisoner of a chief, who carried her to his village and treated her with great kindness. His wife, from jealousy of the favor shown to "the white woman" and her child, always treated them with great hostility. On one occasion she struck the infant with a tomahawk, and barely failed in her attempt to put it to death. Mrs. Burns and her child were not left long in the power of the old squaw after this demonstration, but on the first opportunity were carried to a place of safety.

The family of Mr. Lee had resided in a house on the lake shore, not far from the fort. Mr. Lee was the owner of Lee's Place, which he cultivated as a farm. It was his son who had run down with the discharged soldier to give the alarm of "Indians," at the fort, on the afternoon of April 7.

The father, the son, and all the other members of the family except Mrs. Lee and her young infant had fallen victims to the Indians on August 15. The two survivors were claimed by Black Partridge, and carried by him to his village on the Au Sable. He had been particularly attached to a little twelve-year-old girl of Mrs. Lee's. This child had been placed on horseback for the march; and, as she was unaccustomed to riding, she was tied fast to the saddle, lest she should slip or be thrown off.

She was within reach of the balls at the commencement of the engagement, and was severely wounded. The horse, setting off at a full gallop, partly threw her; but held fast by the bands which confined her, she hung dangling as the animal ran wildly about. In this state she was met by Black Partridge, who caught the horse and disengaged the child from the saddle. Finding her so badly wounded that she could not recover, and seeing that she was in great agony, he at once put an end to her pain with his tomahawk. This, he afterwards said, was the hardest thing he had ever done, but he did it because he could not bear to see the child suffer.

Black Partridge soon became warmly attached to the mother—so much so, that he wished to marry her; and, though she very naturally objected, he continued to treat her with the greatest respect and consideration. He was in no hurry to release her, for he was still in hopes of prevailing upon her to become his wife.

In the course of the winter her child fell ill. Finding that none of the remedies within their reach was effectual, Black Partridge proposed to take the little one to Chicago, to a French trader then living in the house of Mr. Kinzie, and procure medical aid from him. Wrapping up his charge with the greatest care, he set out on his journey.

Arriving at the residence of M. Du Pin, he entered the room where the Frenchman was, and carefully placed his burden on the floor.

"What have you there?" asked M. Du Pin.

"A young raccoon, which I have brought you as a present," was the reply; and, opening the pack, he showed the little sick infant.

When the trader had prescribed for the child, and Black Partridge was about to return to his home, he told his friend of the proposal he had made to Mrs. Lee to become his wife, and the manner in which it had been received.

M. Du Pin entertained some fear that the chief's honorable resolution to allow the lady herself to decide whether or not to accept his addresses might not hold out, and at once entered into a negotiation for her ransom. So effectually were the good feelings of Black Partridge wrought upon that he consented to bring his fair prisoner to Chicago immediately, that she might be restored to her friends.

Whether the kind trader had at the outset any other feeling in the matter than sympathy and brotherly kindness, we cannot say;

we only know that in course of time Mrs. Lee became Madame Du Pin, and that the worthy couple lived together in great happiness for many years after.

The fate of Nau-non-gee, a chief of the Calumet village, deserves to be recorded.

During the battle of August 15, the principal object of his attack was one Sergeant Hays, a man from whom he had accepted many kindnesses.

After Hays had received a ball through the body, this Indian ran up to tomahawk him, when the sergeant, summoning his remaining strength, pierced him through the body with his bayonet. The two fell together. Other Indians running up soon dispatched Hays, and not until then was his bayonet extracted from the body of his adversary.

After the battle the wounded chief was carried to his village on the Calumet, where he survived for several days. Finding his end approaching, he called together his young men, and enjoined them, in the most solemn manner, to regard the safety of their prisoners after his death, and out of respect to his memory to take the lives of none of them; for he himself fully deserved his fate at the hands of the man whose kindness he had so ill requited.

Sources

"Defying the Odds" from *The Devil's Causeway: The True Story of America's First Prisoners of War in the Philippines, and the Heroic Expedition Sent to Their Rescue*. Matthew Westfall. Essex, CT: Lyons Press, an imprint of the Rowman & Littlefield Publishing Group, Inc., 2012.

"My Cave Life in Vicksburg" from *My Cave Life in Vicksburg*. Mary Loughborough. New York: D. Appleton and Company, 1864.

"A Prisoner's Diary" from *Andersonville Diary*. John L. Ransom. Auburn, NY: John L. Ransom, Publisher, 1881.

"Surviving the Jungle" from *Hell Is So Green: Search and Rescue over the Hump in World War II*. William Diebold. Essex, CT: Lyons Press, an imprint of the Rowman & Littlefield Publishing Group, Inc. First paperback edition 2011.

"Shark-Filled Waters" from *The Tragic Fate of the USS* Indianapolis. Raymond B. Lech. New York: Cooper Square Press, a division of the Rowman & Littlefield Publishing Group, 1982.

"Treacherous Passage," from Eight Survived: The Harrowing Story of the USS Flier. Douglas A. Campbell. Essex, CT: Lyons Press, a division of the Rowman & Littlefield Publishing Group, 2010.

"An Arduous Challenge" from *Capturing a Locomotive*. William Pittenger. Washington, DC: The National Tribune, 1885.

"Pearl Harbor, December 7, 1941" from *Eyewitness to Infamy: An Oral History of Pearl Harbor, December 7, 1941*. Paul Joseph Travers. Essex, CT: Lyons Press, a division of the Rowman & Littlefield Publishing Group, 2007.

"Outlasting a Typhoon" from *Sea Cobra: Admiral Halsey's Task Force and the Great Pacific Typhoon*. Buckner Melton Jr. Essex, CT: Lyons Press, a division of the Rowman & Littlefield Publishing Group, 2016.

"Escaping the Chicago Massacre" from *The Fort Dearborn Massacre*. Lanai T. Helm. New York and Chicago: Rand McNally & Company, 1912.